# THE ADVENTURES OF BARRY WEEN BOY GENIUS

# GORILLA WARFARE

# THE ADVENTURES OF BARRY WEEN BOY GENIUS 4

written and illustrated by

## JUDD WINICK

cover colors by

## GUY MAJOR

chapter break gray tones by

## ARTHUR DELA CRUZ

book design by

## KEITH WOOD

edited by

## JAMES LUCAS JONES

original series edited by

## JAMIE S. RICH

ONi PRESS

# GORILLA WARFARE

original logo design by **Chris Eliopoulos**

Published by **Oni Press, Inc.**

**Joe Nozemack**, publisher

**Jamie S. Rich**, editor in chief

**James Lucas Jones**, associate editor

This collects issues 4-6 of the Oni Press comics series
The Adventures of *Barry Ween, Boy Genius 3: Monkey Tales.*

ONI PRESS, INC.
1305 SE Martin Luther King Jr. Blvd.
Suite A
Portland, OR 97214
USA

www.onipress.com
www.barryween.com

First edition: May 2002
ISBN 1-929998-19-8

3 5 7 9 10 8 6 4

PRINTED IN CANADA.

FOR ARMISTEAD MAUPIN
THE BEST STORYTELLER I KNOW.

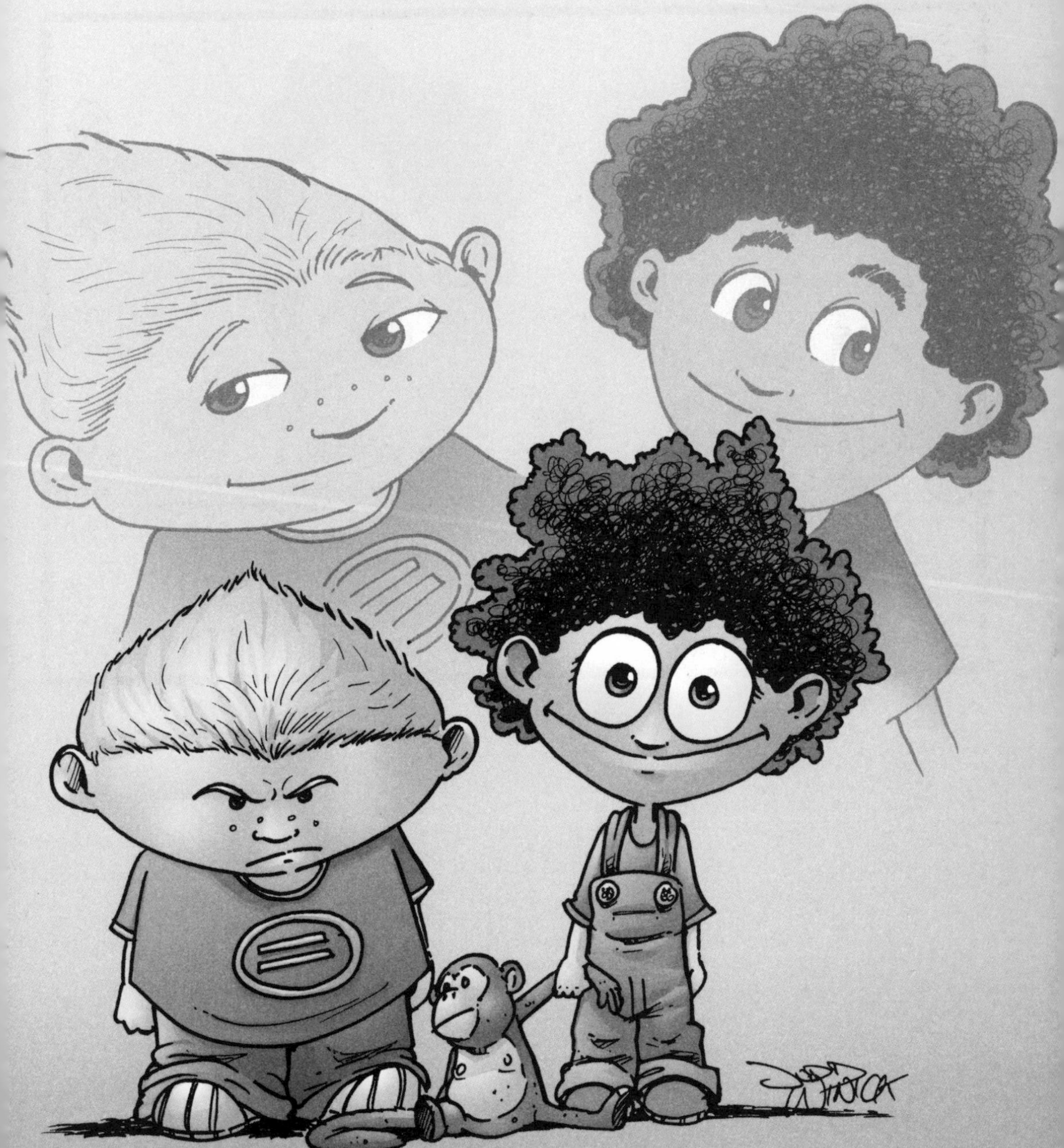

# "ADVENTURES IN BARRYSITTING"

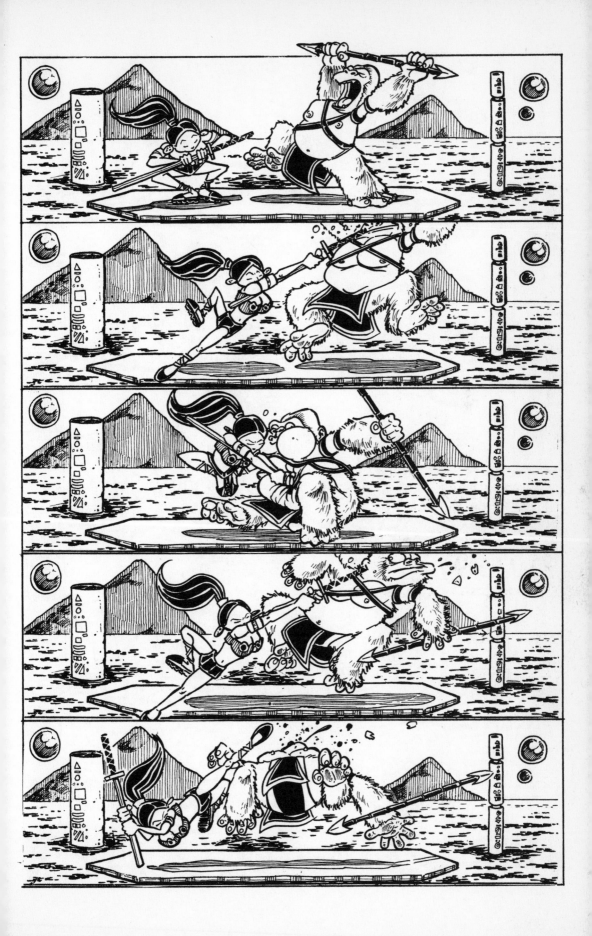

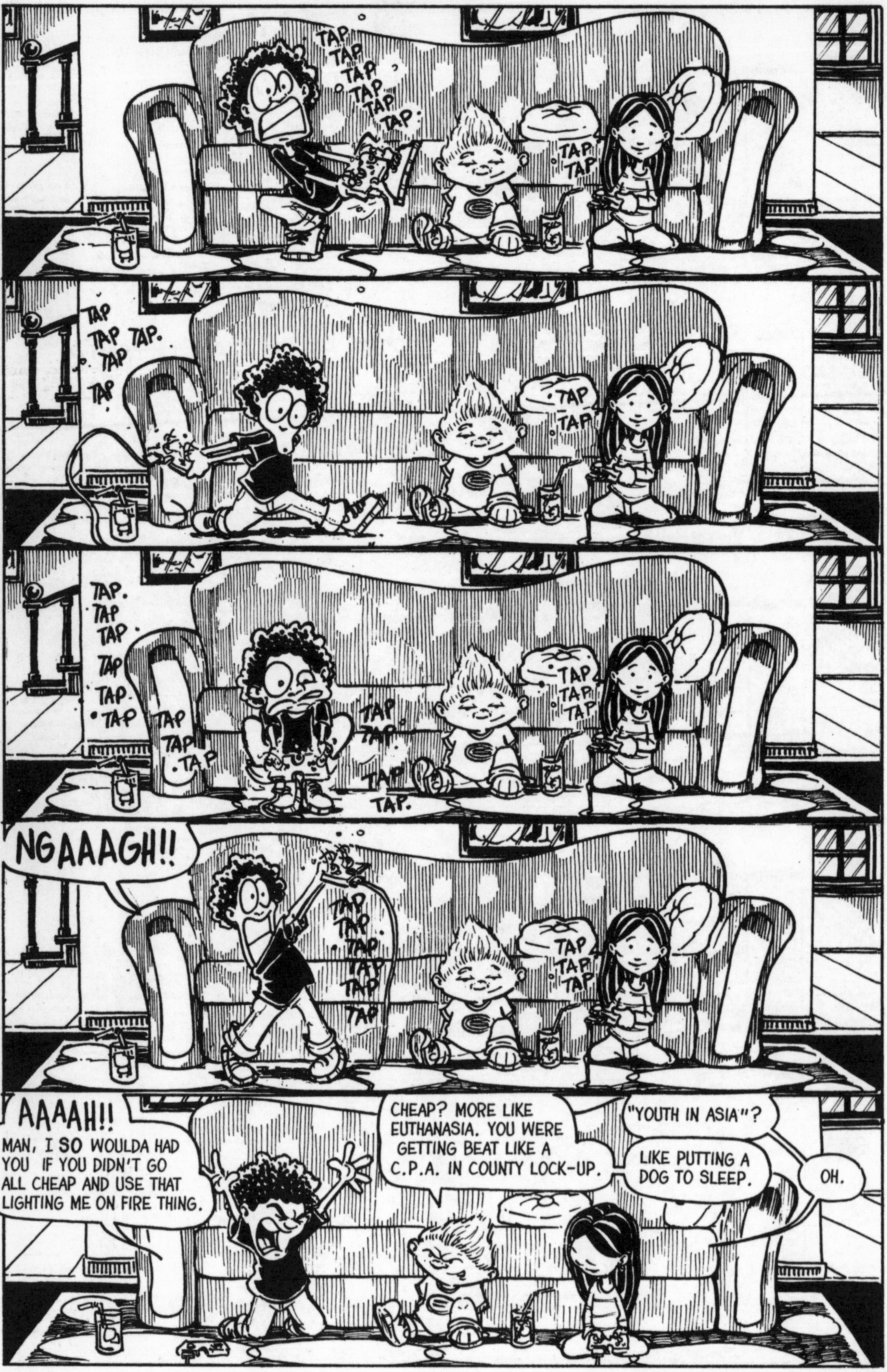

TAP TAP TAP TAP TAP TAP
TAP TAP
TAP TAP TAP. TAP TAP
TAP TAP
TAP. TAP TAP TAP TAP. TAP
TAP TAP TAP
TAP TAP
TAP TAP.
TAP TAP TAP
NGAAAGH!!
TAP TAP TAP TAP TAP TAP
TAP TAP TAP
AAAAH!!
MAN, I SO WOULDA HAD YOU IF YOU DIDN'T GO ALL CHEAP AND USE THAT LIGHTING ME ON FIRE THING.
CHEAP? MORE LIKE EUTHANASIA. YOU WERE GETTING BEAT LIKE A C.P.A. IN COUNTY LOCK-UP.
"YOUTH IN ASIA"?
LIKE PUTTING A DOG TO SLEEP.
OH.

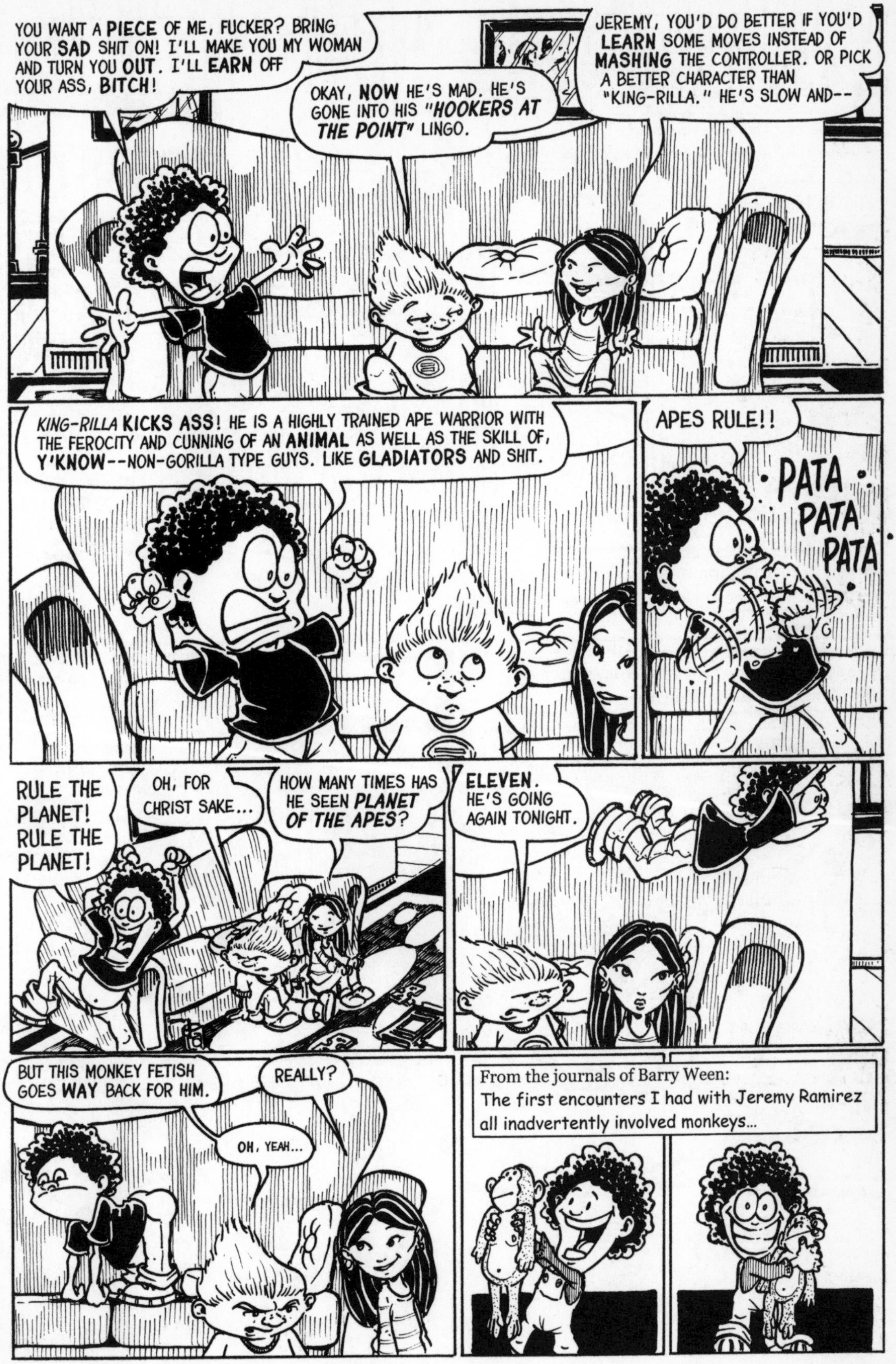
YOU WANT A PIECE OF ME, FUCKER? BRING YOUR SAD SHIT ON! I'LL MAKE YOU MY WOMAN AND TURN YOU OUT. I'LL EARN OFF YOUR ASS, BITCH!
OKAY, NOW HE'S MAD. HE'S GONE INTO HIS "HOOKERS AT THE POINT" LINGO.
JEREMY, YOU'D DO BETTER IF YOU'D LEARN SOME MOVES INSTEAD OF MASHING THE CONTROLLER. OR PICK A BETTER CHARACTER THAN "KING-RILLA." HE'S SLOW AND--
KING-RILLA KICKS ASS! HE IS A HIGHLY TRAINED APE WARRIOR WITH THE FEROCITY AND CUNNING OF AN ANIMAL AS WELL AS THE SKILL OF, Y'KNOW--NON-GORILLA TYPE GUYS. LIKE GLADIATORS AND SHIT.
APES RULE!!
PATA PATA PATA
RULE THE PLANET! RULE THE PLANET!
OH, FOR CHRIST SAKE...
HOW MANY TIMES HAS HE SEEN PLANET OF THE APES?
ELEVEN. HE'S GOING AGAIN TONIGHT.
BUT THIS MONKEY FETISH GOES WAY BACK FOR HIM.
REALLY?
OH, YEAH...
From the journals of Barry Ween:
The first encounters I had with Jeremy Ramirez all inadvertently involved monkeys...

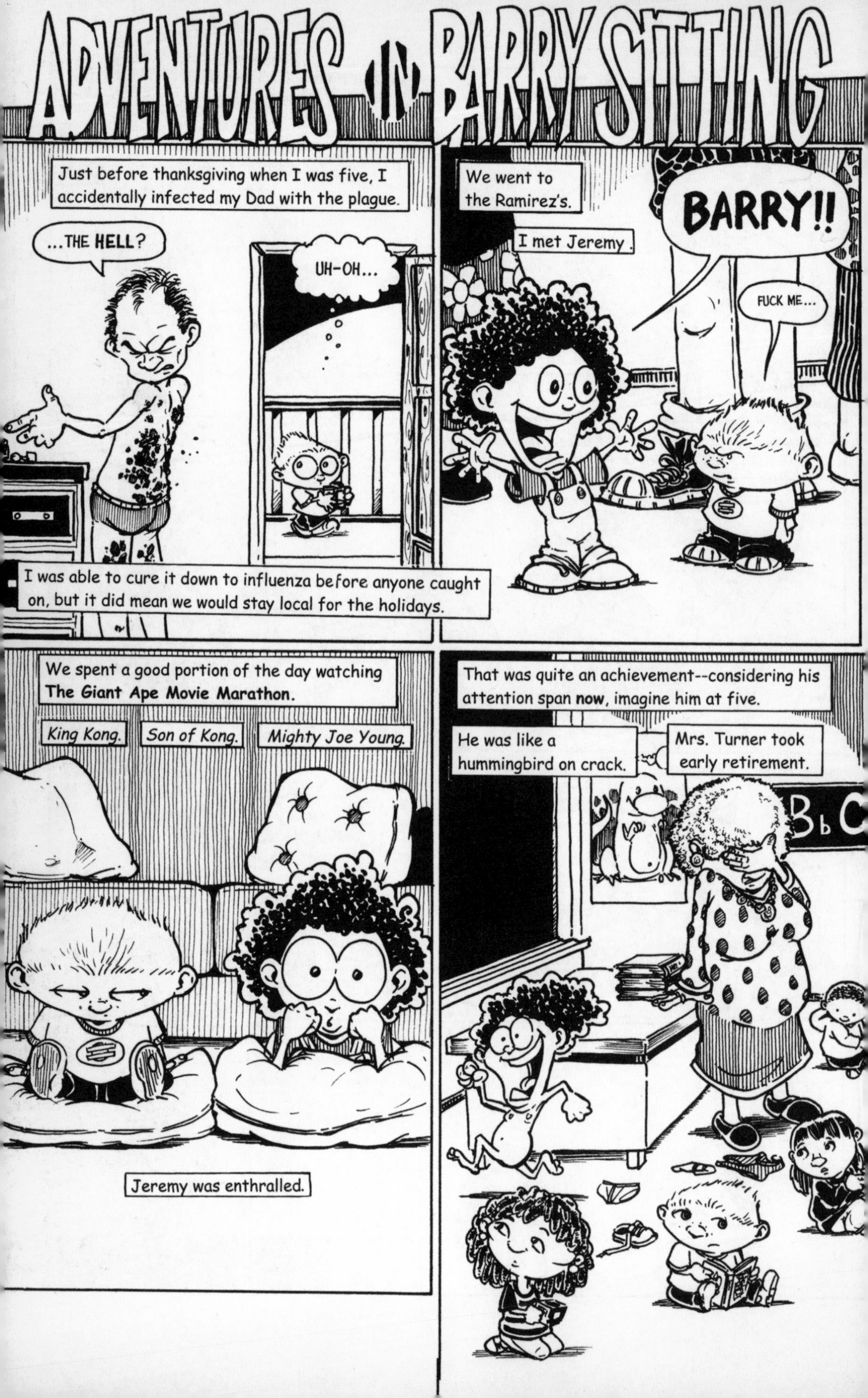
ADVENTURES IN BARRY SITTING
Just before thanksgiving when I was five, I accidentally infected my Dad with the plague.
...THE HELL?
UH-OH...
I was able to cure it down to influenza before anyone caught on, but it did mean we would stay local for the holidays.
We went to the Ramirez's.
I met Jeremy.
BARRY!!
FUCK ME...
We spent a good portion of the day watching The Giant Ape Movie Marathon.
King Kong.
Son of Kong.
Mighty Joe Young.
Jeremy was enthralled.
That was quite an achievement--considering his attention span now, imagine him at five.
He was like a hummingbird on crack.
Mrs. Turner took early retirement.
B b C

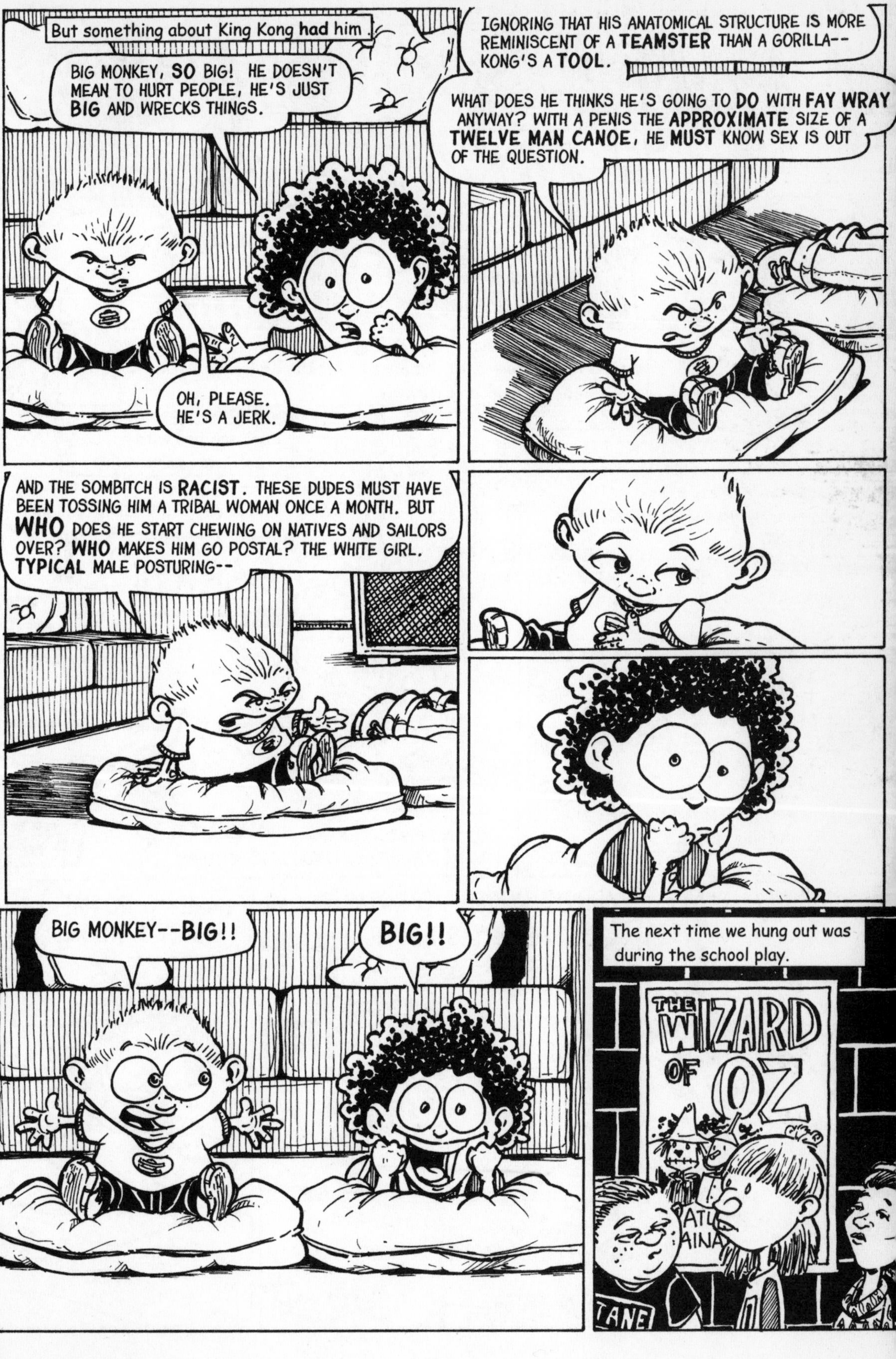
But something about King Kong had him
BIG MONKEY, SO BIG! HE DOESN'T MEAN TO HURT PEOPLE, HE'S JUST BIG AND WRECKS THINGS.
OH, PLEASE. HE'S A JERK.
IGNORING THAT HIS ANATOMICAL STRUCTURE IS MORE REMINISCENT OF A TEAMSTER THAN A GORILLA-- KONG'S A TOOL.
WHAT DOES HE THINKS HE'S GOING TO DO WITH FAY WRAY ANYWAY? WITH A PENIS THE APPROXIMATE SIZE OF A TWELVE MAN CANOE, HE MUST KNOW SEX IS OUT OF THE QUESTION.
AND THE SOMBITCH IS RACIST. THESE DUDES MUST HAVE BEEN TOSSING HIM A TRIBAL WOMAN ONCE A MONTH. BUT WHO DOES HE START CHEWING ON NATIVES AND SAILORS OVER? WHO MAKES HIM GO POSTAL? THE WHITE GIRL. TYPICAL MALE POSTURING--
BIG MONKEY--BIG!!
BIG!!
The next time we hung out was during the school play.
THE WIZARD OF OZ

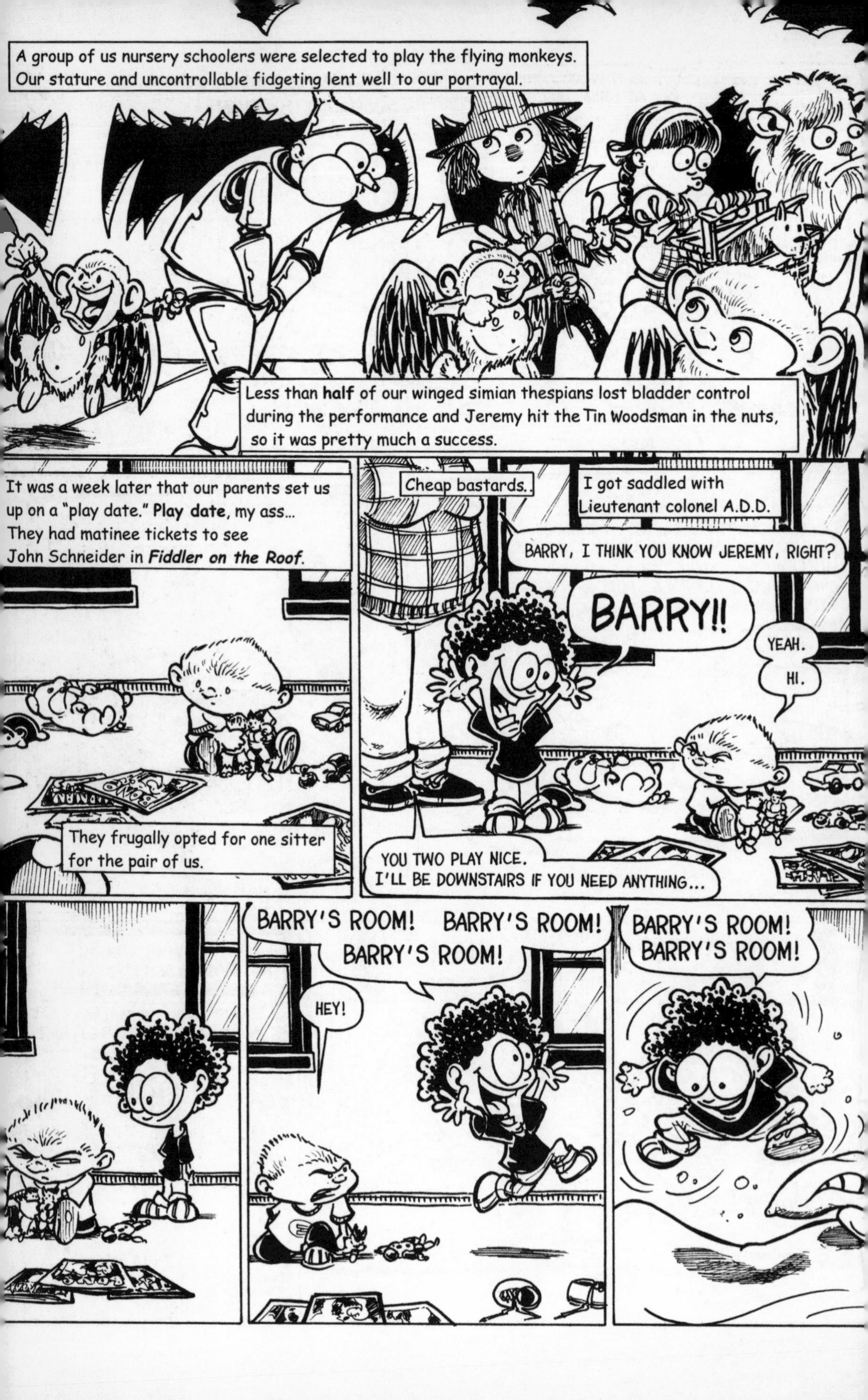
A group of us nursery schoolers were selected to play the flying monkeys.
Our stature and uncontrollable fidgeting lent well to our portrayal.
Less than **half** of our winged simian thespians lost bladder control during the performance and Jeremy hit the Tin Woodsman in the nuts, so it was pretty much a success.
It was a week later that our parents set us up on a "play date." **Play date**, my ass... They had matinee tickets to see John Schneider in ***Fiddler on the Roof***.
They frugally opted for one sitter for the pair of us.
Cheap bastards.
I got saddled with Lieutenant colonel A.D.D.
BARRY, I THINK YOU KNOW JEREMY, RIGHT?
BARRY!!
YEAH.
HI.
YOU TWO PLAY NICE.
I'LL BE DOWNSTAIRS IF YOU NEED ANYTHING...
BARRY'S ROOM! BARRY'S ROOM!
BARRY'S ROOM!
HEY!
BARRY'S ROOM!
BARRY'S ROOM!

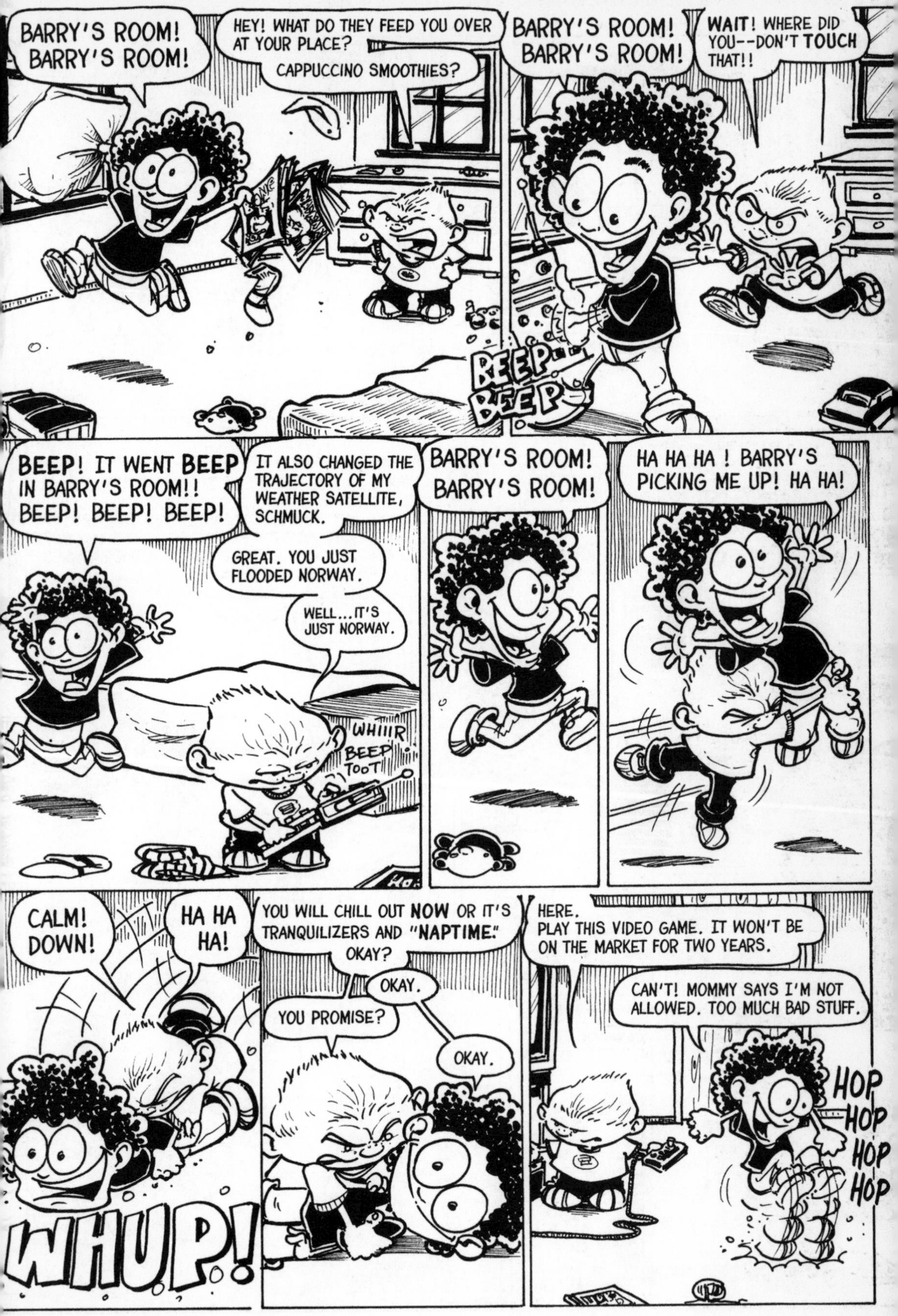
BARRY'S ROOM! BARRY'S ROOM!
HEY! WHAT DO THEY FEED YOU OVER AT YOUR PLACE?
CAPPUCCINO SMOOTHIES?
BARRY'S ROOM! BARRY'S ROOM!
WAIT! WHERE DID YOU--DON'T TOUCH THAT!!
BEEP BEEP
BEEP! IT WENT BEEP IN BARRY'S ROOM!! BEEP! BEEP! BEEP!
IT ALSO CHANGED THE TRAJECTORY OF MY WEATHER SATELLITE, SCHMUCK.
GREAT. YOU JUST FLOODED NORWAY.
WELL... IT'S JUST NORWAY.
WHIIIR
BEEP
TOOT
BARRY'S ROOM! BARRY'S ROOM!
HA HA HA ! BARRY'S PICKING ME UP! HA HA!
CALM! DOWN!
HA HA HA!
WHUP!
YOU WILL CHILL OUT NOW OR IT'S TRANQUILIZERS AND "NAPTIME." OKAY?
OKAY.
YOU PROMISE?
OKAY.
HERE. PLAY THIS VIDEO GAME. IT WON'T BE ON THE MARKET FOR TWO YEARS.
CAN'T! MOMMY SAYS I'M NOT ALLOWED. TOO MUCH BAD STUFF.
HOP
HOP
HOP
HOP

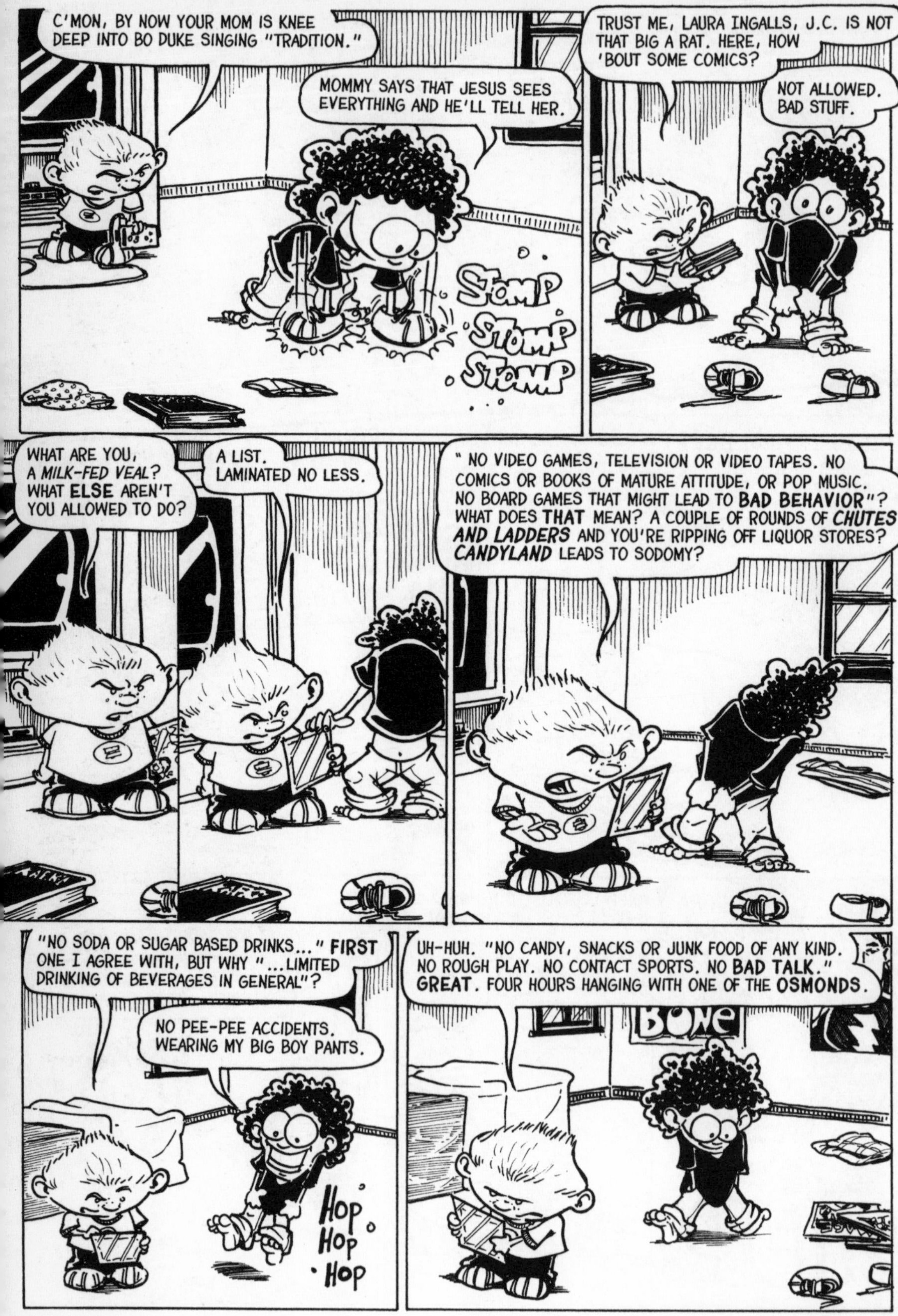

C'MON, BY NOW YOUR MOM IS KNEE DEEP INTO BO DUKE SINGING "TRADITION."
MOMMY SAYS THAT JESUS SEES EVERYTHING AND HE'LL TELL HER.
STOMP
STOMP
STOMP
TRUST ME, LAURA INGALLS, J.C. IS NOT THAT BIG A RAT. HERE, HOW 'BOUT SOME COMICS?
NOT ALLOWED. BAD STUFF.
WHAT ARE YOU, A *MILK-FED VEAL*? WHAT **ELSE** AREN'T YOU ALLOWED TO DO?
A LIST. LAMINATED NO LESS.
" NO VIDEO GAMES, TELEVISION OR VIDEO TAPES. NO COMICS OR BOOKS OF MATURE ATTITUDE, OR POP MUSIC. NO BOARD GAMES THAT MIGHT LEAD TO **BAD BEHAVIOR**"? WHAT DOES **THAT** MEAN? A COUPLE OF ROUNDS OF ***CHUTES AND LADDERS*** AND YOU'RE RIPPING OFF LIQUOR STORES? ***CANDYLAND*** LEADS TO SODOMY?
"NO SODA OR SUGAR BASED DRINKS..." **FIRST** ONE I AGREE WITH, BUT WHY "...LIMITED DRINKING OF BEVERAGES IN GENERAL"?
NO PEE-PEE ACCIDENTS. WEARING MY BIG BOY PANTS.
HOP
HOP
HOP
UH-HUH. "NO CANDY, SNACKS OR JUNK FOOD OF ANY KIND. NO ROUGH PLAY. NO CONTACT SPORTS. NO **BAD TALK**." **GREAT**. FOUR HOURS HANGING WITH ONE OF THE **OSMONDS**.
BONE

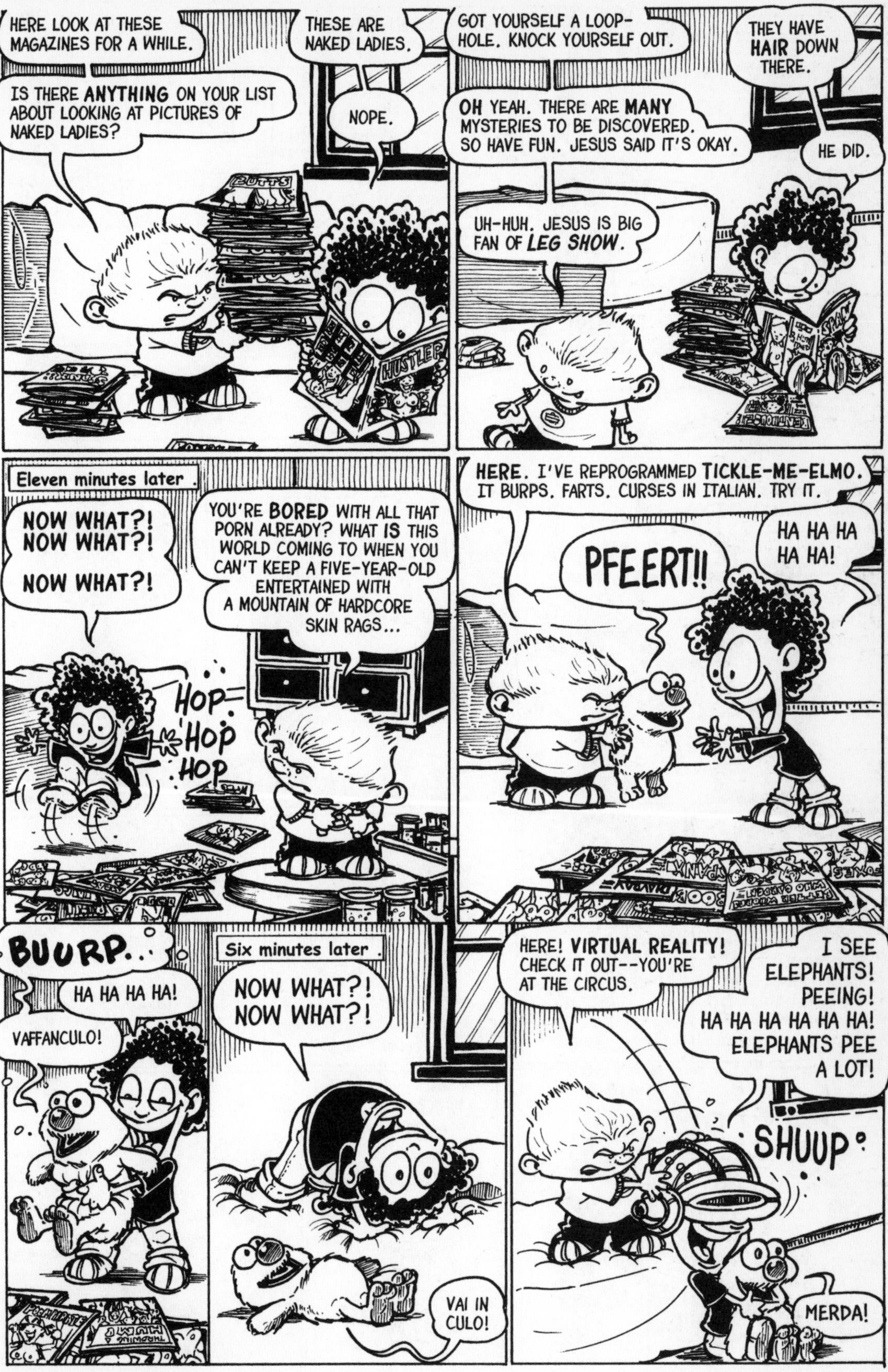
HERE LOOK AT THESE MAGAZINES FOR A WHILE.
IS THERE ANYTHING ON YOUR LIST ABOUT LOOKING AT PICTURES OF NAKED LADIES?
THESE ARE NAKED LADIES.
NOPE.
HUSTLER
GOT YOURSELF A LOOP-HOLE. KNOCK YOURSELF OUT.
OH YEAH. THERE ARE MANY MYSTERIES TO BE DISCOVERED. SO HAVE FUN. JESUS SAID IT'S OKAY.
THEY HAVE HAIR DOWN THERE.
HE DID.
UH-HUH. JESUS IS BIG FAN OF LEG SHOW.
Eleven minutes later.
NOW WHAT?! NOW WHAT?!
NOW WHAT?!
YOU'RE BORED WITH ALL THAT PORN ALREADY? WHAT IS THIS WORLD COMING TO WHEN YOU CAN'T KEEP A FIVE-YEAR-OLD ENTERTAINED WITH A MOUNTAIN OF HARDCORE SKIN RAGS...
HOP HOP HOP
HERE. I'VE REPROGRAMMED TICKLE-ME-ELMO. IT BURPS. FARTS. CURSES IN ITALIAN. TRY IT.
PFEERT!!
HA HA HA HA HA!
BUURP...
HA HA HA HA!
VAFFANCULO!
Six minutes later.
NOW WHAT?! NOW WHAT?!
VAI IN CULO!
HERE! VIRTUAL REALITY! CHECK IT OUT--YOU'RE AT THE CIRCUS.
I SEE ELEPHANTS! PEEING! HA HA HA HA HA HA! ELEPHANTS PEE A LOT!
SHUUP
MERDA!

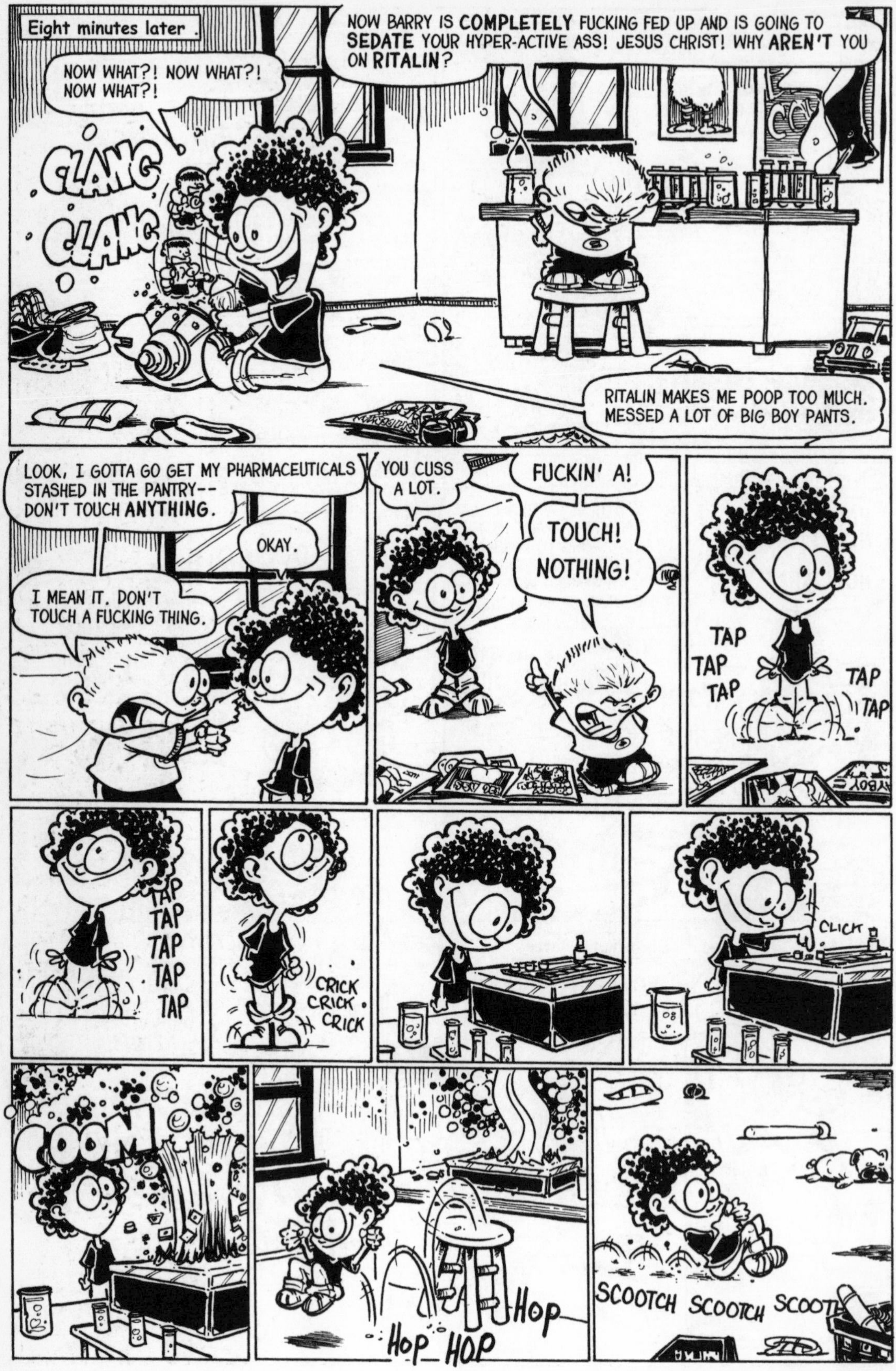
Eight minutes later.
NOW WHAT?! NOW WHAT?! NOW WHAT?!
NOW BARRY IS COMPLETELY FUCKING FED UP AND IS GOING TO SEDATE YOUR HYPER-ACTIVE ASS! JESUS CHRIST! WHY AREN'T YOU ON RITALIN?
CLANG
CLANG
RITALIN MAKES ME POOP TOO MUCH. MESSED A LOT OF BIG BOY PANTS.
LOOK, I GOTTA GO GET MY PHARMACEUTICALS STASHED IN THE PANTRY-- DON'T TOUCH ANYTHING.
OKAY.
I MEAN IT. DON'T TOUCH A FUCKING THING.
YOU CUSS A LOT.
FUCKIN' A!
TOUCH! NOTHING!
TAP TAP TAP TAP TAP
TAP TAP TAP TAP TAP
CRICK CRICK CRICK
CLICK
COOM
HOP HOP HOP
SCOOTCH SCOOTCH SCOOT

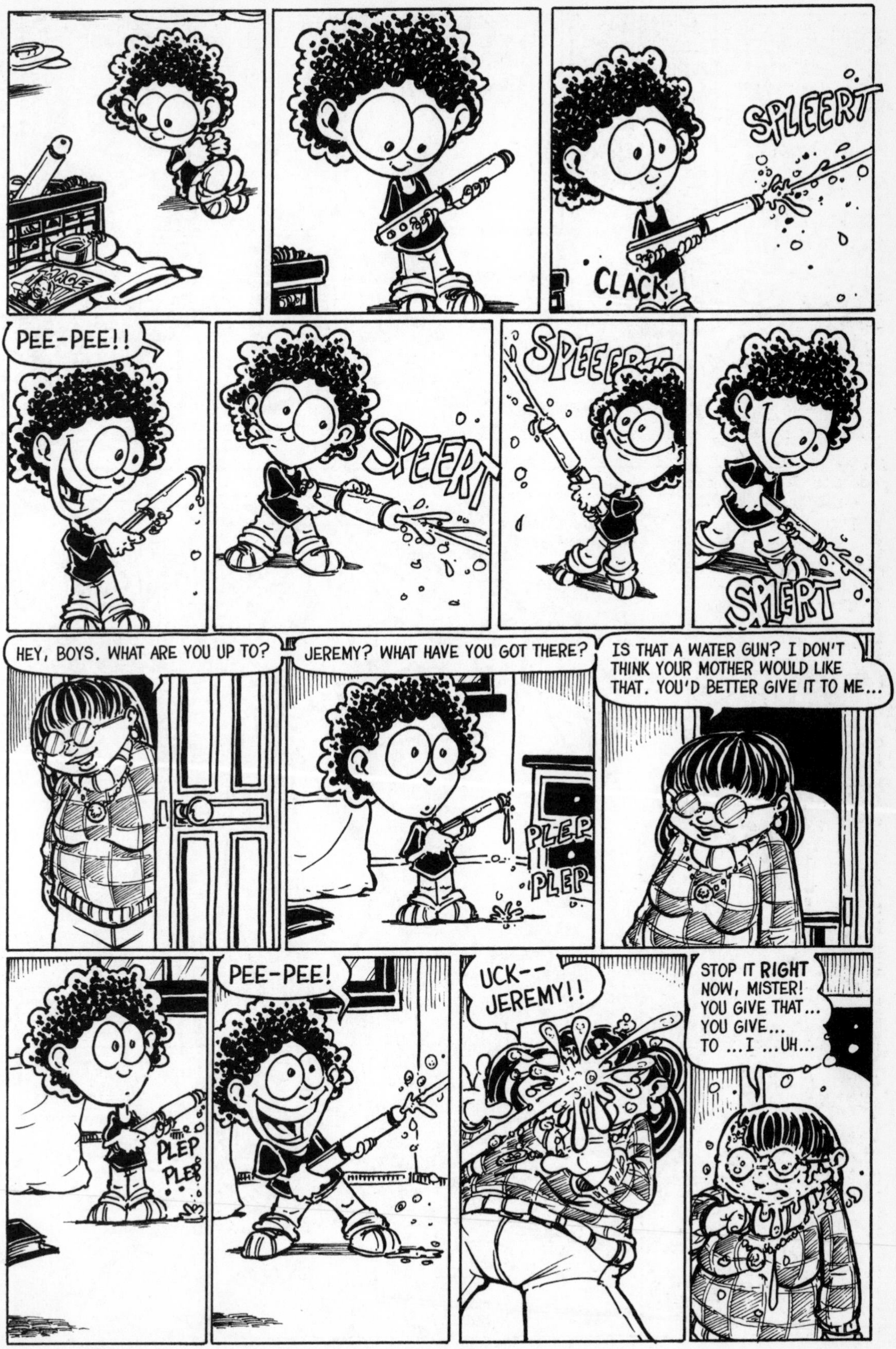
CLACK
SPLEERT
PEE-PEE!!
SPEERT
SPEEERT
SPLERT
HEY, BOYS. WHAT ARE YOU UP TO?
JEREMY? WHAT HAVE YOU GOT THERE?
PLEP
PLEP
IS THAT A WATER GUN? I DON'T THINK YOUR MOTHER WOULD LIKE THAT. YOU'D BETTER GIVE IT TO ME...
PLEP
PLEP
PEE-PEE!
UCK-- JEREMY!!
STOP IT **RIGHT** NOW, MISTER! YOU GIVE THAT... YOU GIVE... TO ... I ... UH...

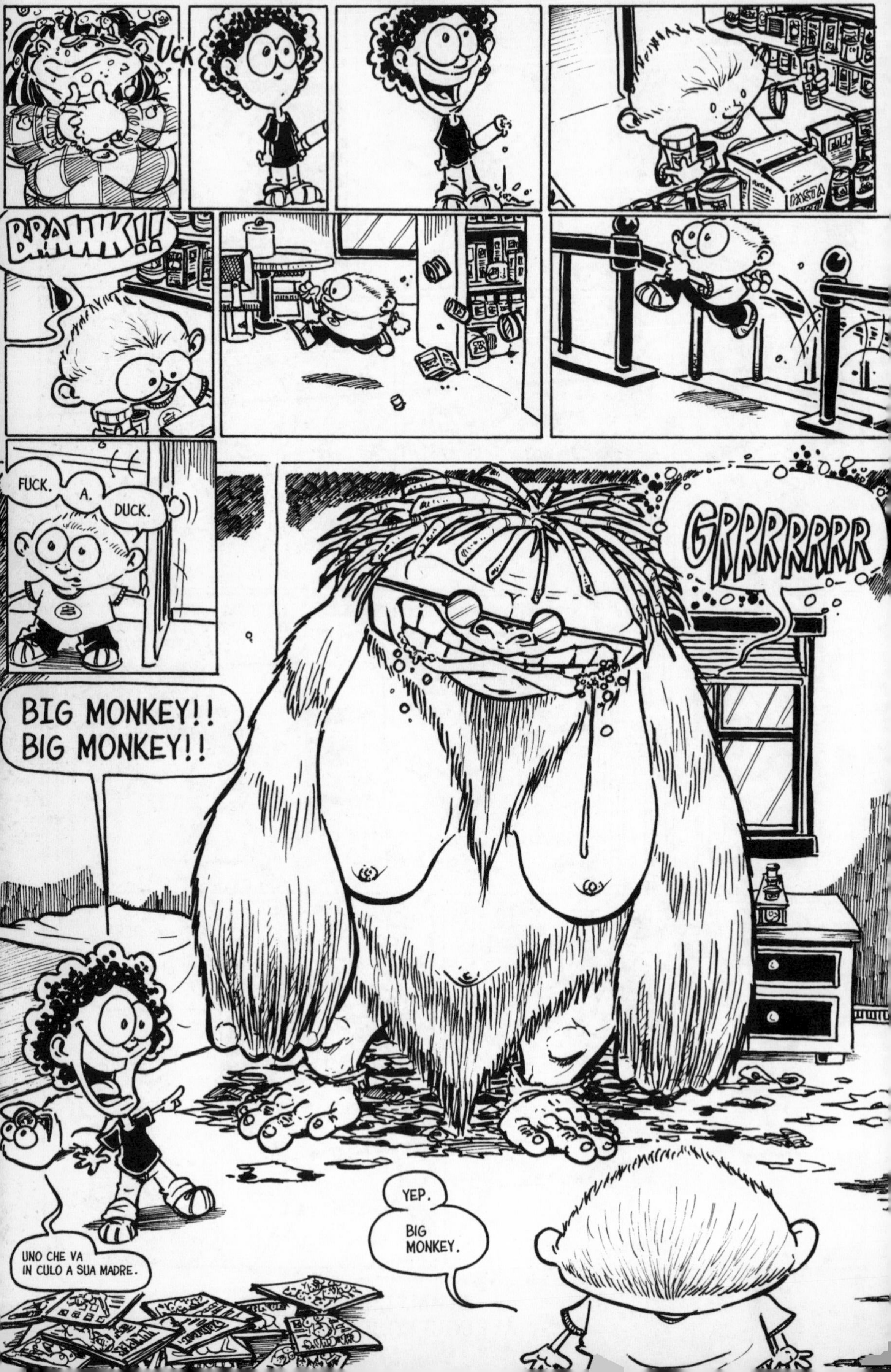
UCK
BRAWK!!
FUCK.
A.
DUCK.
GRRRRRRR
BIG MONKEY!!
BIG MONKEY!!
UNO CHE VA
IN CULO A SUA MADRE.
YEP.
BIG
MONKEY.

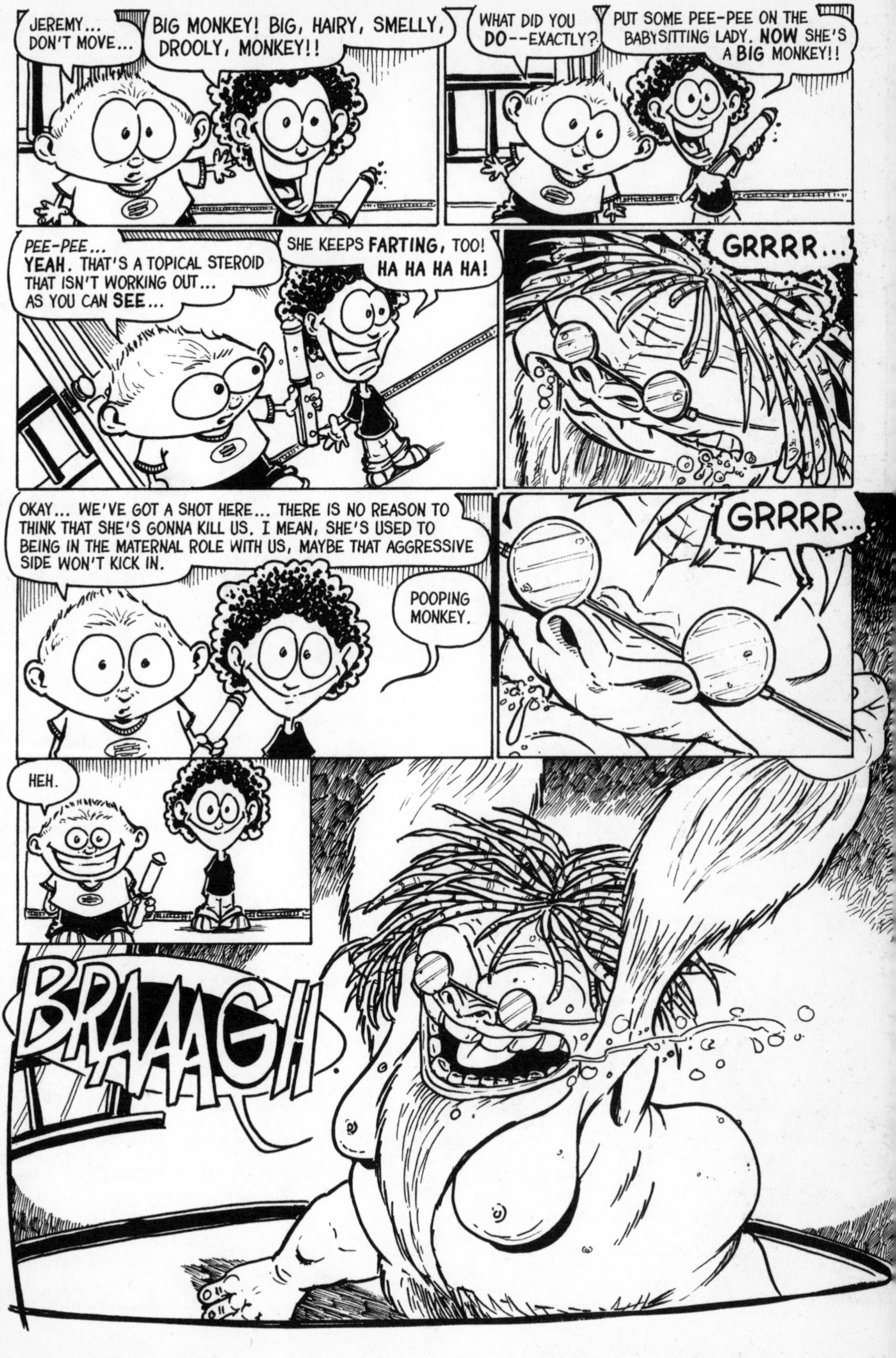

JEREMY... DON'T MOVE...
BIG MONKEY! BIG, HAIRY, SMELLY, DROOLY, MONKEY!!
WHAT DID YOU DO--EXACTLY?
PUT SOME PEE-PEE ON THE BABYSITTING LADY. NOW SHE'S A BIG MONKEY!!
PEE-PEE... YEAH. THAT'S A TOPICAL STEROID THAT ISN'T WORKING OUT... AS YOU CAN SEE...
SHE KEEPS FARTING, TOO! HA HA HA HA!
GRRRR...
OKAY... WE'VE GOT A SHOT HERE... THERE IS NO REASON TO THINK THAT SHE'S GONNA KILL US. I MEAN, SHE'S USED TO BEING IN THE MATERNAL ROLE WITH US, MAYBE THAT AGGRESSIVE SIDE WON'T KICK IN.
POOPING MONKEY.
GRRRR...
HEH.
BRAAAGH

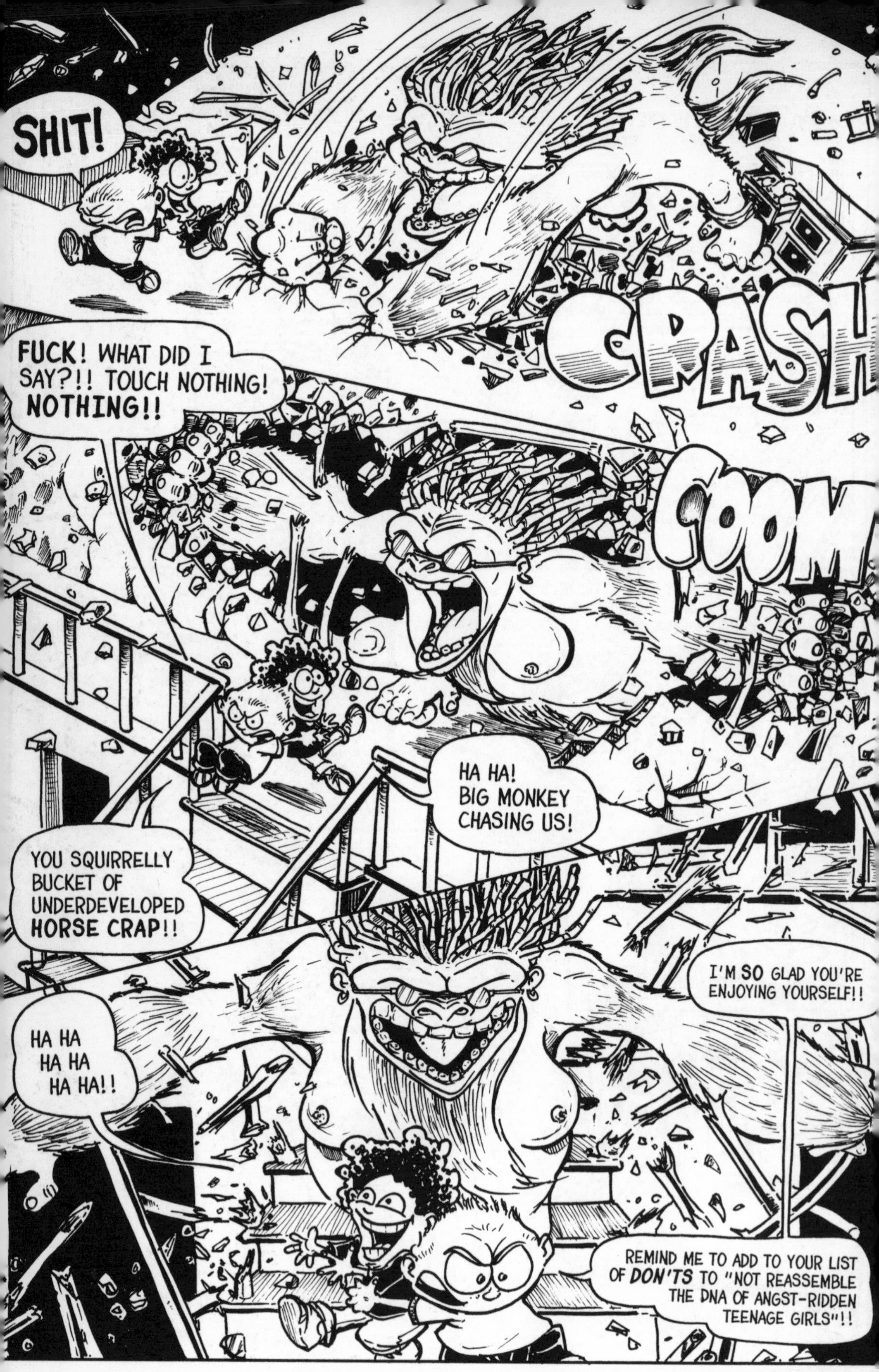
SHIT!
CRASH
FUCK! WHAT DID I SAY?!! TOUCH NOTHING! NOTHING!!
COOM
HA HA! BIG MONKEY CHASING US!
YOU SQUIRRELLY BUCKET OF UNDERDEVELOPED HORSE CRAP!!
I'M SO GLAD YOU'RE ENJOYING YOURSELF!!
HA HA HA HA HA HA!!
REMIND ME TO ADD TO YOUR LIST OF DON'TS TO "NOT REASSEMBLE THE DNA OF ANGST-RIDDEN TEENAGE GIRLS"!!

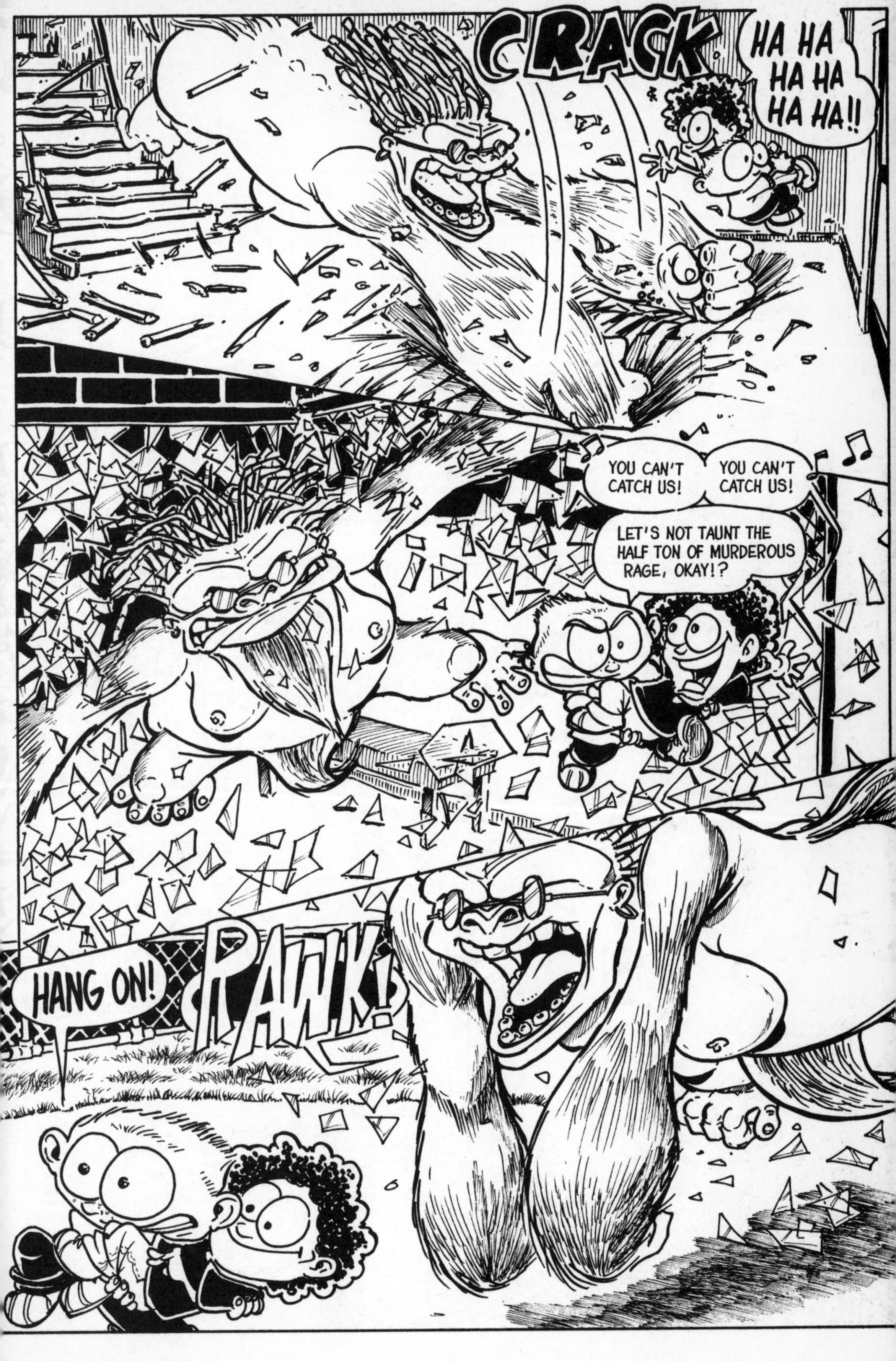
CRACK
HA HA HA HA HA HA!!
YOU CAN'T CATCH US!
YOU CAN'T CATCH US!
LET'S NOT TAUNT THE HALF TON OF MURDEROUS RAGE, OKAY!?
HANG ON!
PANK!

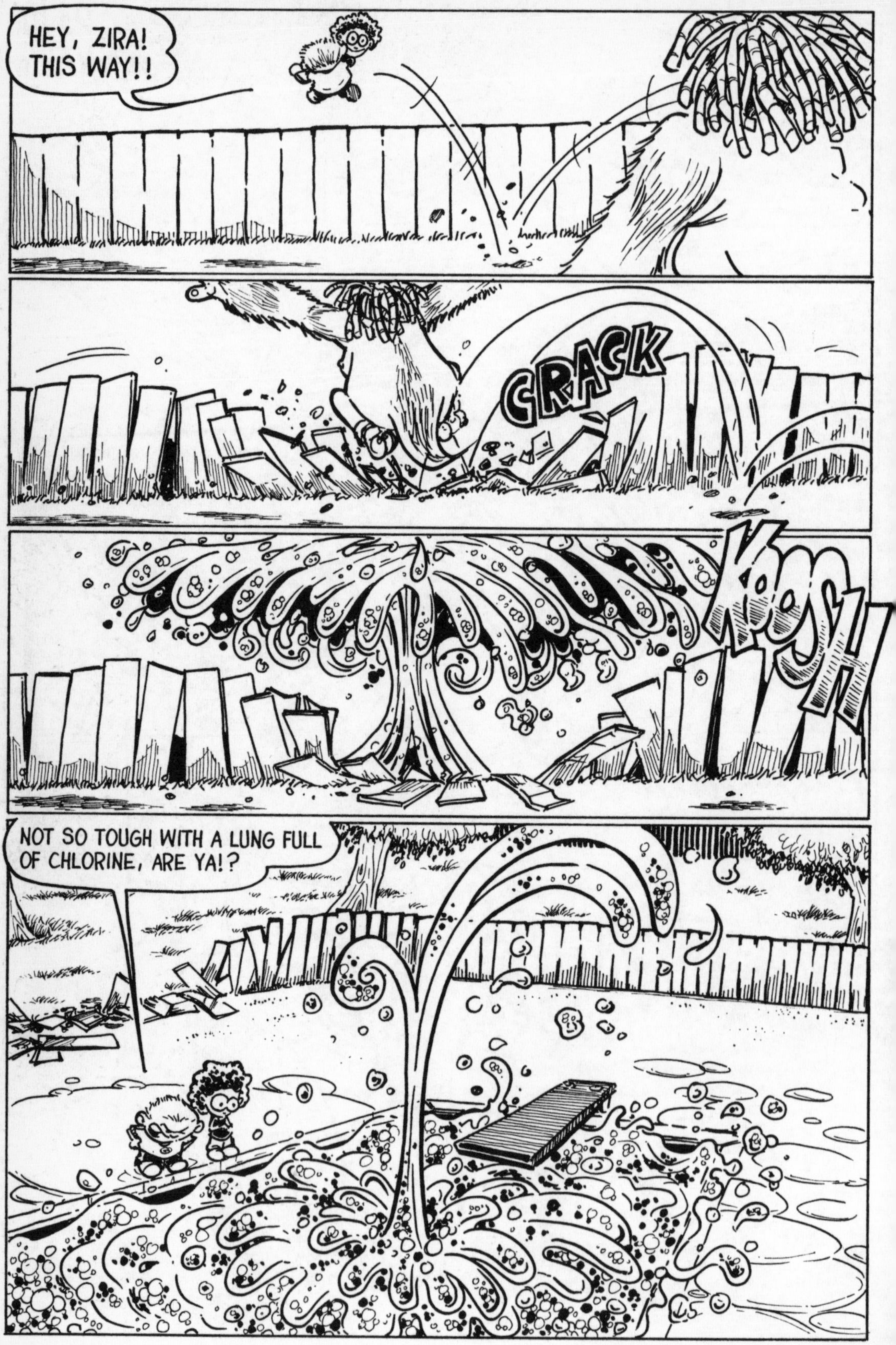
HEY, ZIRA! THIS WAY!!
CRACK
KOOSH
NOT SO TOUGH WITH A LUNG FULL OF CHLORINE, ARE YA!?

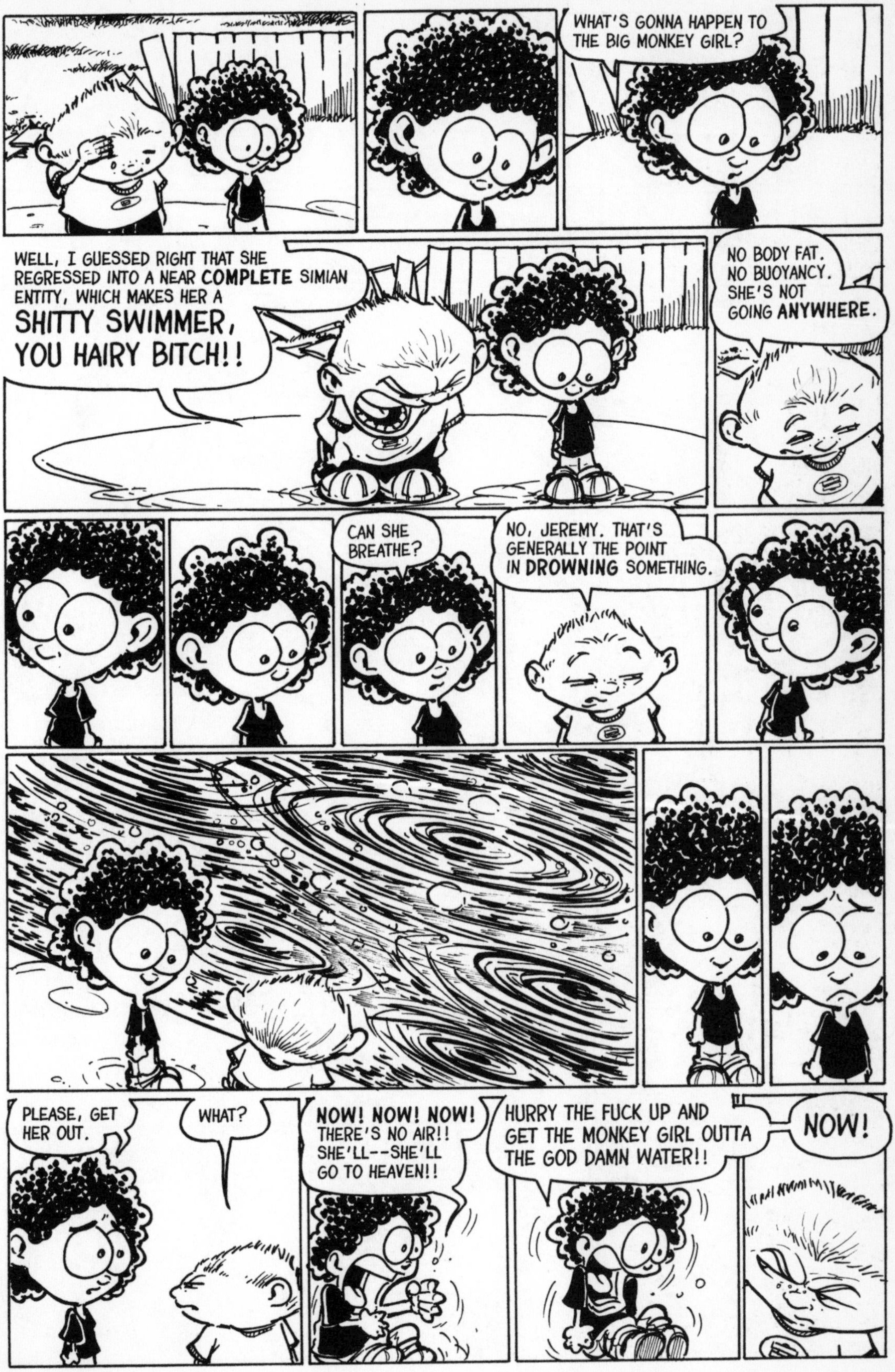
WHAT'S GONNA HAPPEN TO THE BIG MONKEY GIRL?
WELL, I GUESSED RIGHT THAT SHE REGRESSED INTO A NEAR COMPLETE SIMIAN ENTITY, WHICH MAKES HER A SHITTY SWIMMER, YOU HAIRY BITCH!!
NO BODY FAT. NO BUOYANCY. SHE'S NOT GOING ANYWHERE.
CAN SHE BREATHE?
NO, JEREMY. THAT'S GENERALLY THE POINT IN DROWNING SOMETHING.
PLEASE, GET HER OUT.
WHAT?
NOW! NOW! NOW! THERE'S NO AIR!! SHE'LL--SHE'LL GO TO HEAVEN!!
HURRY THE FUCK UP AND GET THE MONKEY GIRL OUTTA THE GOD DAMN WATER!!
NOW!

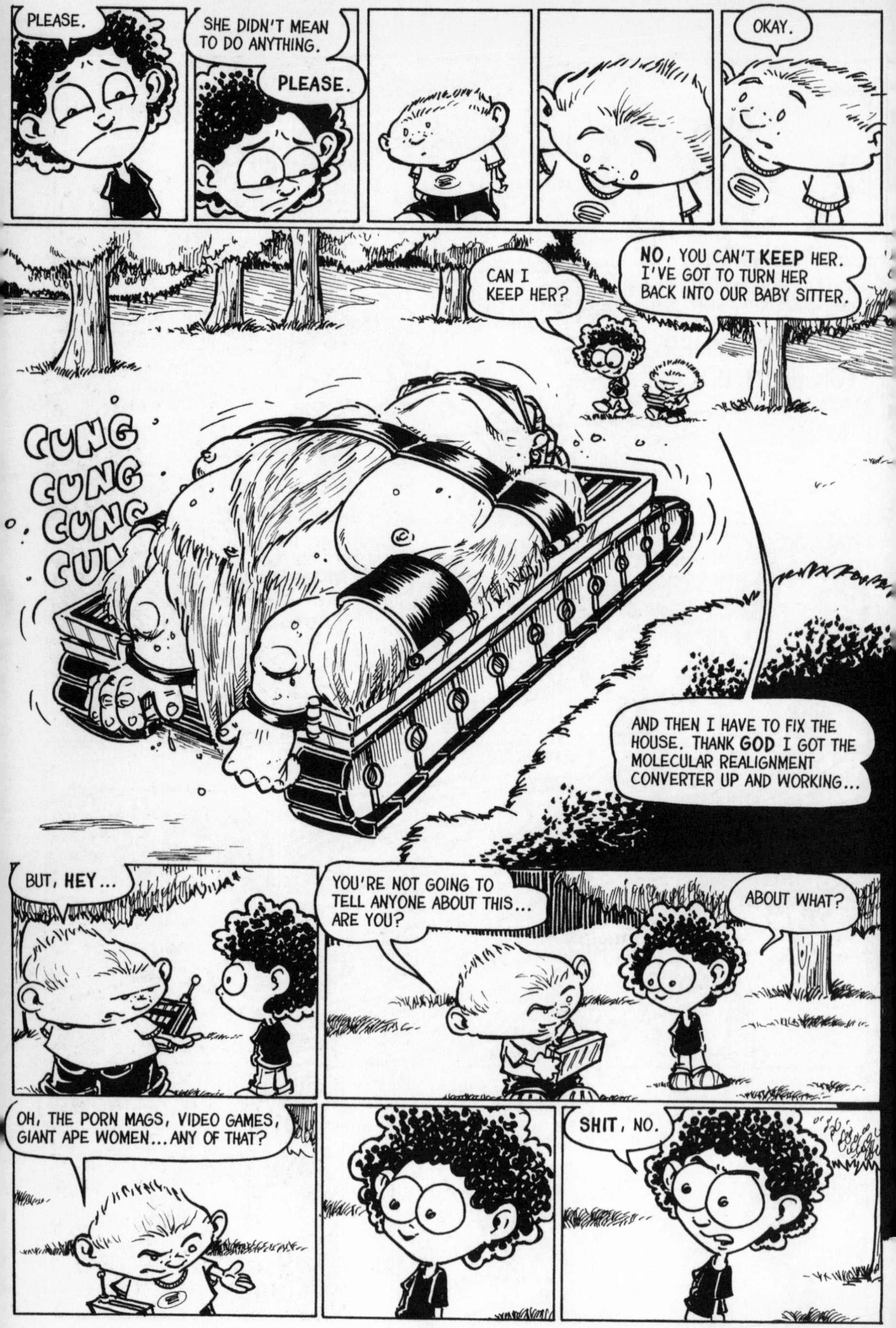
PLEASE.
SHE DIDN'T MEAN TO DO ANYTHING.
PLEASE.
OKAY.
CAN I KEEP HER?
NO, YOU CAN'T KEEP HER. I'VE GOT TO TURN HER BACK INTO OUR BABY SITTER.
GUNG GUNG GUNG GU
AND THEN I HAVE TO FIX THE HOUSE. THANK GOD I GOT THE MOLECULAR REALIGNMENT CONVERTER UP AND WORKING...
BUT, HEY...
YOU'RE NOT GOING TO TELL ANYONE ABOUT THIS... ARE YOU?
ABOUT WHAT?
OH, THE PORN MAGS, VIDEO GAMES, GIANT APE WOMEN... ANY OF THAT?
SHIT, NO.

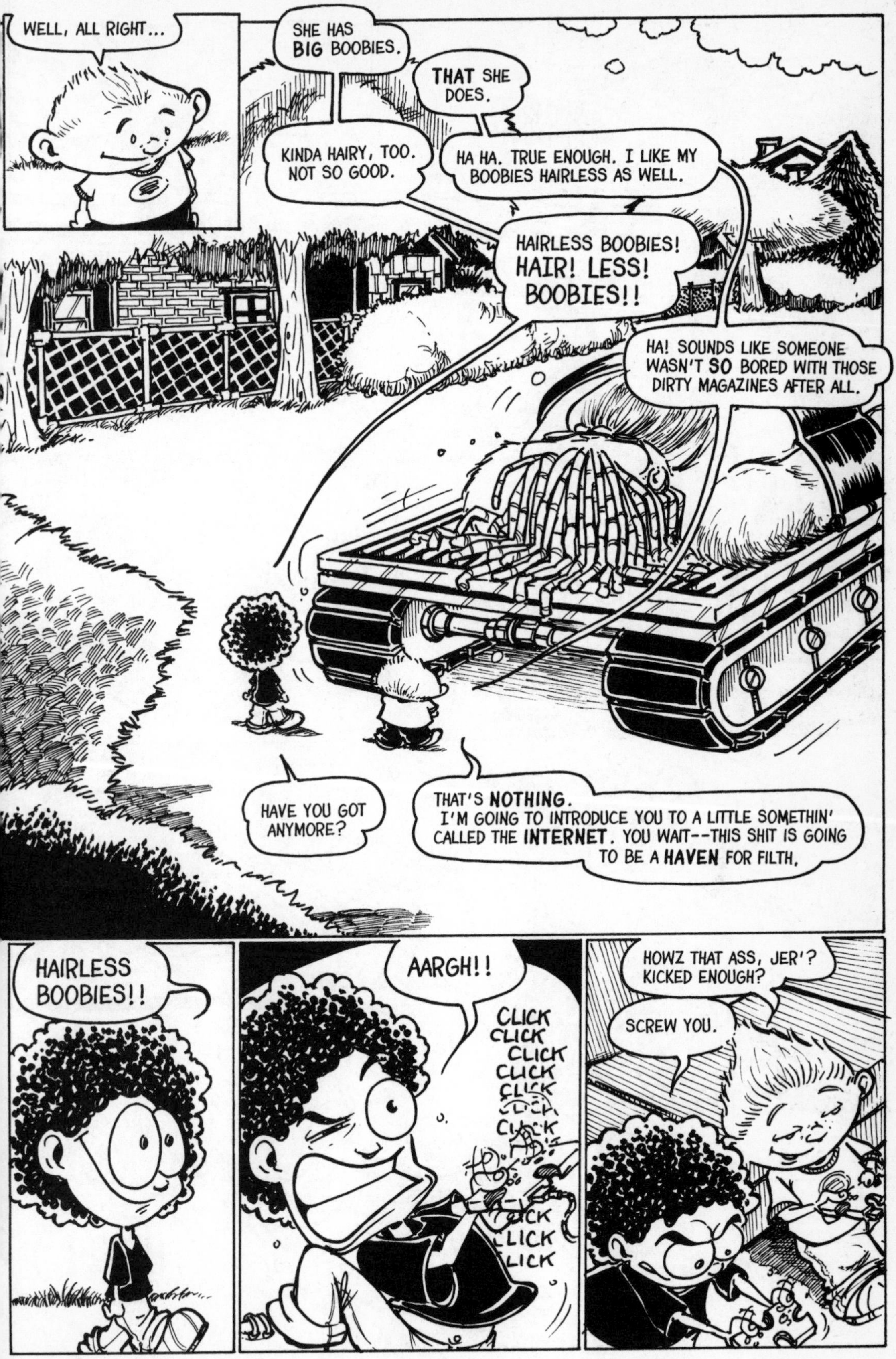
WELL, ALL RIGHT...
SHE HAS BIG BOOBIES.
THAT SHE DOES.
KINDA HAIRY, TOO. NOT SO GOOD.
HA HA. TRUE ENOUGH. I LIKE MY BOOBIES HAIRLESS AS WELL.
HAIRLESS BOOBIES! HAIR! LESS! BOOBIES!!
HA! SOUNDS LIKE SOMEONE WASN'T SO BORED WITH THOSE DIRTY MAGAZINES AFTER ALL.
HAVE YOU GOT ANYMORE?
THAT'S NOTHING. I'M GOING TO INTRODUCE YOU TO A LITTLE SOMETHIN' CALLED THE INTERNET. YOU WAIT--THIS SHIT IS GOING TO BE A HAVEN FOR FILTH.
HAIRLESS BOOBIES!!
AARGH!!
CLICK CLICK CLICK CLICK
HOWZ THAT ASS, JER'? KICKED ENOUGH?
SCREW YOU.

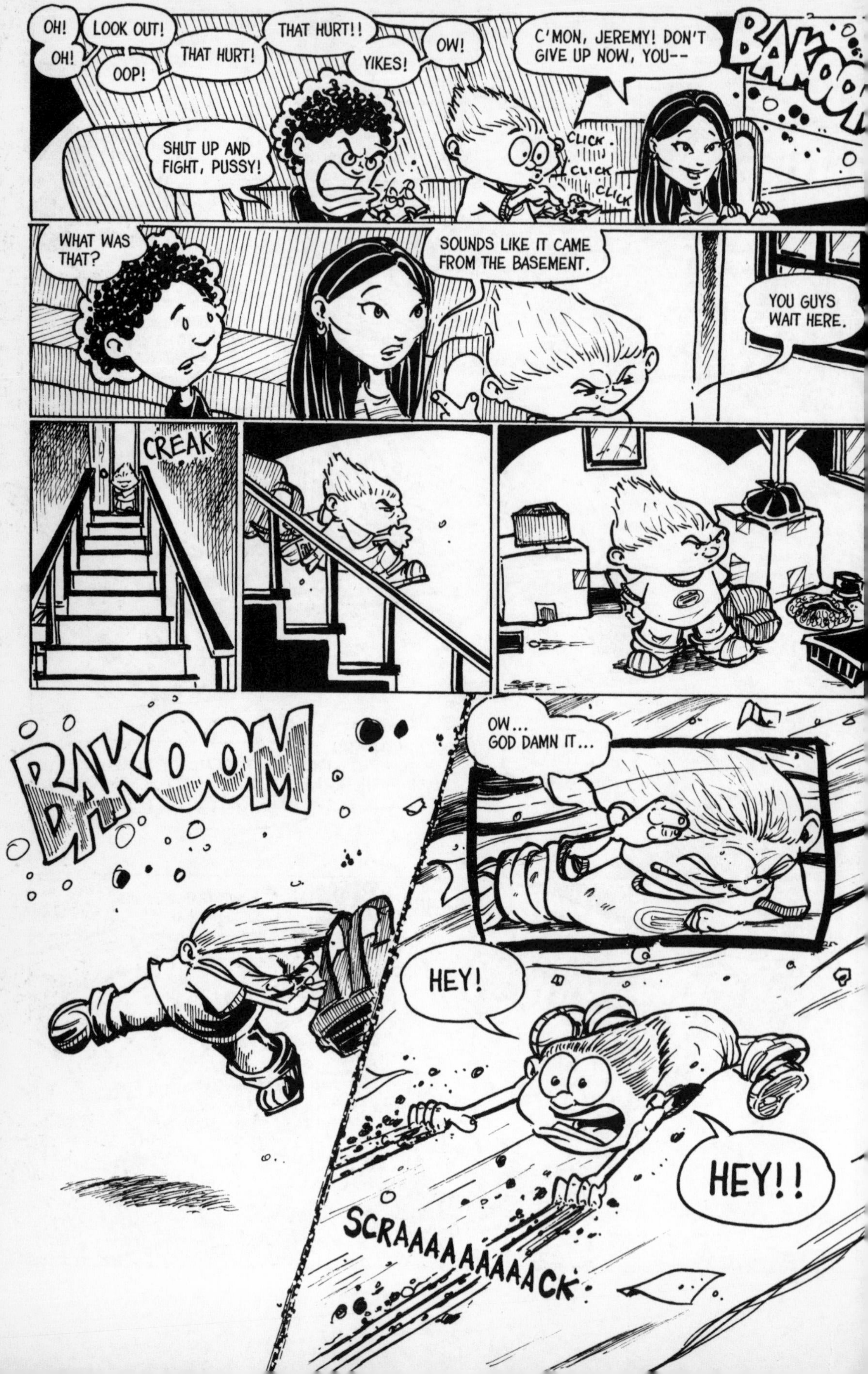
OH!
OH!
LOOK OUT!
OOP!
THAT HURT!
THAT HURT!!
YIKES!
OW!
SHUT UP AND FIGHT, PUSSY!
C'MON, JEREMY! DON'T GIVE UP NOW, YOU--
CLICK
CLICK
CLICK
BAKOOM
WHAT WAS THAT?
SOUNDS LIKE IT CAME FROM THE BASEMENT.
YOU GUYS WAIT HERE.
CREAK
BAKOOM
OW... GOD DAMN IT...
HEY!
HEY!!
SCRAAAAAAAAACK

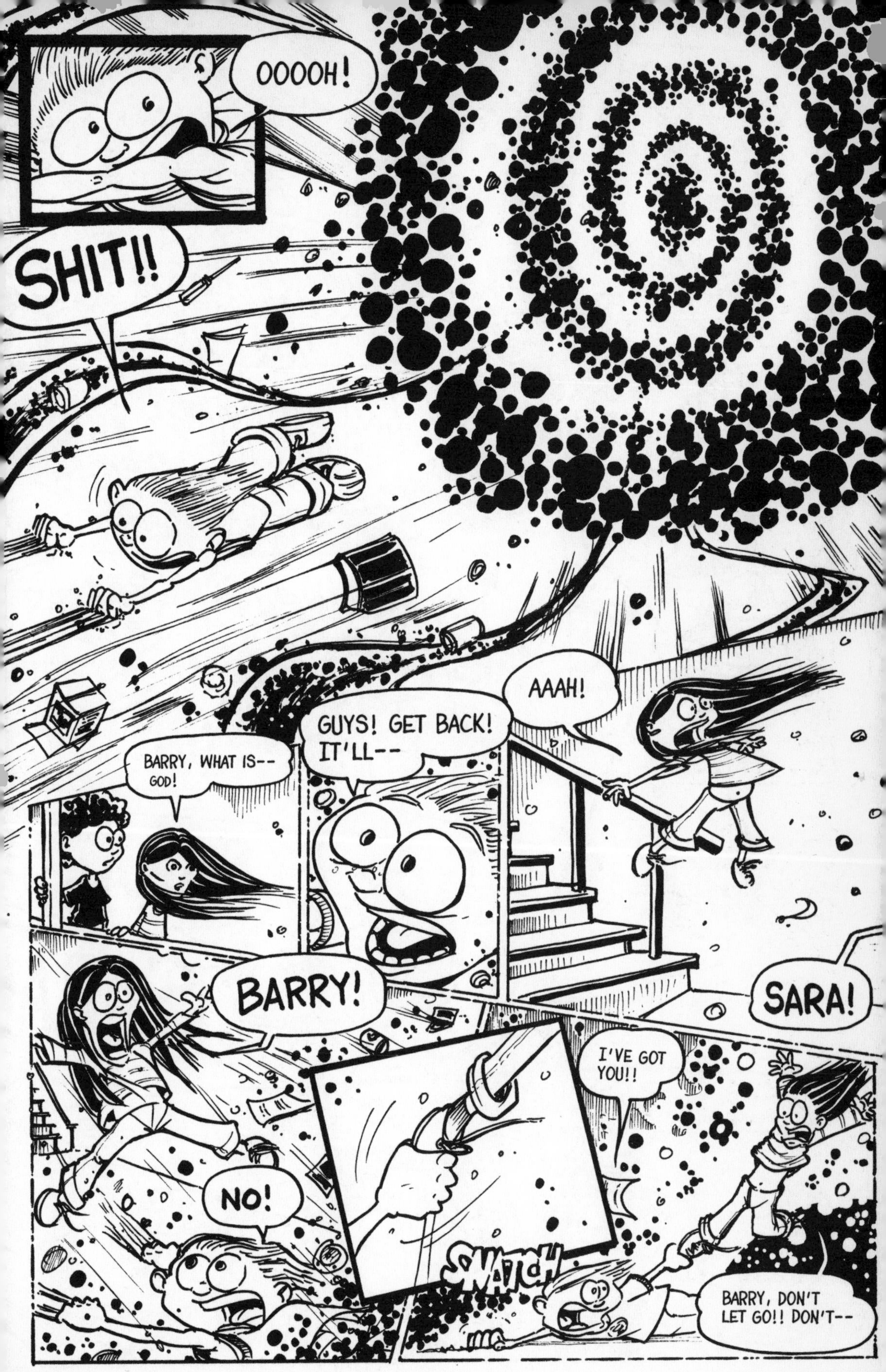
OOOOH!
SHIT!!
AAAH!
GUYS! GET BACK! IT'LL--
BARRY, WHAT IS-- GOD!
BARRY!
SARA!
I'VE GOT YOU!!
NO!
SNATCH
BARRY, DON'T LET GO!! DON'T--

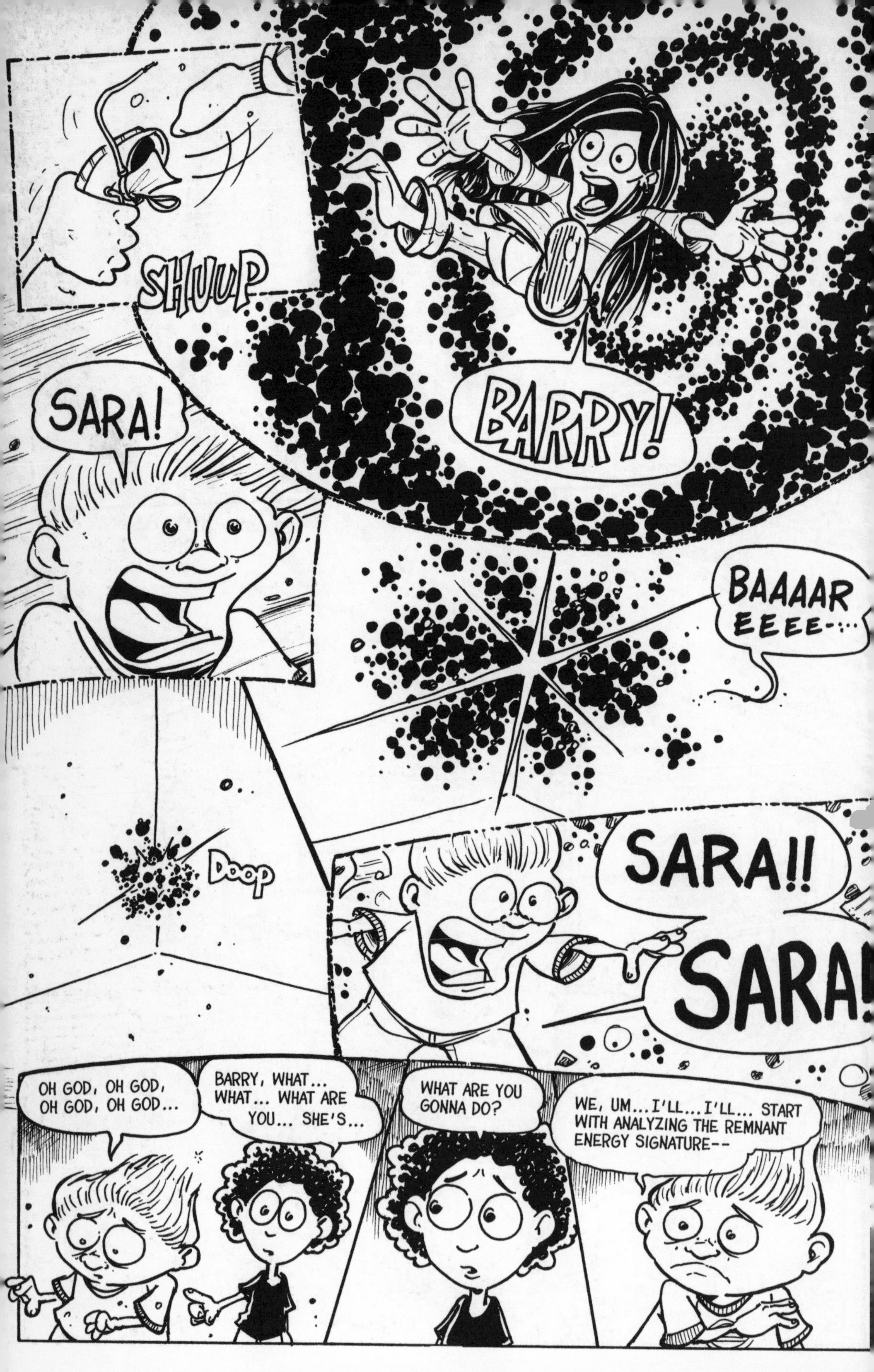
SHUUP
BARRY!
SARA!
BAAAAR EEEE-...
Doop
SARA!!
SARA!
OH GOD, OH GOD, OH GOD, OH GOD...
BARRY, WHAT... WHAT... WHAT ARE YOU... SHE'S...
WHAT ARE YOU GONNA DO?
WE, UM... I'LL... I'LL... START WITH ANALYZING THE REMNANT ENERGY SIGNATURE--

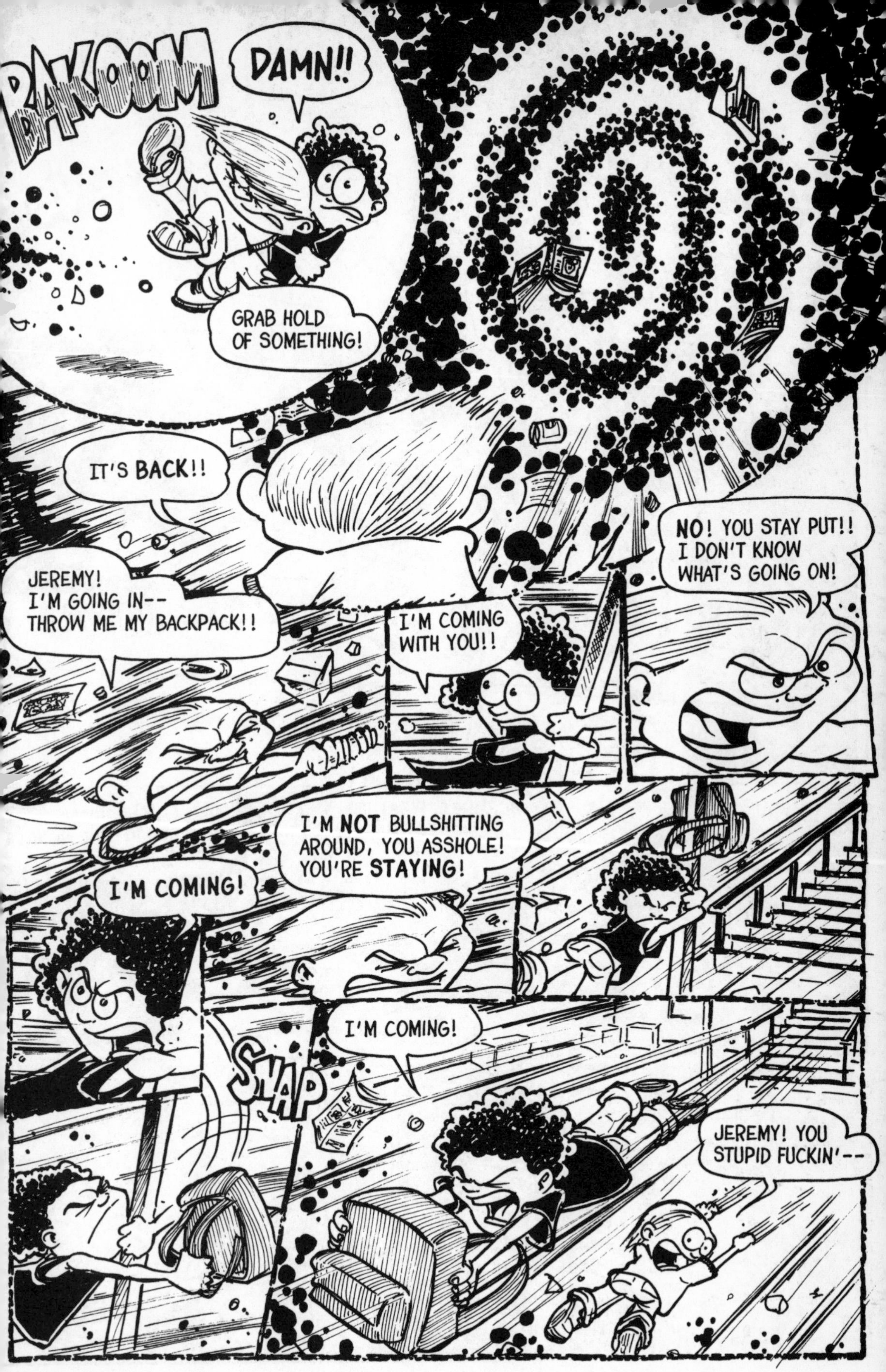

BAKOOM
DAMN!!
GRAB HOLD OF SOMETHING!
IT'S BACK!!
JEREMY! I'M GOING IN-- THROW ME MY BACKPACK!!
I'M COMING WITH YOU!!
NO! YOU STAY PUT!! I DON'T KNOW WHAT'S GOING ON!
I'M COMING!
I'M NOT BULLSHITTING AROUND, YOU ASSHOLE! YOU'RE STAYING!
SNAP
I'M COMING!
JEREMY! YOU STUPID FUCKIN'--

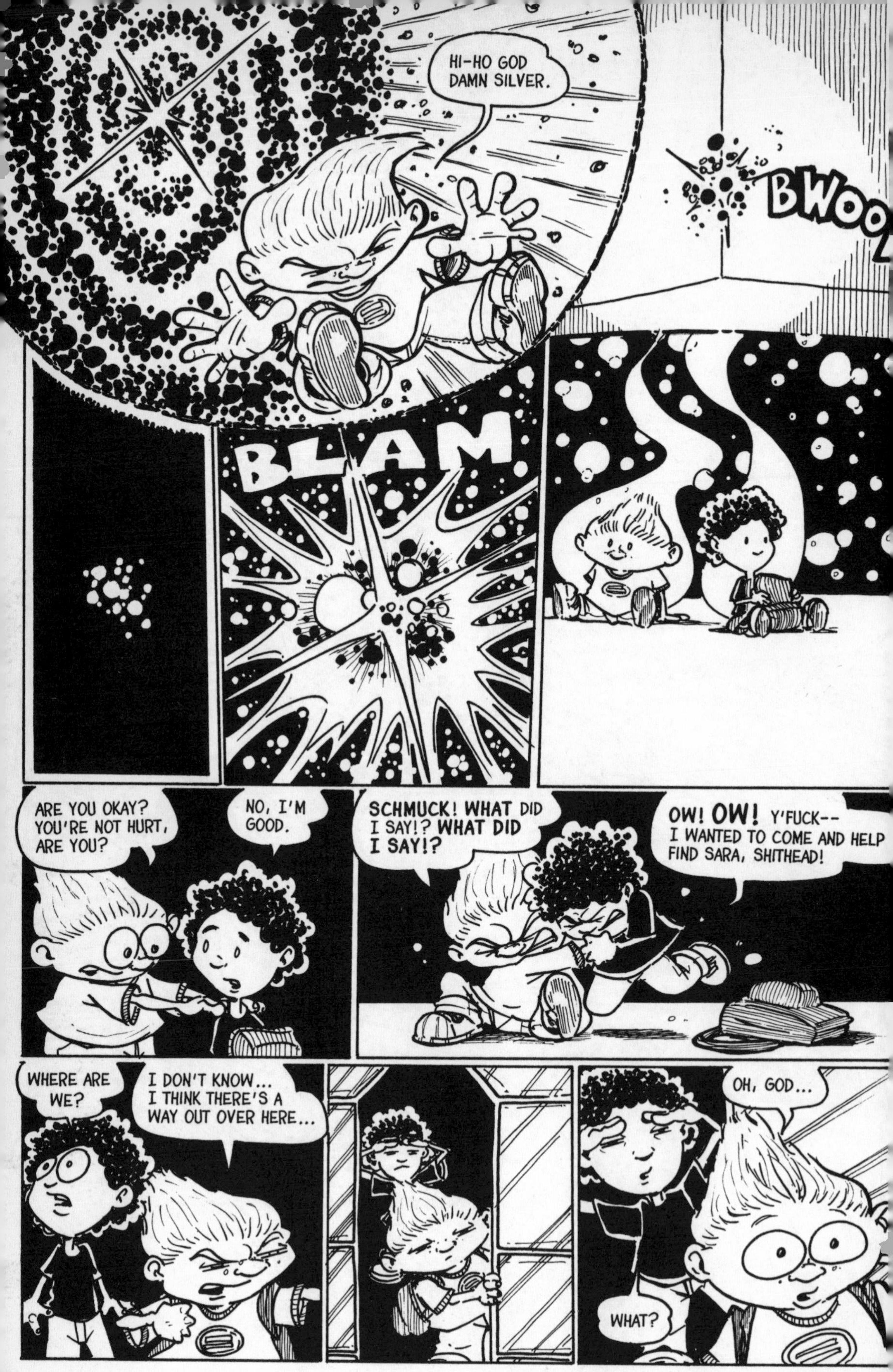
HI-HO GOD DAMN SILVER.
BWOO
BLAM
ARE YOU OKAY? YOU'RE NOT HURT, ARE YOU?
NO, I'M GOOD.
SCHMUCK! WHAT DID I SAY!? WHAT DID I SAY!?
OW! OW! Y'FUCK-- I WANTED TO COME AND HELP FIND SARA, SHITHEAD!
WHERE ARE WE?
I DON'T KNOW... I THINK THERE'S A WAY OUT OVER HERE...
OH, GOD...
WHAT?

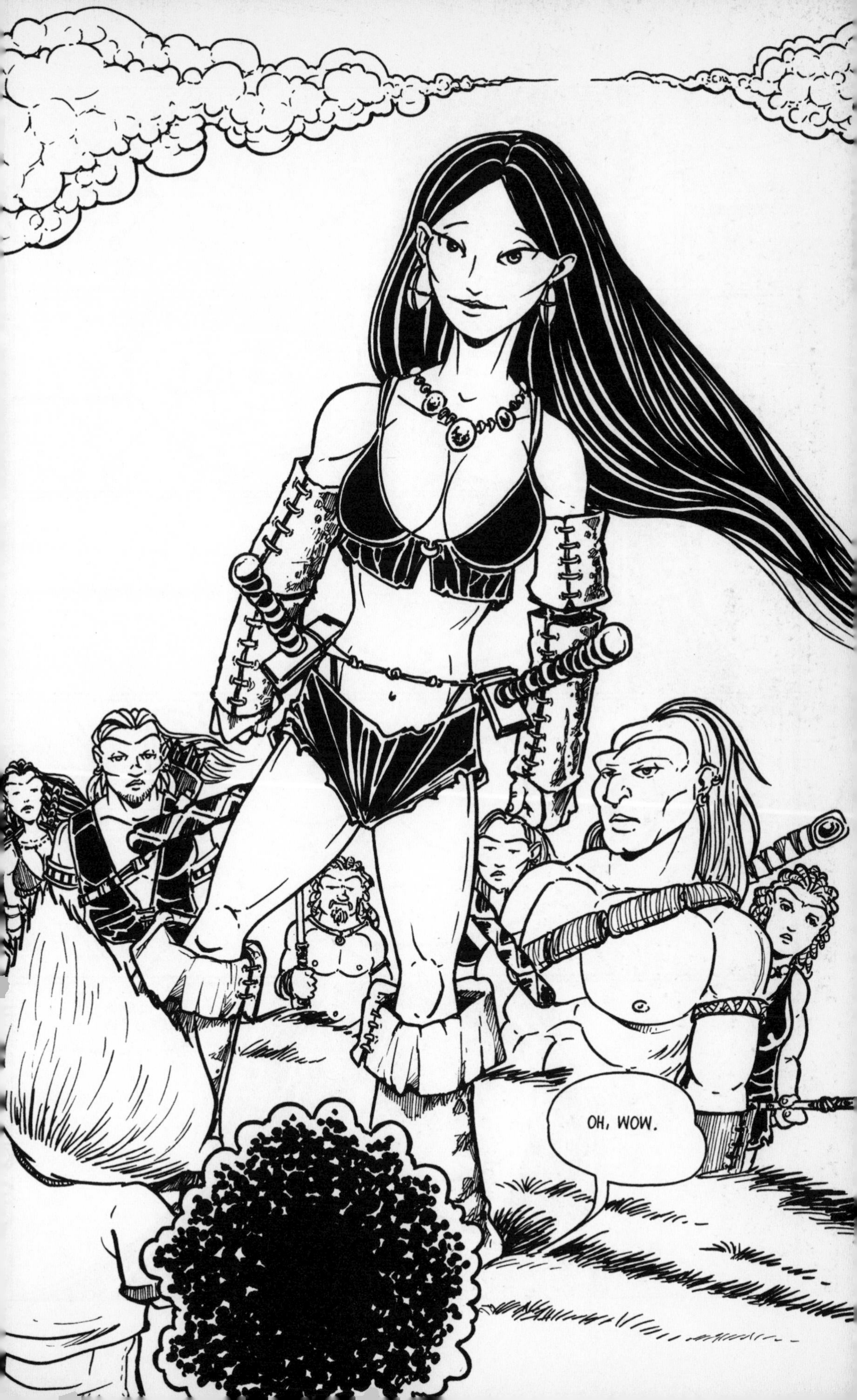
OH, WOW.

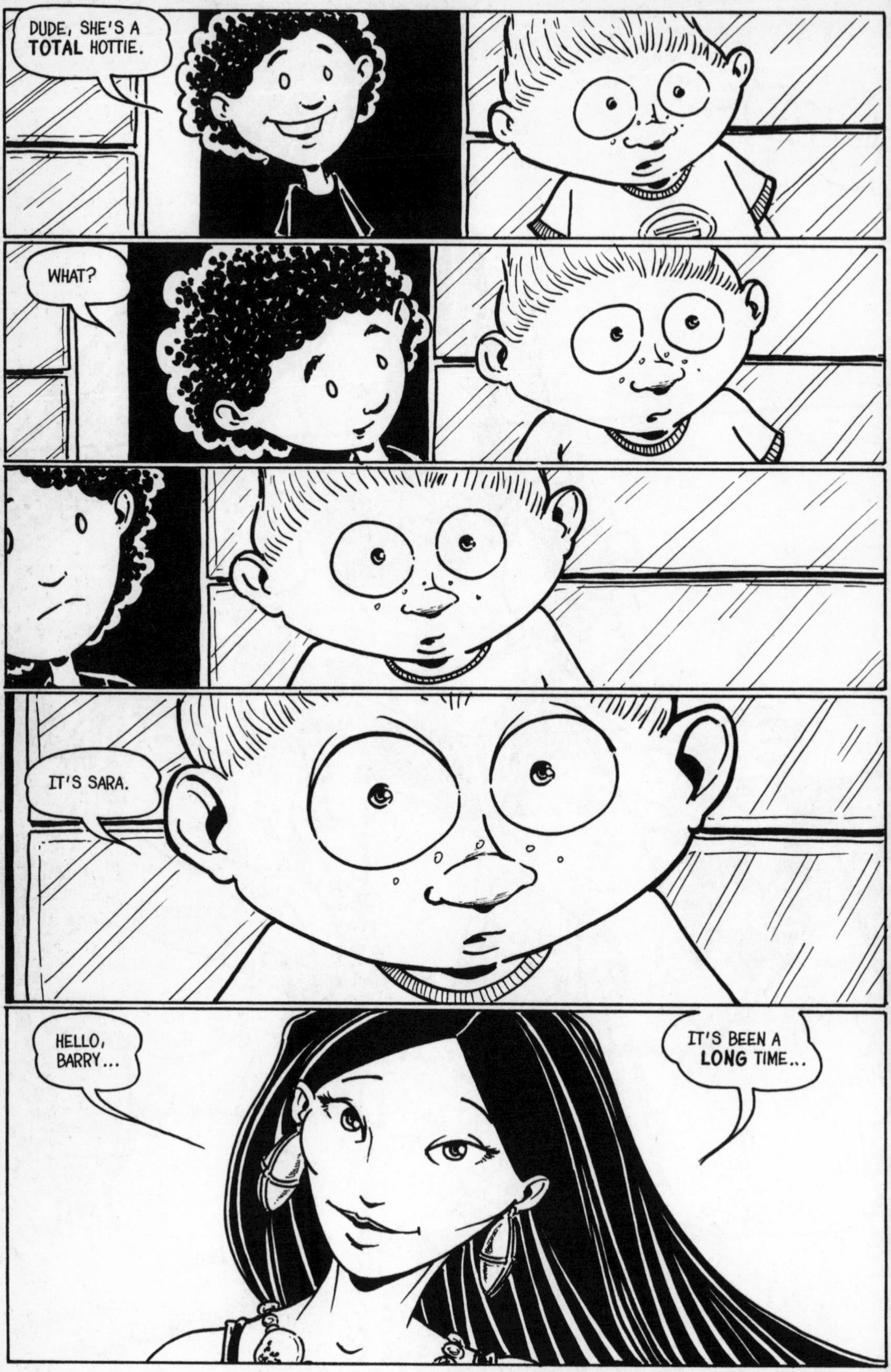
DUDE, SHE'S A TOTAL HOTTIE.
WHAT?
IT'S SARA.
HELLO, BARRY...
IT'S BEEN A LONG TIME...

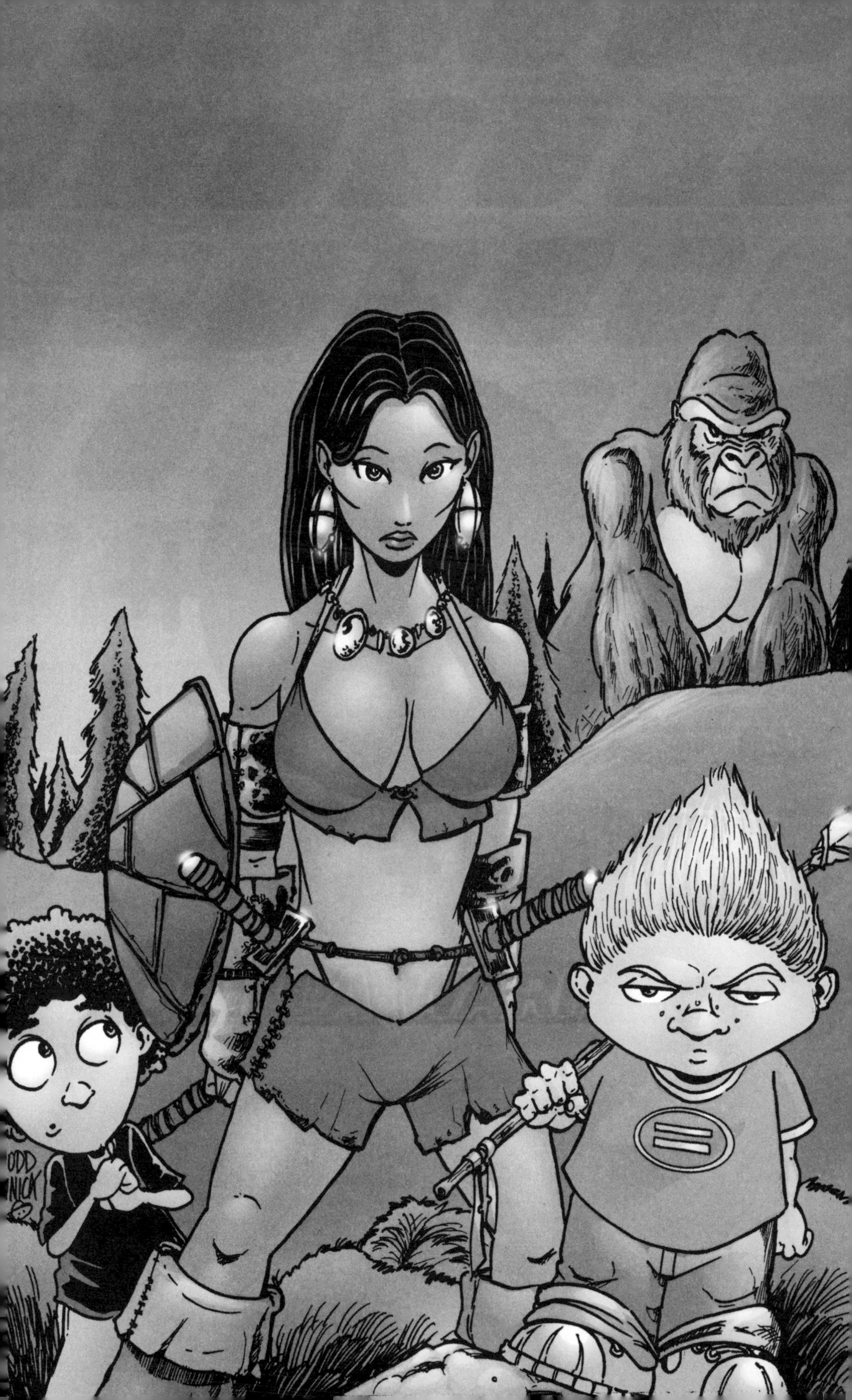

# "Our Little Girl's All Grown Up"

## "The Tale of the Great Ape—part two"

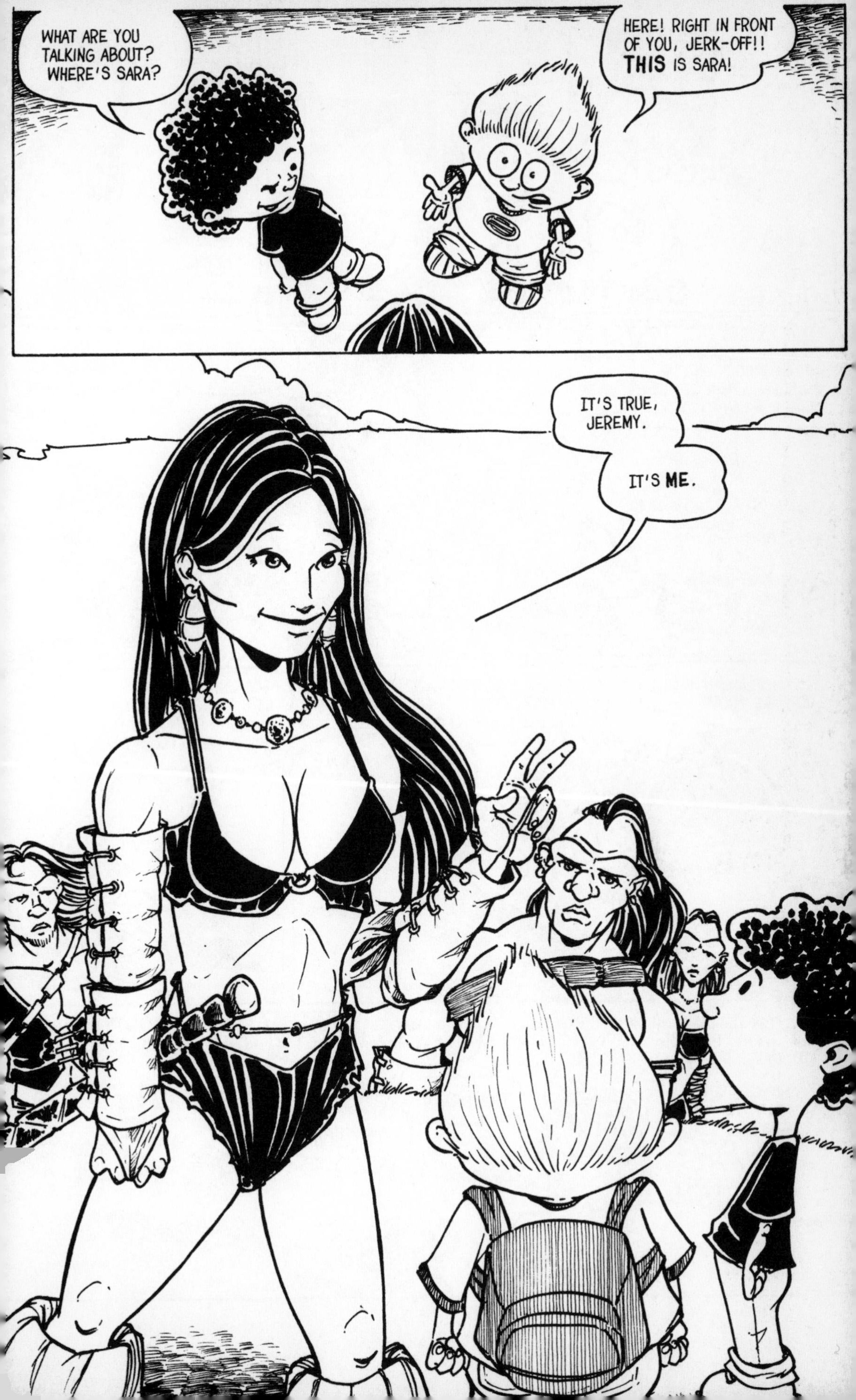
WHAT ARE YOU TALKING ABOUT? WHERE'S SARA?
HERE! RIGHT IN FRONT OF YOU, JERK-OFF!! **THIS** IS SARA!
IT'S TRUE, JEREMY.
IT'S **ME**.

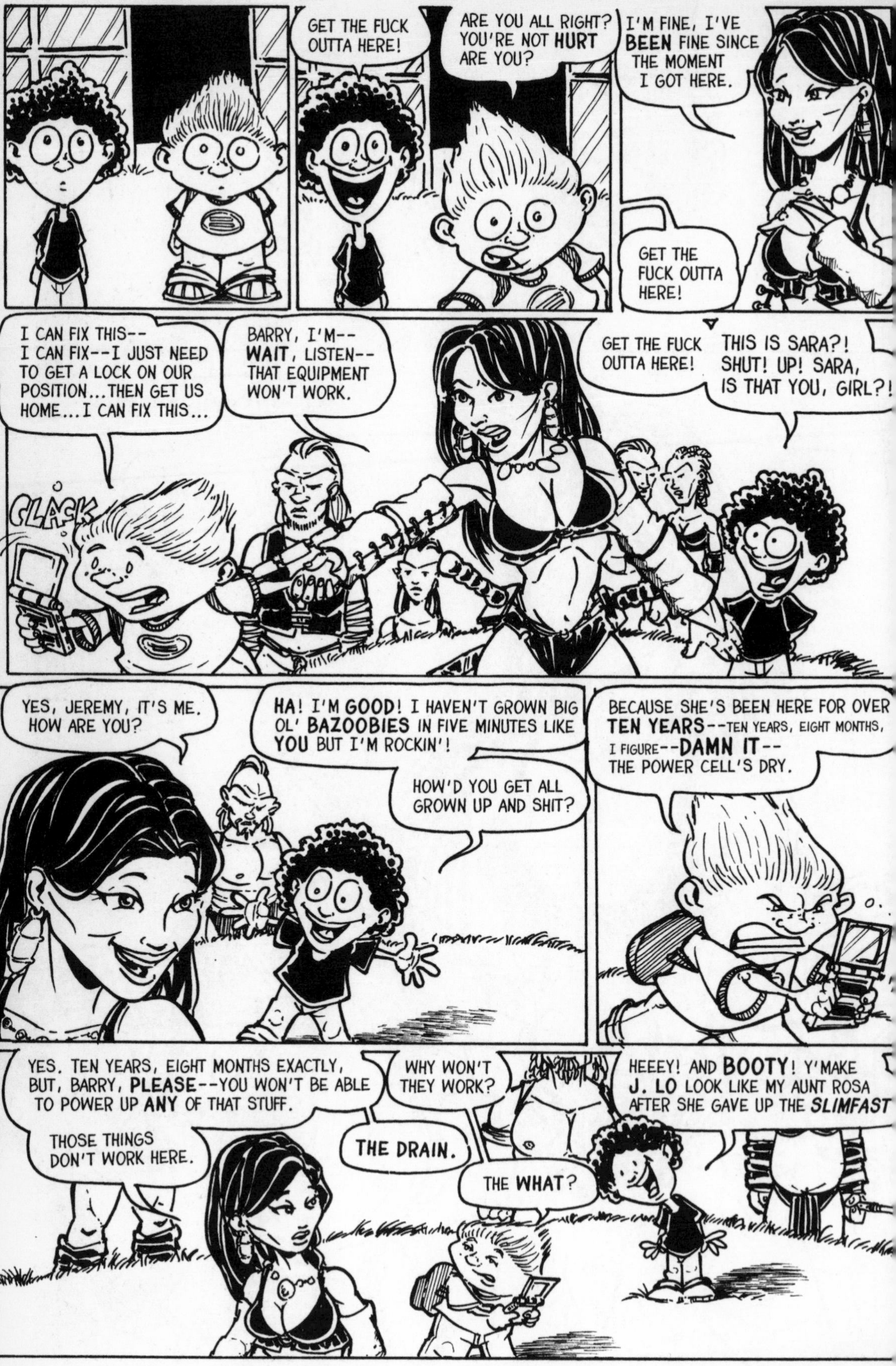
GET THE FUCK OUTTA HERE!
ARE YOU ALL RIGHT? YOU'RE NOT HURT ARE YOU?
I'M FINE, I'VE BEEN FINE SINCE THE MOMENT I GOT HERE.
GET THE FUCK OUTTA HERE!
I CAN FIX THIS-- I CAN FIX--I JUST NEED TO GET A LOCK ON OUR POSITION...THEN GET US HOME...I CAN FIX THIS...
BARRY, I'M-- WAIT, LISTEN-- THAT EQUIPMENT WON'T WORK.
GET THE FUCK OUTTA HERE!
THIS IS SARA?! SHUT! UP! SARA, IS THAT YOU, GIRL?!
CLACK
YES, JEREMY, IT'S ME. HOW ARE YOU?
HA! I'M GOOD! I HAVEN'T GROWN BIG OL' BAZOOBIES IN FIVE MINUTES LIKE YOU BUT I'M ROCKIN'!
HOW'D YOU GET ALL GROWN UP AND SHIT?
BECAUSE SHE'S BEEN HERE FOR OVER TEN YEARS--TEN YEARS, EIGHT MONTHS, I FIGURE--DAMN IT-- THE POWER CELL'S DRY.
YES. TEN YEARS, EIGHT MONTHS EXACTLY, BUT, BARRY, PLEASE--YOU WON'T BE ABLE TO POWER UP ANY OF THAT STUFF.
THOSE THINGS DON'T WORK HERE.
WHY WON'T THEY WORK?
THE DRAIN.
THE WHAT?
HEEEY! AND BOOTY! Y'MAKE J. LO LOOK LIKE MY AUNT ROSA AFTER SHE GAVE UP THE SLIMFAST

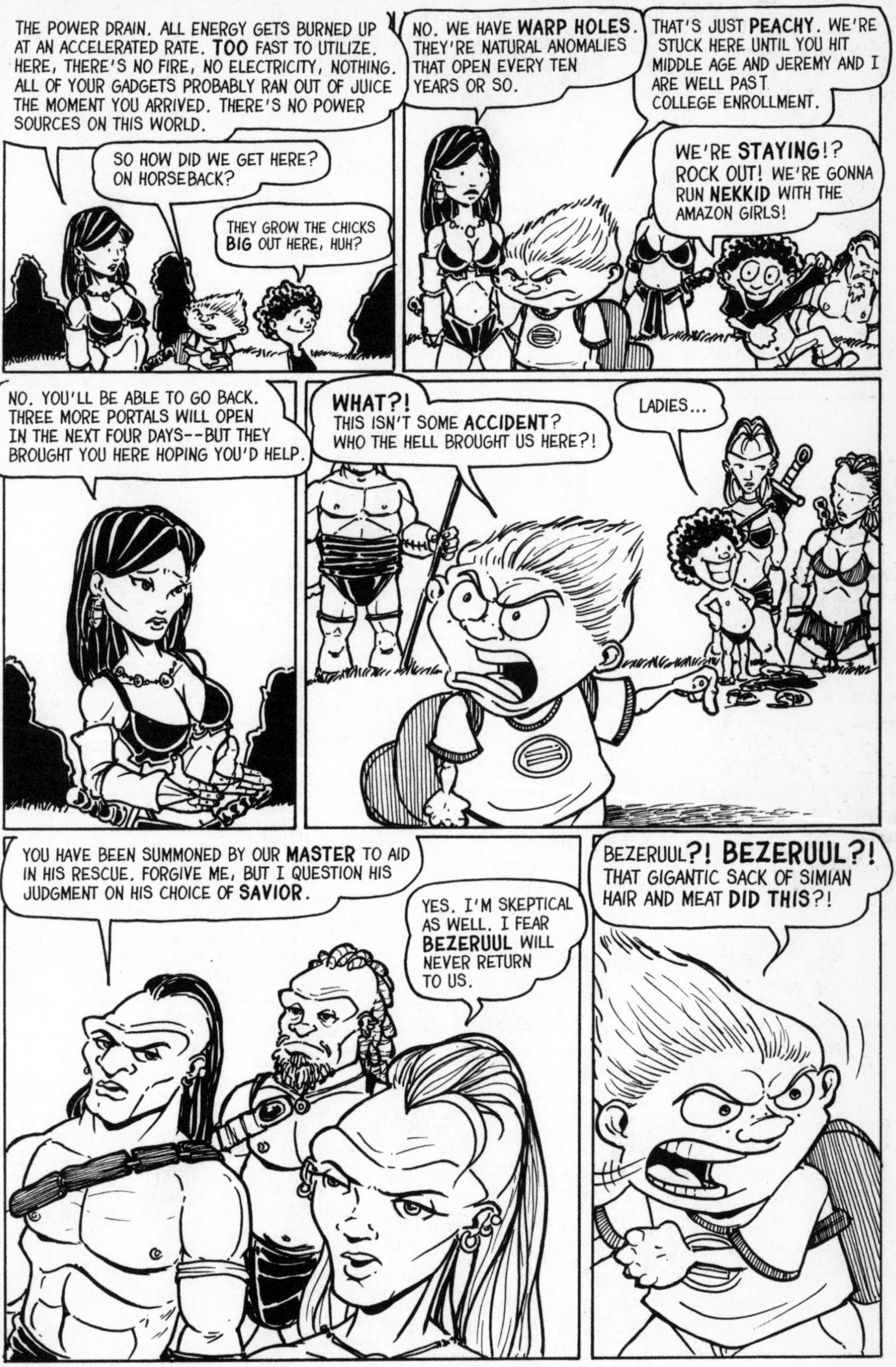
THE POWER DRAIN. ALL ENERGY GETS BURNED UP AT AN ACCELERATED RATE. **TOO** FAST TO UTILIZE. HERE, THERE'S NO FIRE, NO ELECTRICITY, NOTHING. ALL OF YOUR GADGETS PROBABLY RAN OUT OF JUICE THE MOMENT YOU ARRIVED. THERE'S NO POWER SOURCES ON THIS WORLD.
SO HOW DID WE GET HERE? ON HORSEBACK?
THEY GROW THE CHICKS **BIG** OUT HERE, HUH?
NO. WE HAVE **WARP HOLES**. THEY'RE NATURAL ANOMALIES THAT OPEN EVERY TEN YEARS OR SO.
THAT'S JUST **PEACHY**. WE'RE STUCK HERE UNTIL YOU HIT MIDDLE AGE AND JEREMY AND I ARE WELL PAST COLLEGE ENROLLMENT.
WE'RE **STAYING**!? ROCK OUT! WE'RE GONNA RUN **NEKKID** WITH THE AMAZON GIRLS!
NO. YOU'LL BE ABLE TO GO BACK. THREE MORE PORTALS WILL OPEN IN THE NEXT FOUR DAYS--BUT THEY BROUGHT YOU HERE HOPING YOU'D HELP.
**WHAT?!** THIS ISN'T SOME **ACCIDENT**? WHO THE HELL BROUGHT US HERE?!
LADIES...
YOU HAVE BEEN SUMMONED BY OUR **MASTER** TO AID IN HIS RESCUE. FORGIVE ME, BUT I QUESTION HIS JUDGMENT ON HIS CHOICE OF **SAVIOR**.
YES. I'M SKEPTICAL AS WELL. I FEAR **BEZERUUL** WILL NEVER RETURN TO US.
BEZERUUL?! **BEZERUUL?!** THAT GIGANTIC SACK OF SIMIAN HAIR AND MEAT **DID THIS**?!

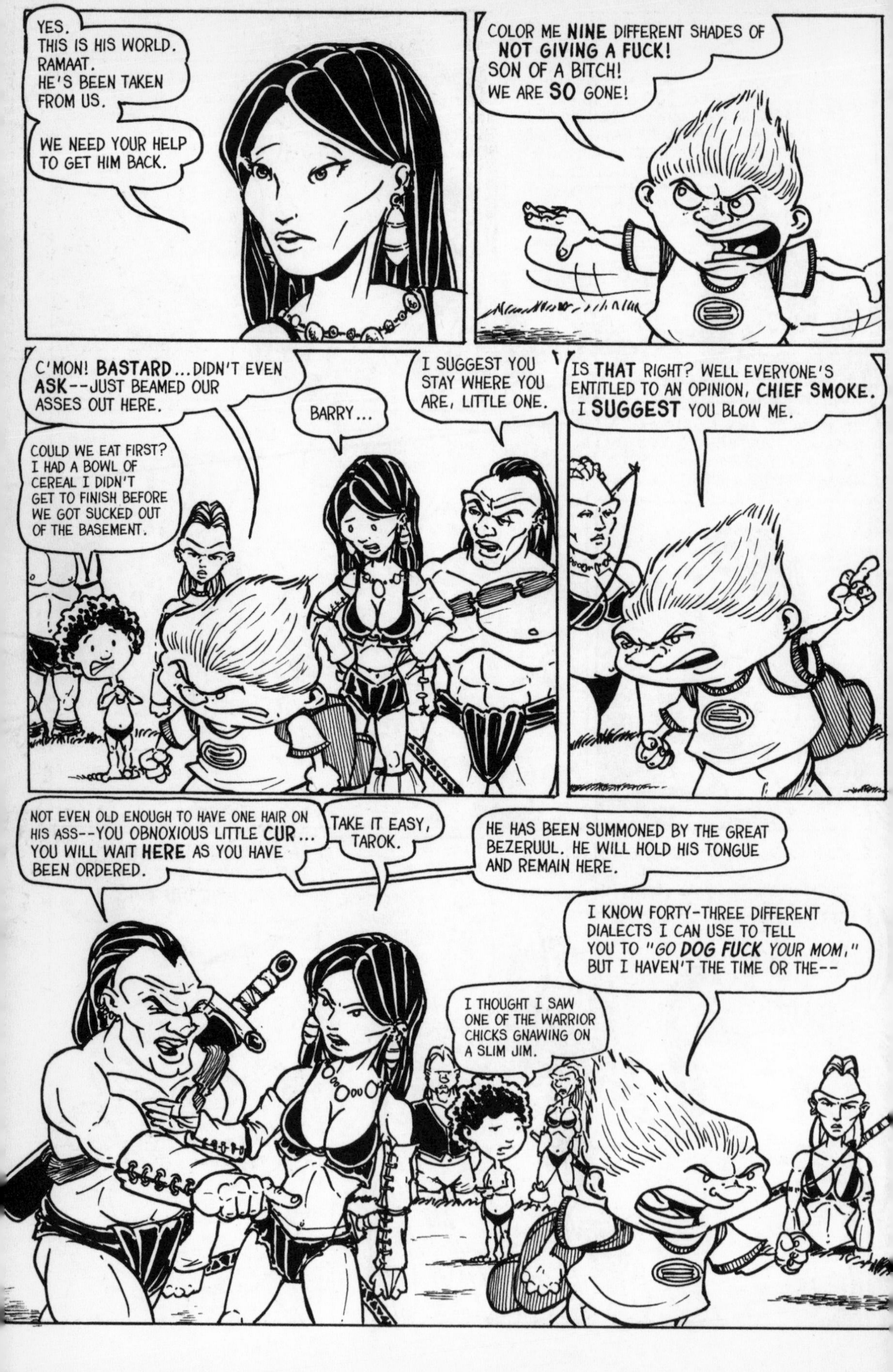

YES.
THIS IS HIS WORLD.
RAMAAT.
HE'S BEEN TAKEN FROM US.
WE NEED YOUR HELP TO GET HIM BACK.
COLOR ME NINE DIFFERENT SHADES OF NOT GIVING A FUCK! SON OF A BITCH! WE ARE SO GONE!
C'MON! BASTARD...DIDN'T EVEN ASK--JUST BEAMED OUR ASSES OUT HERE.
COULD WE EAT FIRST? I HAD A BOWL OF CEREAL I DIDN'T GET TO FINISH BEFORE WE GOT SUCKED OUT OF THE BASEMENT.
BARRY...
I SUGGEST YOU STAY WHERE YOU ARE, LITTLE ONE.
IS THAT RIGHT? WELL EVERYONE'S ENTITLED TO AN OPINION, CHIEF SMOKE. I SUGGEST YOU BLOW ME.
NOT EVEN OLD ENOUGH TO HAVE ONE HAIR ON HIS ASS--YOU OBNOXIOUS LITTLE CUR... YOU WILL WAIT HERE AS YOU HAVE BEEN ORDERED.
TAKE IT EASY, TAROK.
HE HAS BEEN SUMMONED BY THE GREAT BEZERUUL. HE WILL HOLD HIS TONGUE AND REMAIN HERE.
I KNOW FORTY-THREE DIFFERENT DIALECTS I CAN USE TO TELL YOU TO "GO DOG FUCK YOUR MOM," BUT I HAVEN'T THE TIME OR THE--
I THOUGHT I SAW ONE OF THE WARRIOR CHICKS GNAWING ON A SLIM JIM.

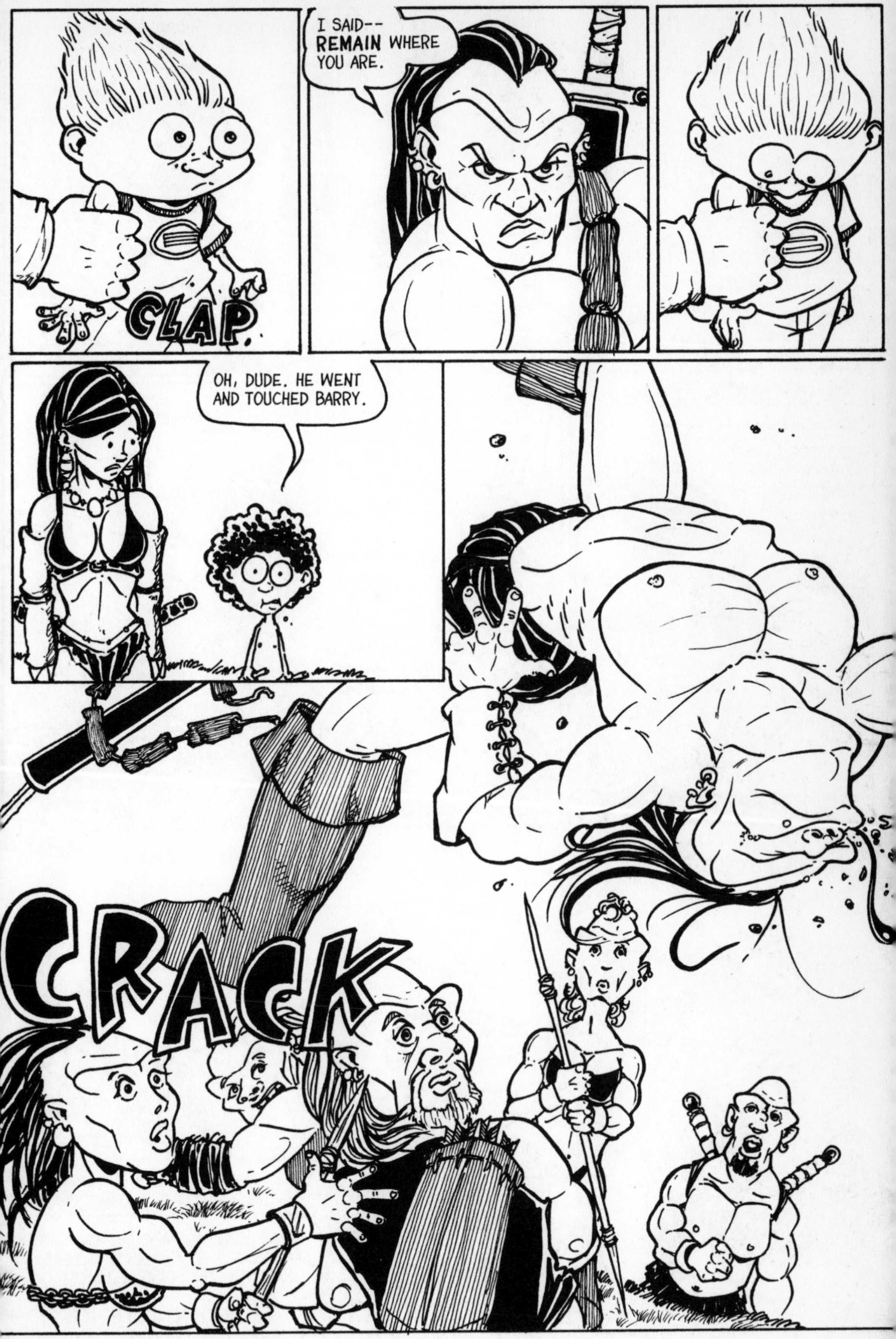
CLAP
I SAID--
REMAIN WHERE YOU ARE.
OH, DUDE. HE WENT AND TOUCHED BARRY.
CRACK

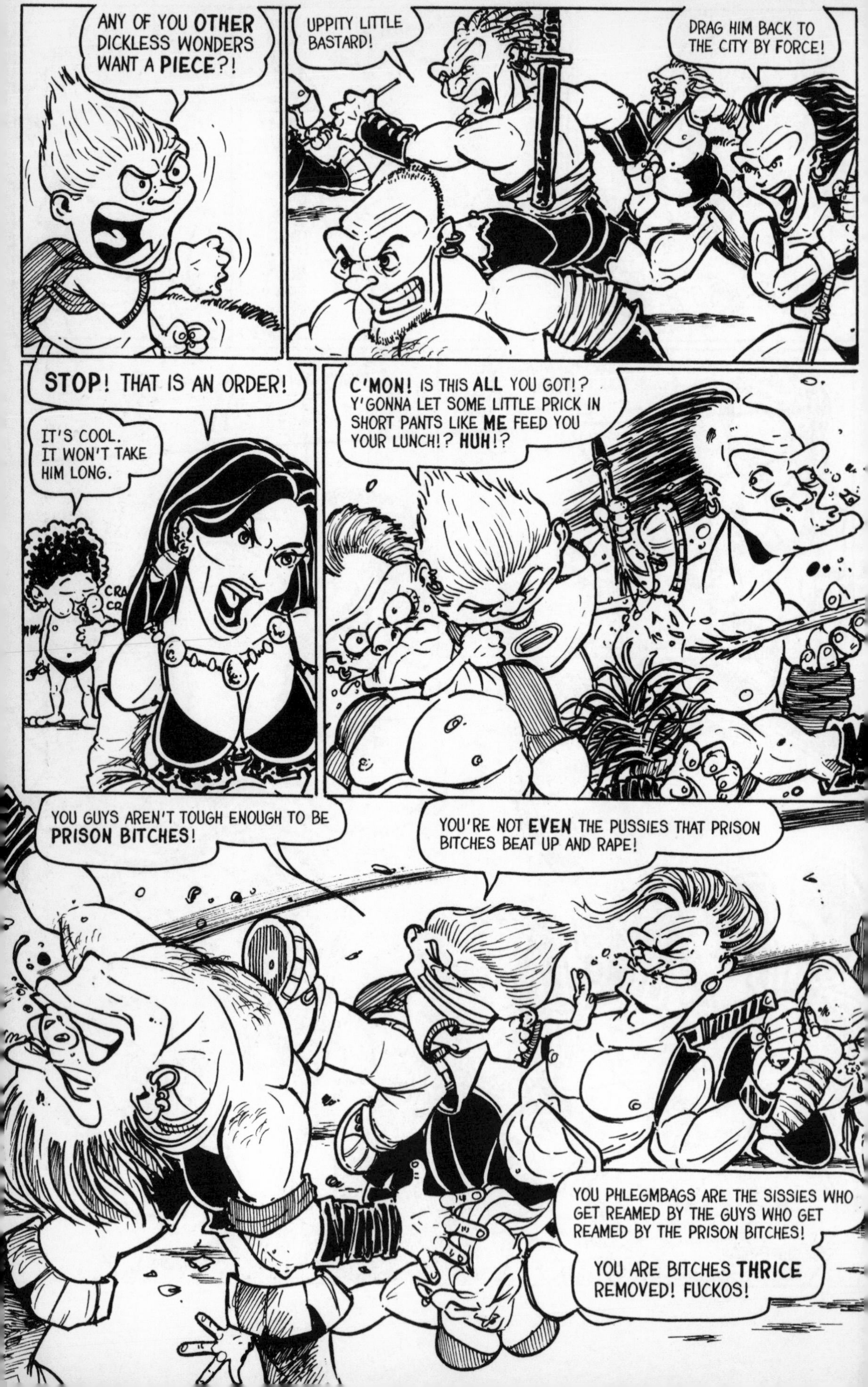
ANY OF YOU OTHER DICKLESS WONDERS WANT A PIECE?!
UPPITY LITTLE BASTARD!
DRAG HIM BACK TO THE CITY BY FORCE!
STOP! THAT IS AN ORDER!
IT'S COOL. IT WON'T TAKE HIM LONG.
C'MON! IS THIS ALL YOU GOT!? Y'GONNA LET SOME LITTLE PRICK IN SHORT PANTS LIKE ME FEED YOU YOUR LUNCH!? HUH!?
YOU GUYS AREN'T TOUGH ENOUGH TO BE PRISON BITCHES!
YOU'RE NOT EVEN THE PUSSIES THAT PRISON BITCHES BEAT UP AND RAPE!
YOU PHLEGMBAGS ARE THE SISSIES WHO GET REAMED BY THE GUYS WHO GET REAMED BY THE PRISON BITCHES!
YOU ARE BITCHES THRICE REMOVED! FUCKOS!

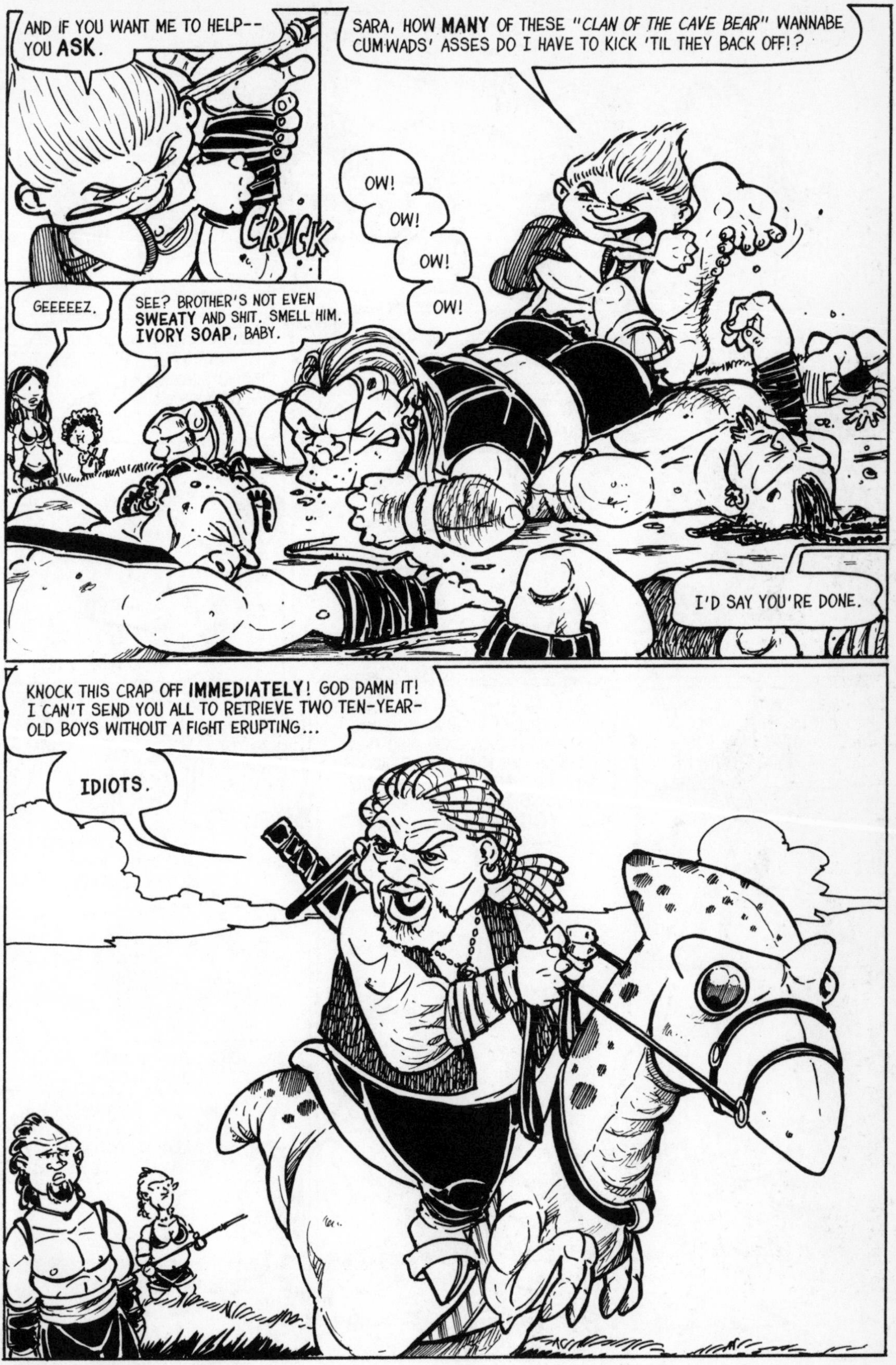
AND IF YOU WANT ME TO HELP-- YOU ASK.
CRICK
SARA, HOW MANY OF THESE "CLAN OF THE CAVE BEAR" WANNABE CUM-WADS' ASSES DO I HAVE TO KICK 'TIL THEY BACK OFF!?
OW!
OW!
OW!
OW!
GEEEEEZ.
SEE? BROTHER'S NOT EVEN SWEATY AND SHIT. SMELL HIM. IVORY SOAP, BABY.
I'D SAY YOU'RE DONE.
KNOCK THIS CRAP OFF IMMEDIATELY! GOD DAMN IT! I CAN'T SEND YOU ALL TO RETRIEVE TWO TEN-YEAR-OLD BOYS WITHOUT A FIGHT ERUPTING...
IDIOTS.

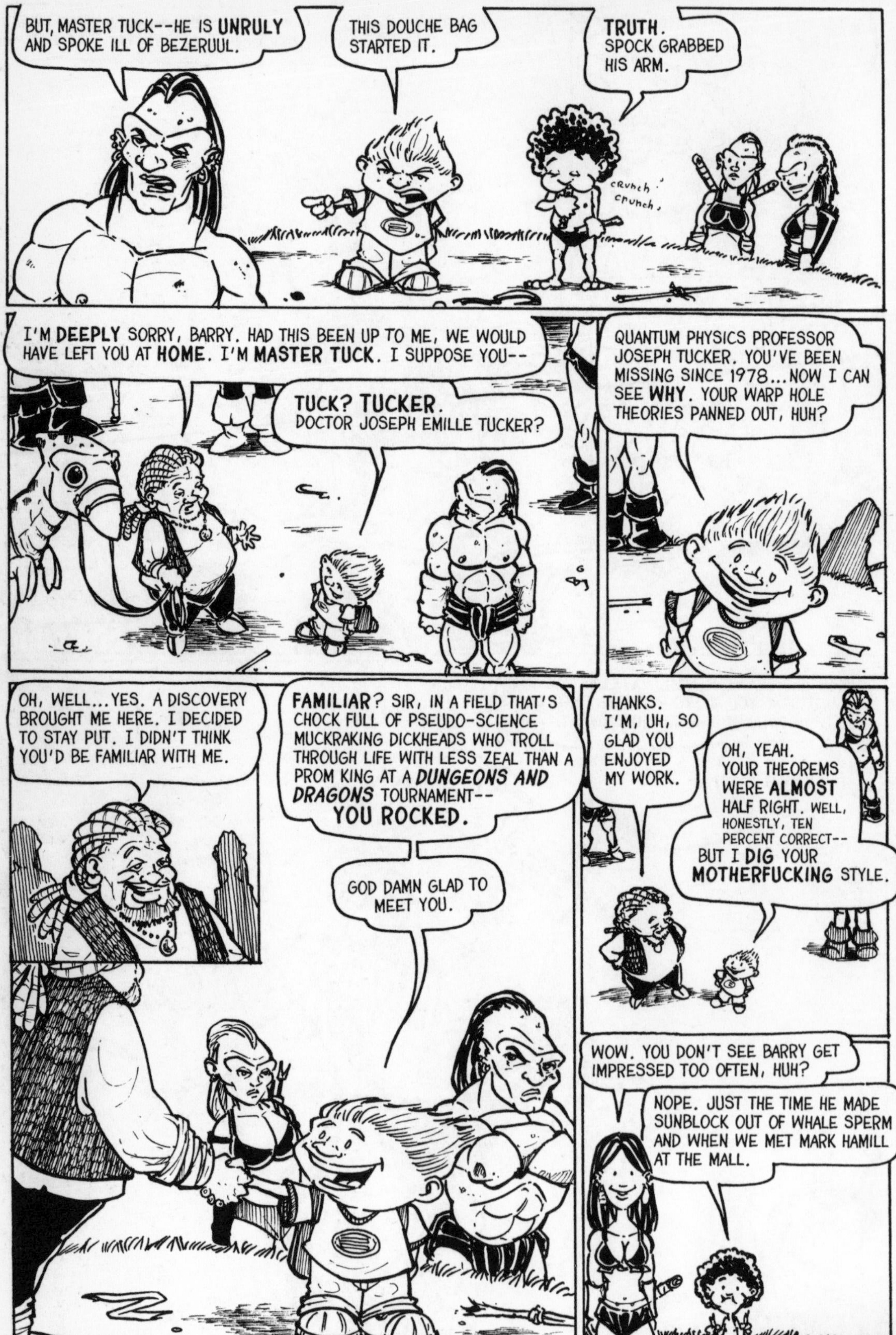
BUT, MASTER TUCK--HE IS UNRULY AND SPOKE ILL OF BEZERUUL.
THIS DOUCHE BAG STARTED IT.
TRUTH. SPOCK GRABBED HIS ARM.
crunch crunch
I'M DEEPLY SORRY, BARRY. HAD THIS BEEN UP TO ME, WE WOULD HAVE LEFT YOU AT HOME. I'M MASTER TUCK. I SUPPOSE YOU--
TUCK? TUCKER. DOCTOR JOSEPH EMILLE TUCKER?
QUANTUM PHYSICS PROFESSOR JOSEPH TUCKER. YOU'VE BEEN MISSING SINCE 1978...NOW I CAN SEE WHY. YOUR WARP HOLE THEORIES PANNED OUT, HUH?
OH, WELL...YES. A DISCOVERY BROUGHT ME HERE. I DECIDED TO STAY PUT. I DIDN'T THINK YOU'D BE FAMILIAR WITH ME.
FAMILIAR? SIR, IN A FIELD THAT'S CHOCK FULL OF PSEUDO-SCIENCE MUCKRAKING DICKHEADS WHO TROLL THROUGH LIFE WITH LESS ZEAL THAN A PROM KING AT A DUNGEONS AND DRAGONS TOURNAMENT-- YOU ROCKED.
GOD DAMN GLAD TO MEET YOU.
THANKS. I'M, UH, SO GLAD YOU ENJOYED MY WORK.
OH, YEAH. YOUR THEOREMS WERE ALMOST HALF RIGHT. WELL, HONESTLY, TEN PERCENT CORRECT-- BUT I DIG YOUR MOTHERFUCKING STYLE.
WOW. YOU DON'T SEE BARRY GET IMPRESSED TOO OFTEN, HUH?
NOPE. JUST THE TIME HE MADE SUNBLOCK OUT OF WHALE SPERM AND WHEN WE MET MARK HAMILL AT THE MALL.

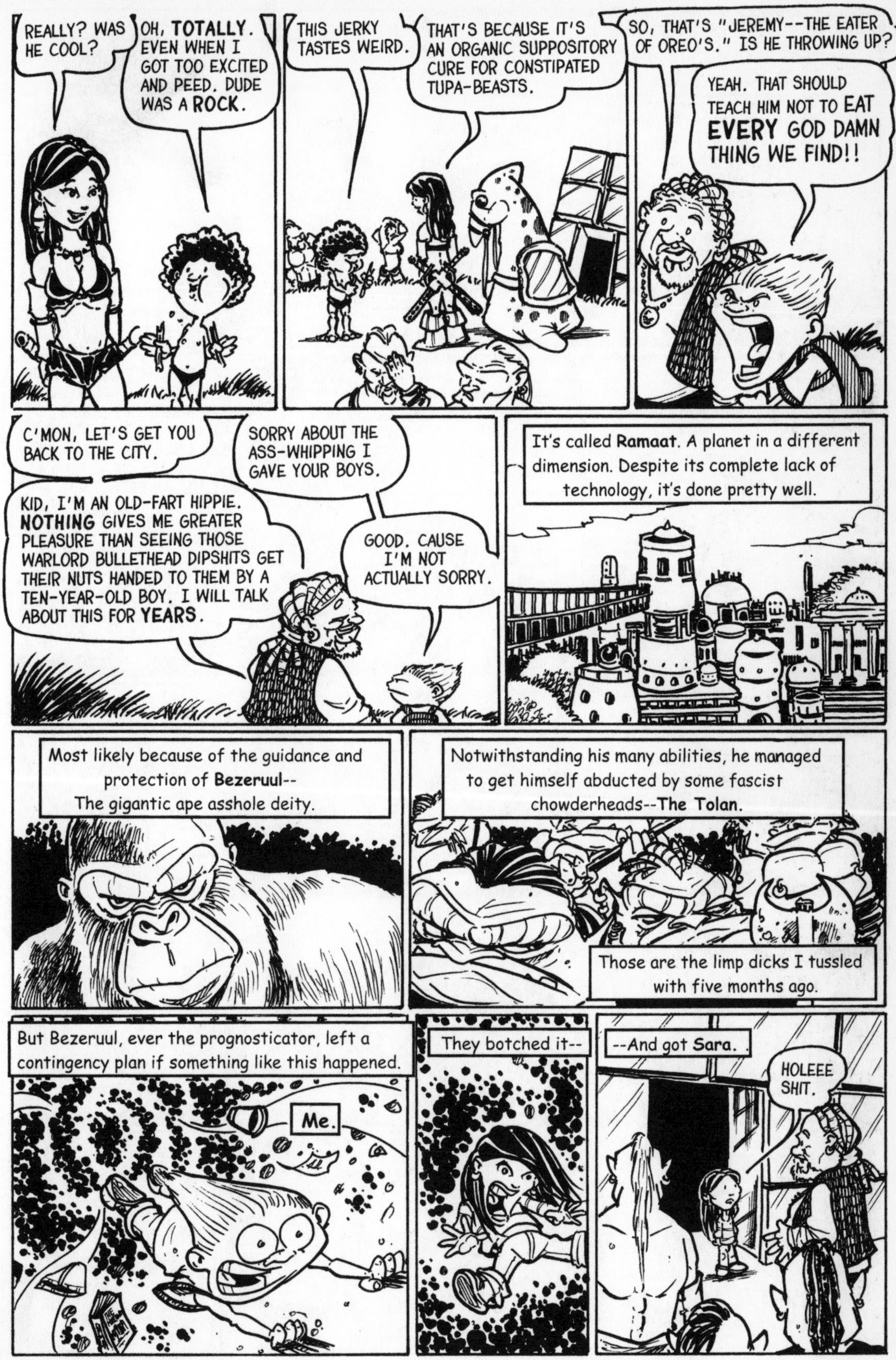

REALLY? WAS HE COOL?
OH, TOTALLY. EVEN WHEN I GOT TOO EXCITED AND PEED. DUDE WAS A ROCK.
THIS JERKY TASTES WEIRD.
THAT'S BECAUSE IT'S AN ORGANIC SUPPOSITORY CURE FOR CONSTIPATED TUPA-BEASTS.
SO, THAT'S "JEREMY--THE EATER OF OREO'S." IS HE THROWING UP?
YEAH. THAT SHOULD TEACH HIM NOT TO EAT EVERY GOD DAMN THING WE FIND!!
C'MON, LET'S GET YOU BACK TO THE CITY.
SORRY ABOUT THE ASS-WHIPPING I GAVE YOUR BOYS.
KID, I'M AN OLD-FART HIPPIE. NOTHING GIVES ME GREATER PLEASURE THAN SEEING THOSE WARLORD BULLETHEAD DIPSHITS GET THEIR NUTS HANDED TO THEM BY A TEN-YEAR-OLD BOY. I WILL TALK ABOUT THIS FOR YEARS.
GOOD. CAUSE I'M NOT ACTUALLY SORRY.
It's called Ramaat. A planet in a different dimension. Despite its complete lack of technology, it's done pretty well.
Most likely because of the guidance and protection of Bezeruul-- The gigantic ape asshole deity.
Notwithstanding his many abilities, he managed to get himself abducted by some fascist chowderheads--The Tolan.
Those are the limp dicks I tussled with five months ago.
But Bezeruul, ever the prognosticator, left a contingency plan if something like this happened.
Me.
They botched it--
--And got Sara.
HOLEEE SHIT.

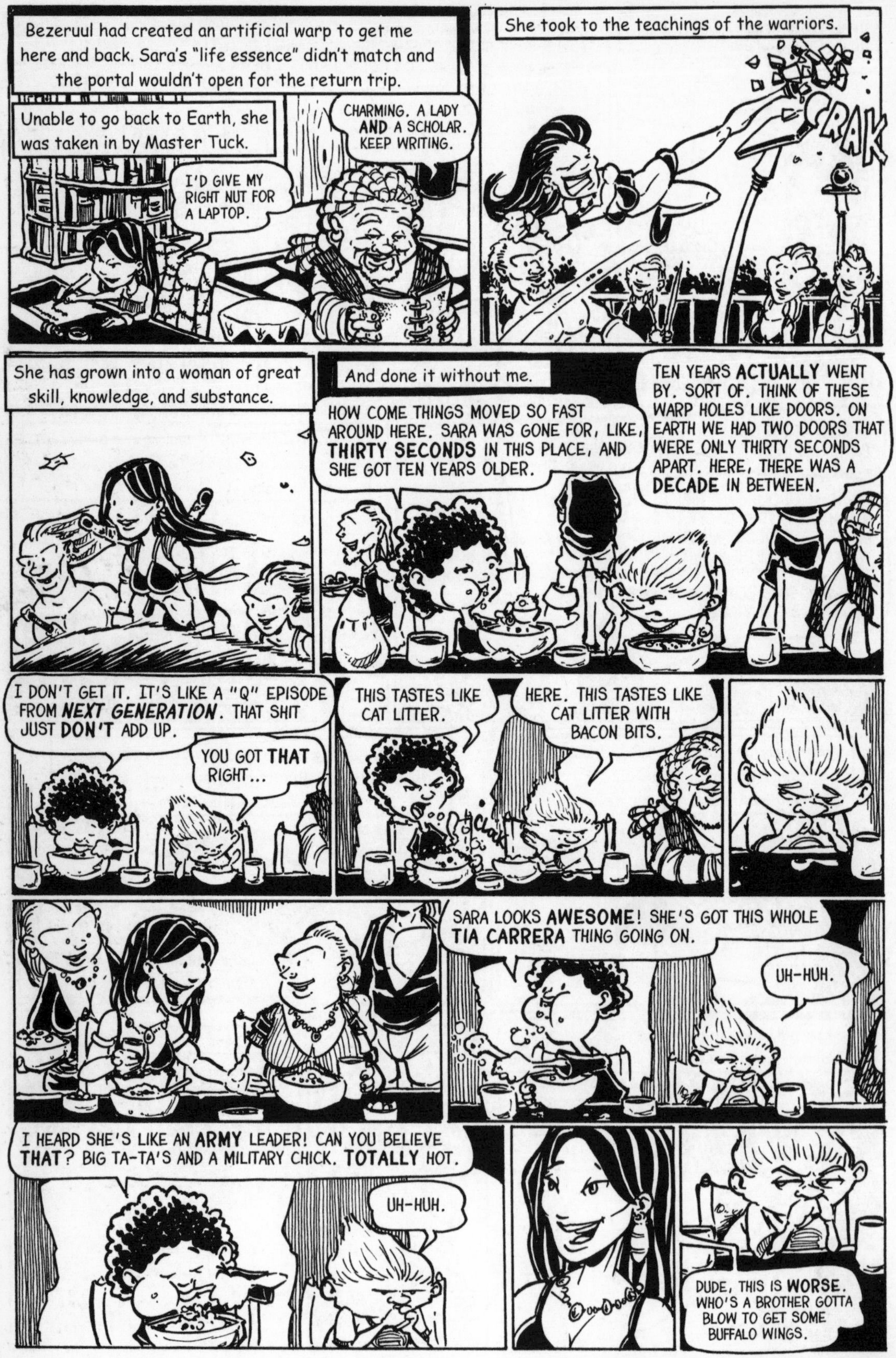
Bezeruul had created an artificial warp to get me here and back. Sara's "life essence" didn't match and the portal wouldn't open for the return trip.
Unable to go back to Earth, she was taken in by Master Tuck.
CHARMING. A LADY AND A SCHOLAR. KEEP WRITING.
I'D GIVE MY RIGHT NUT FOR A LAPTOP.
She took to the teachings of the warriors.
CRAK
She has grown into a woman of great skill, knowledge, and substance.
And done it without me.
HOW COME THINGS MOVED SO FAST AROUND HERE. SARA WAS GONE FOR, LIKE, THIRTY SECONDS IN THIS PLACE, AND SHE GOT TEN YEARS OLDER.
TEN YEARS ACTUALLY WENT BY. SORT OF. THINK OF THESE WARP HOLES LIKE DOORS. ON EARTH WE HAD TWO DOORS THAT WERE ONLY THIRTY SECONDS APART. HERE, THERE WAS A DECADE IN BETWEEN.
I DON'T GET IT. IT'S LIKE A "Q" EPISODE FROM NEXT GENERATION. THAT SHIT JUST DON'T ADD UP.
YOU GOT THAT RIGHT...
THIS TASTES LIKE CAT LITTER.
HERE. THIS TASTES LIKE CAT LITTER WITH BACON BITS.
CLOCK
SARA LOOKS AWESOME! SHE'S GOT THIS WHOLE TIA CARRERA THING GOING ON.
UH-HUH.
I HEARD SHE'S LIKE AN ARMY LEADER! CAN YOU BELIEVE THAT? BIG TA-TA'S AND A MILITARY CHICK. TOTALLY HOT.
UH-HUH.
DUDE, THIS IS WORSE. WHO'S A BROTHER GOTTA BLOW TO GET SOME BUFFALO WINGS.

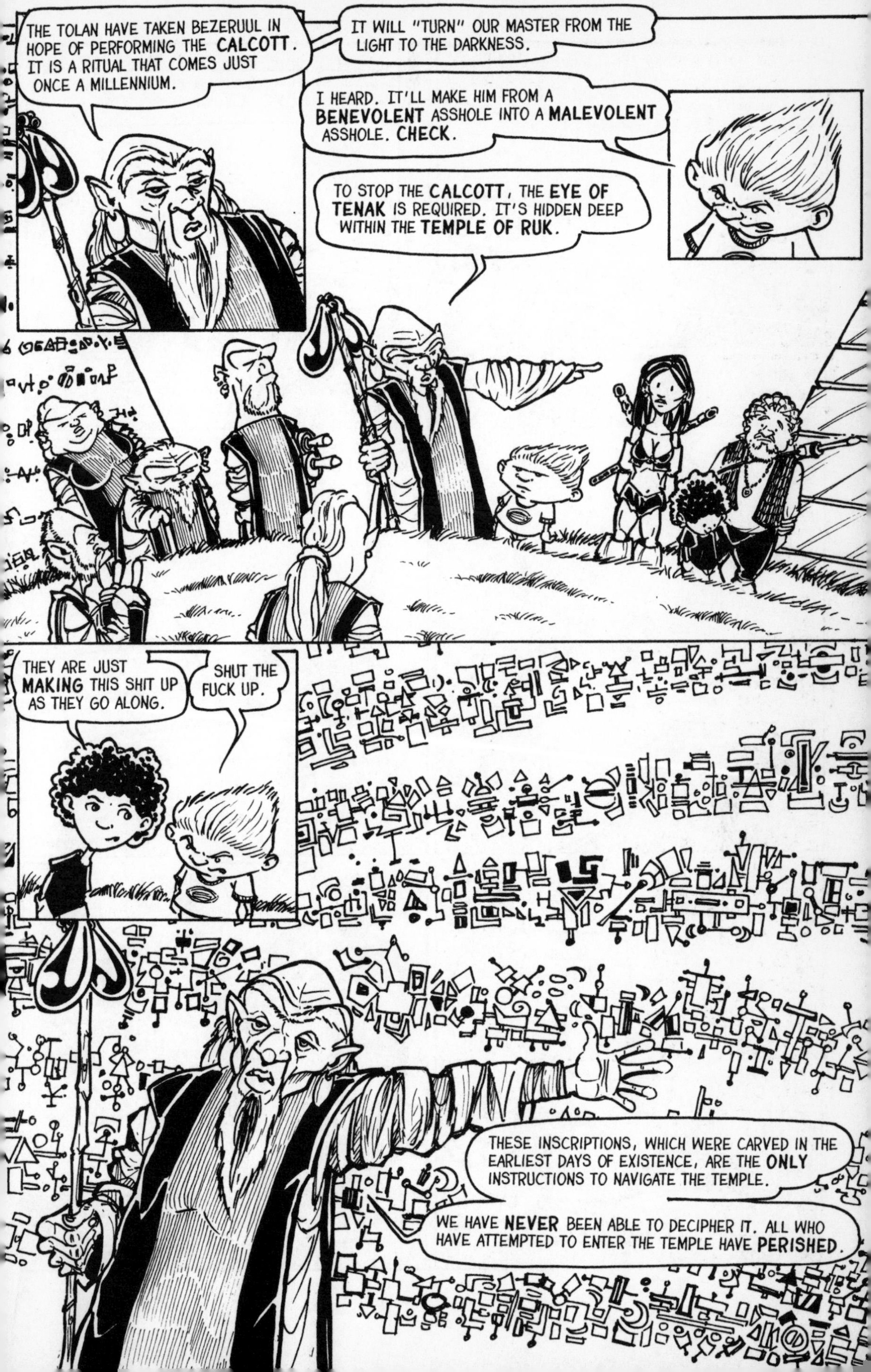

THE TOLAN HAVE TAKEN BEZERUUL IN HOPE OF PERFORMING THE **CALCOTT**. IT IS A RITUAL THAT COMES JUST ONCE A MILLENNIUM.
IT WILL "TURN" OUR MASTER FROM THE LIGHT TO THE DARKNESS.
I HEARD. IT'LL MAKE HIM FROM A **BENEVOLENT** ASSHOLE INTO A **MALEVOLENT** ASSHOLE. **CHECK**.
TO STOP THE **CALCOTT**, THE **EYE OF TENAK** IS REQUIRED. IT'S HIDDEN DEEP WITHIN THE **TEMPLE OF RUK**.
THEY ARE JUST **MAKING** THIS SHIT UP AS THEY GO ALONG.
SHUT THE FUCK UP.
THESE INSCRIPTIONS, WHICH WERE CARVED IN THE EARLIEST DAYS OF EXISTENCE, ARE THE **ONLY** INSTRUCTIONS TO NAVIGATE THE TEMPLE.
WE HAVE **NEVER** BEEN ABLE TO DECIPHER IT. ALL WHO HAVE ATTEMPTED TO ENTER THE TEMPLE HAVE **PERISHED**.

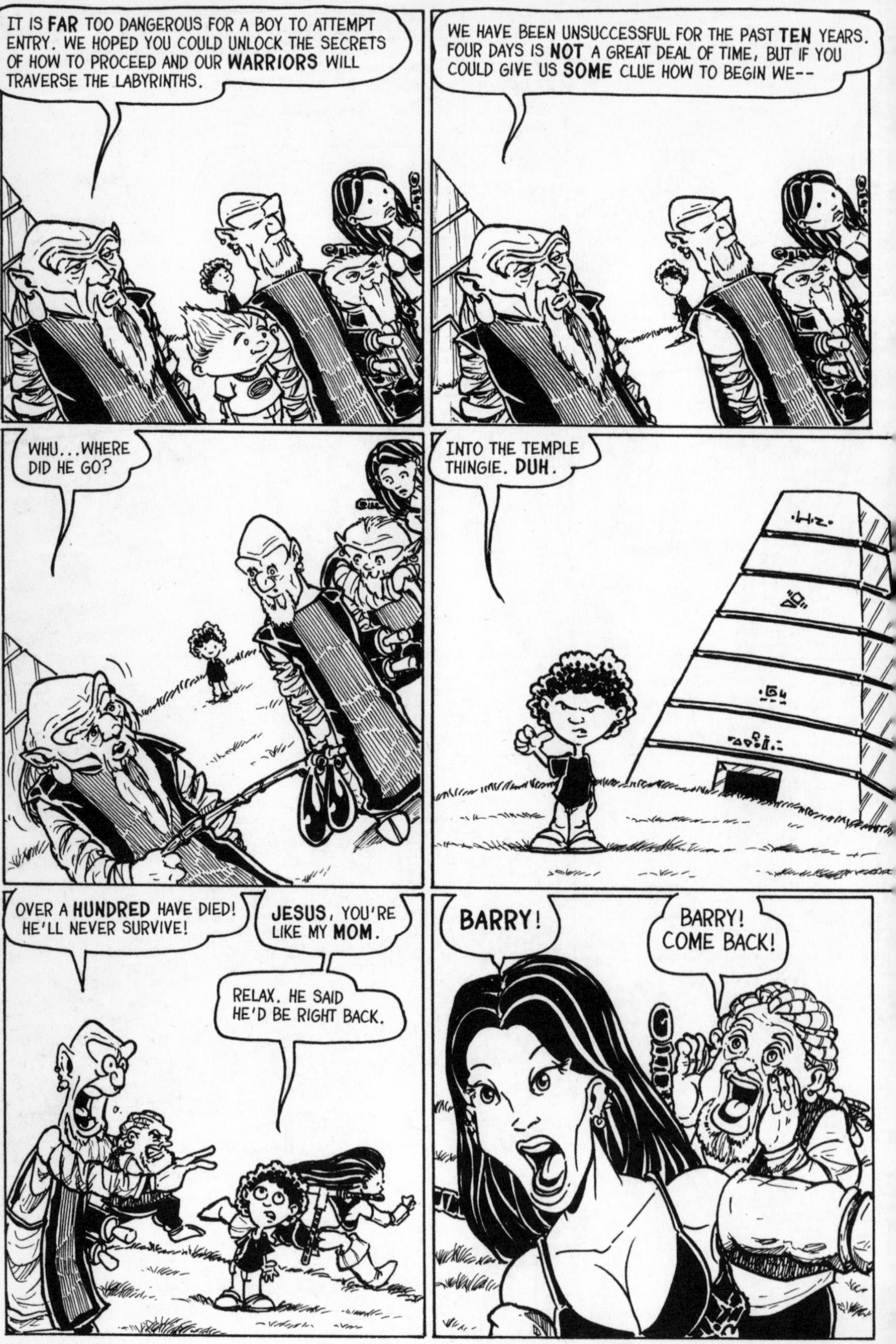
IT IS FAR TOO DANGEROUS FOR A BOY TO ATTEMPT ENTRY. WE HOPED YOU COULD UNLOCK THE SECRETS OF HOW TO PROCEED AND OUR WARRIORS WILL TRAVERSE THE LABYRINTHS.
WE HAVE BEEN UNSUCCESSFUL FOR THE PAST TEN YEARS. FOUR DAYS IS NOT A GREAT DEAL OF TIME, BUT IF YOU COULD GIVE US SOME CLUE HOW TO BEGIN WE--
WHU...WHERE DID HE GO?
INTO THE TEMPLE THINGIE. DUH.
OVER A HUNDRED HAVE DIED! HE'LL NEVER SURVIVE!
JESUS, YOU'RE LIKE MY MOM.
RELAX. HE SAID HE'D BE RIGHT BACK.
BARRY!
BARRY! COME BACK!

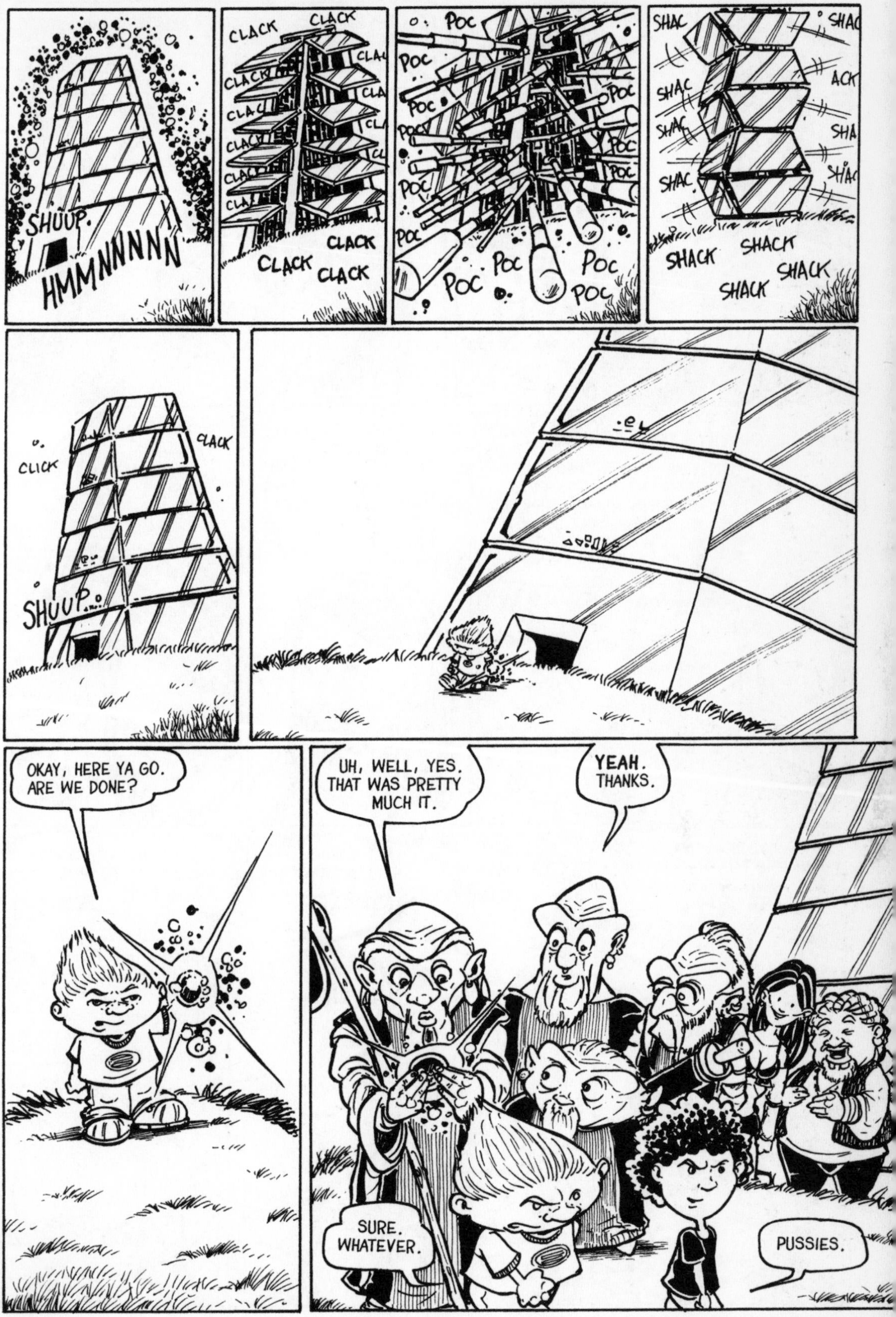
SHUUP.
HMMNNNNN
CLACK
CLACK
CLACK
CLACK
CLACK
POC
POC
POC
POC
POC
POC
SHAC
SHAC
SHACK
SHACK
SHACK
SHACK
CLICK
CLACK
SHUUP.
OKAY, HERE YA GO. ARE WE DONE?
UH, WELL, YES. THAT WAS PRETTY MUCH IT.
YEAH. THANKS.
SURE. WHATEVER.
PUSSIES.

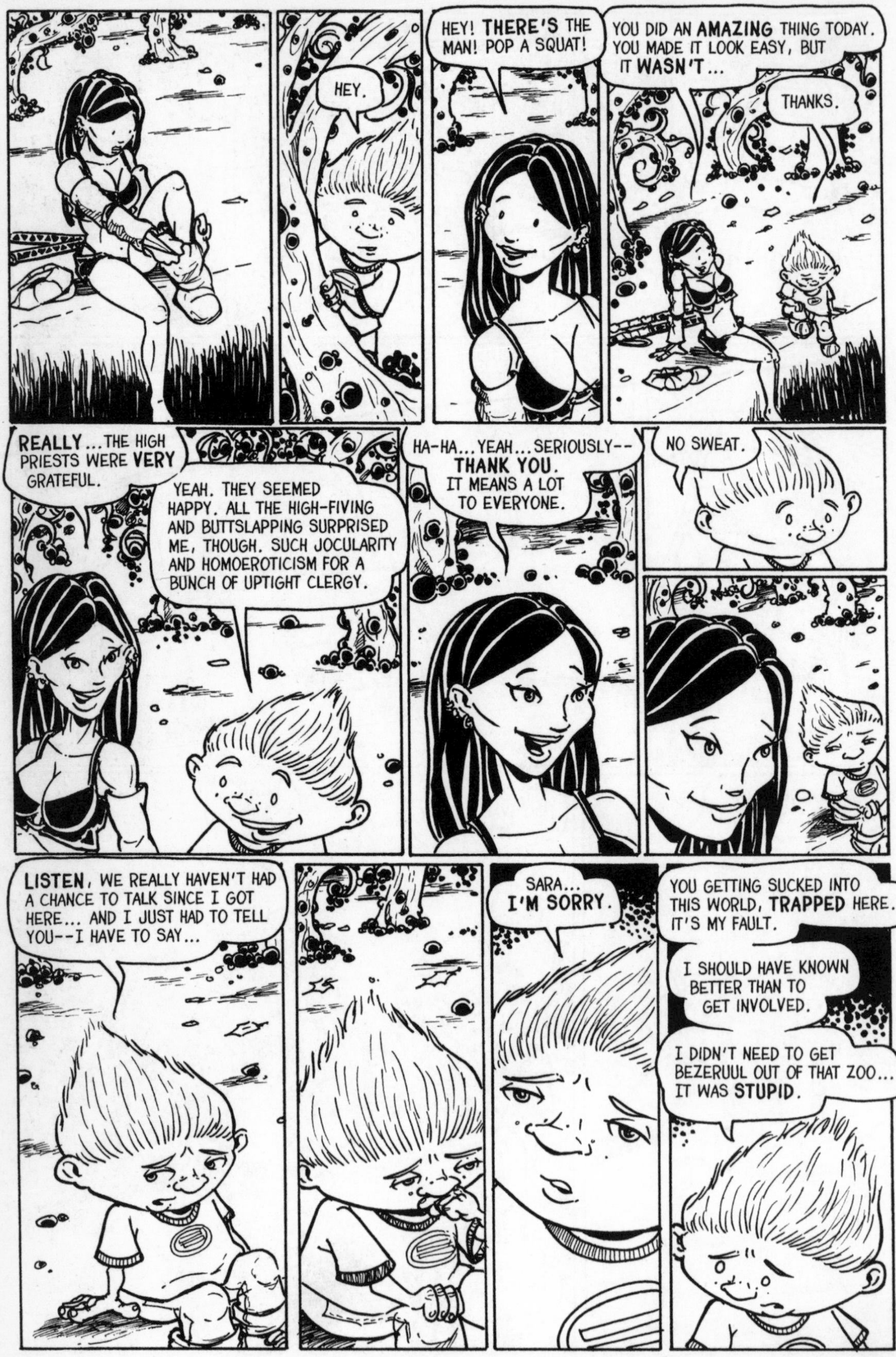
HEY.
HEY! **THERE'S** THE MAN! POP A SQUAT!
YOU DID AN **AMAZING** THING TODAY. YOU MADE IT LOOK EASY, BUT IT **WASN'T**...
THANKS.
**REALLY**...THE HIGH PRIESTS WERE **VERY** GRATEFUL.
YEAH. THEY SEEMED HAPPY. ALL THE HIGH-FIVING AND BUTTSLAPPING SURPRISED ME, THOUGH. SUCH JOCULARITY AND HOMOEROTICISM FOR A BUNCH OF UPTIGHT CLERGY.
HA-HA...YEAH...SERIOUSLY-- **THANK YOU**. IT MEANS A LOT TO EVERYONE.
NO SWEAT.
**LISTEN**, WE REALLY HAVEN'T HAD A CHANCE TO TALK SINCE I GOT HERE... AND I JUST HAD TO TELL YOU--I HAVE TO SAY...
SARA... **I'M SORRY**.
YOU GETTING SUCKED INTO THIS WORLD, **TRAPPED** HERE... IT'S MY FAULT.
I SHOULD HAVE KNOWN BETTER THAN TO GET INVOLVED.
I DIDN'T NEED TO GET BEZERUUL OUT OF THAT ZOO... IT WAS **STUPID**.

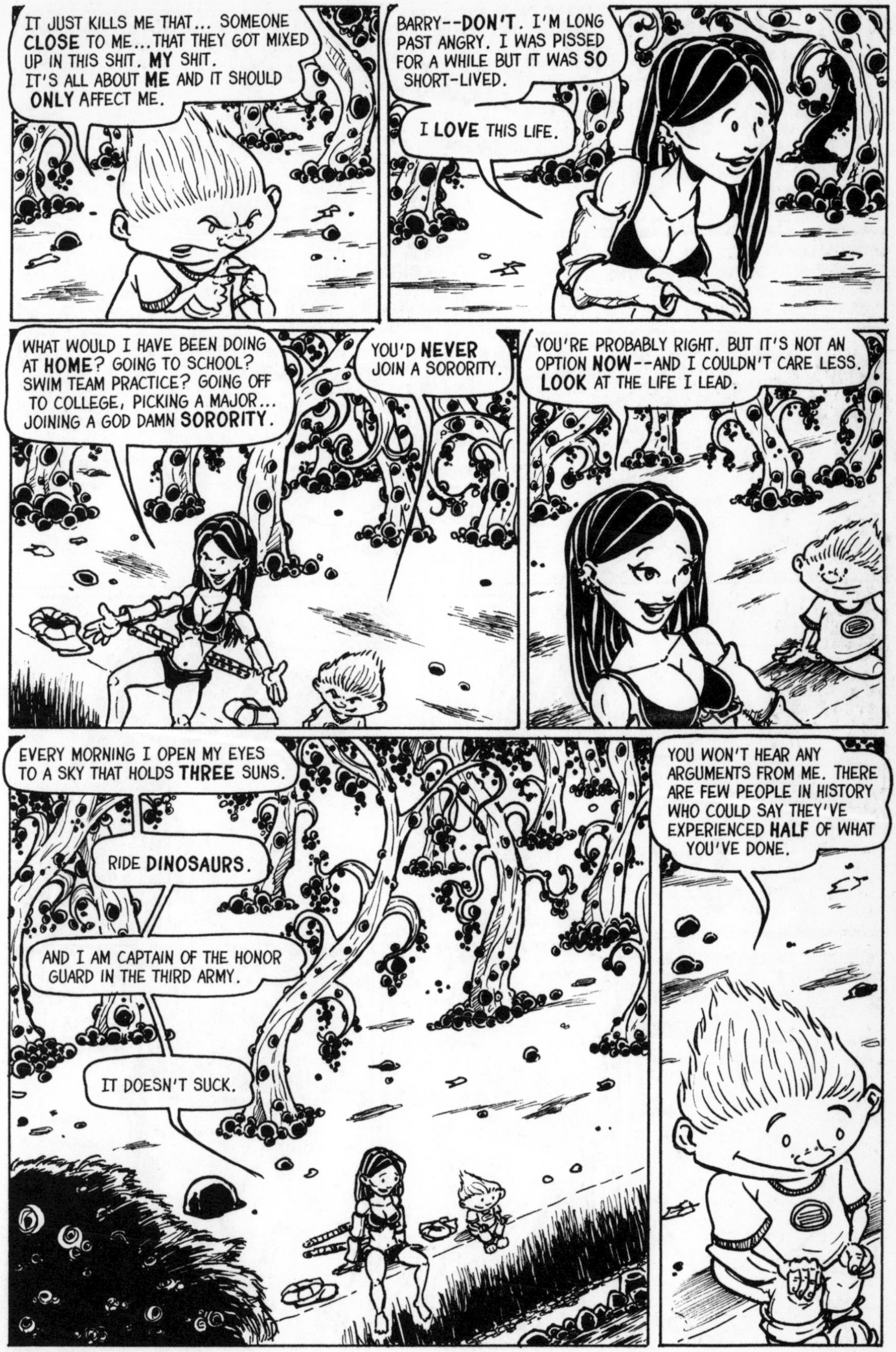
IT JUST KILLS ME THAT... SOMEONE CLOSE TO ME...THAT THEY GOT MIXED UP IN THIS SHIT. MY SHIT. IT'S ALL ABOUT ME AND IT SHOULD ONLY AFFECT ME.
BARRY--DON'T. I'M LONG PAST ANGRY. I WAS PISSED FOR A WHILE BUT IT WAS SO SHORT-LIVED.
I LOVE THIS LIFE.
WHAT WOULD I HAVE BEEN DOING AT HOME? GOING TO SCHOOL? SWIM TEAM PRACTICE? GOING OFF TO COLLEGE, PICKING A MAJOR... JOINING A GOD DAMN SORORITY.
YOU'D NEVER JOIN A SORORITY.
YOU'RE PROBABLY RIGHT. BUT IT'S NOT AN OPTION NOW--AND I COULDN'T CARE LESS. LOOK AT THE LIFE I LEAD.
EVERY MORNING I OPEN MY EYES TO A SKY THAT HOLDS THREE SUNS.
RIDE DINOSAURS.
AND I AM CAPTAIN OF THE HONOR GUARD IN THE THIRD ARMY.
IT DOESN'T SUCK.
YOU WON'T HEAR ANY ARGUMENTS FROM ME. THERE ARE FEW PEOPLE IN HISTORY WHO COULD SAY THEY'VE EXPERIENCED HALF OF WHAT YOU'VE DONE.

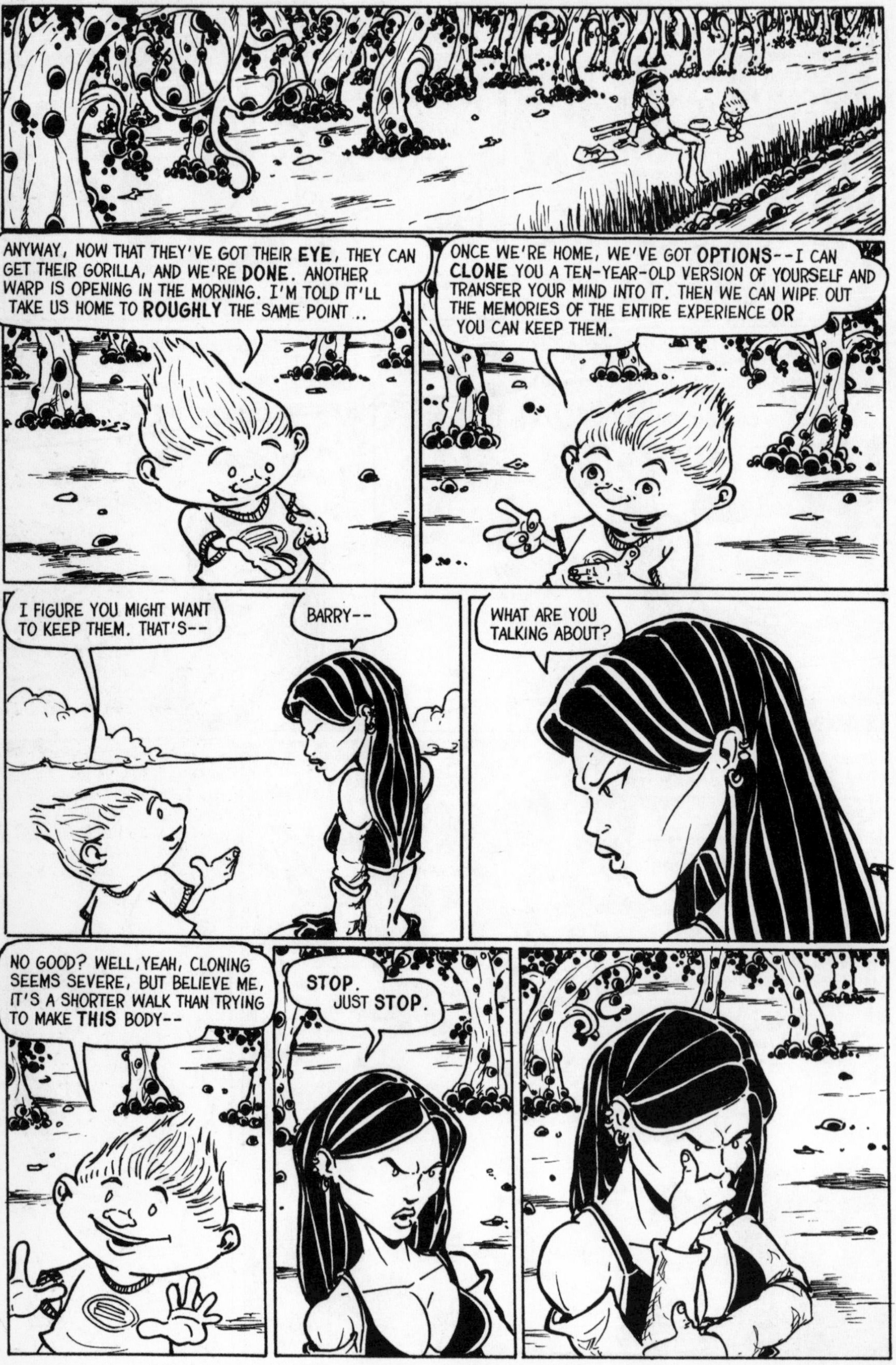
ANYWAY, NOW THAT THEY'VE GOT THEIR EYE, THEY CAN GET THEIR GORILLA, AND WE'RE DONE. ANOTHER WARP IS OPENING IN THE MORNING. I'M TOLD IT'LL TAKE US HOME TO ROUGHLY THE SAME POINT...
ONCE WE'RE HOME, WE'VE GOT OPTIONS--I CAN CLONE YOU A TEN-YEAR-OLD VERSION OF YOURSELF AND TRANSFER YOUR MIND INTO IT. THEN WE CAN WIPE OUT THE MEMORIES OF THE ENTIRE EXPERIENCE OR YOU CAN KEEP THEM.
I FIGURE YOU MIGHT WANT TO KEEP THEM. THAT'S--
BARRY--
WHAT ARE YOU TALKING ABOUT?
NO GOOD? WELL, YEAH, CLONING SEEMS SEVERE, BUT BELIEVE ME, IT'S A SHORTER WALK THAN TRYING TO MAKE THIS BODY--
STOP. JUST STOP.

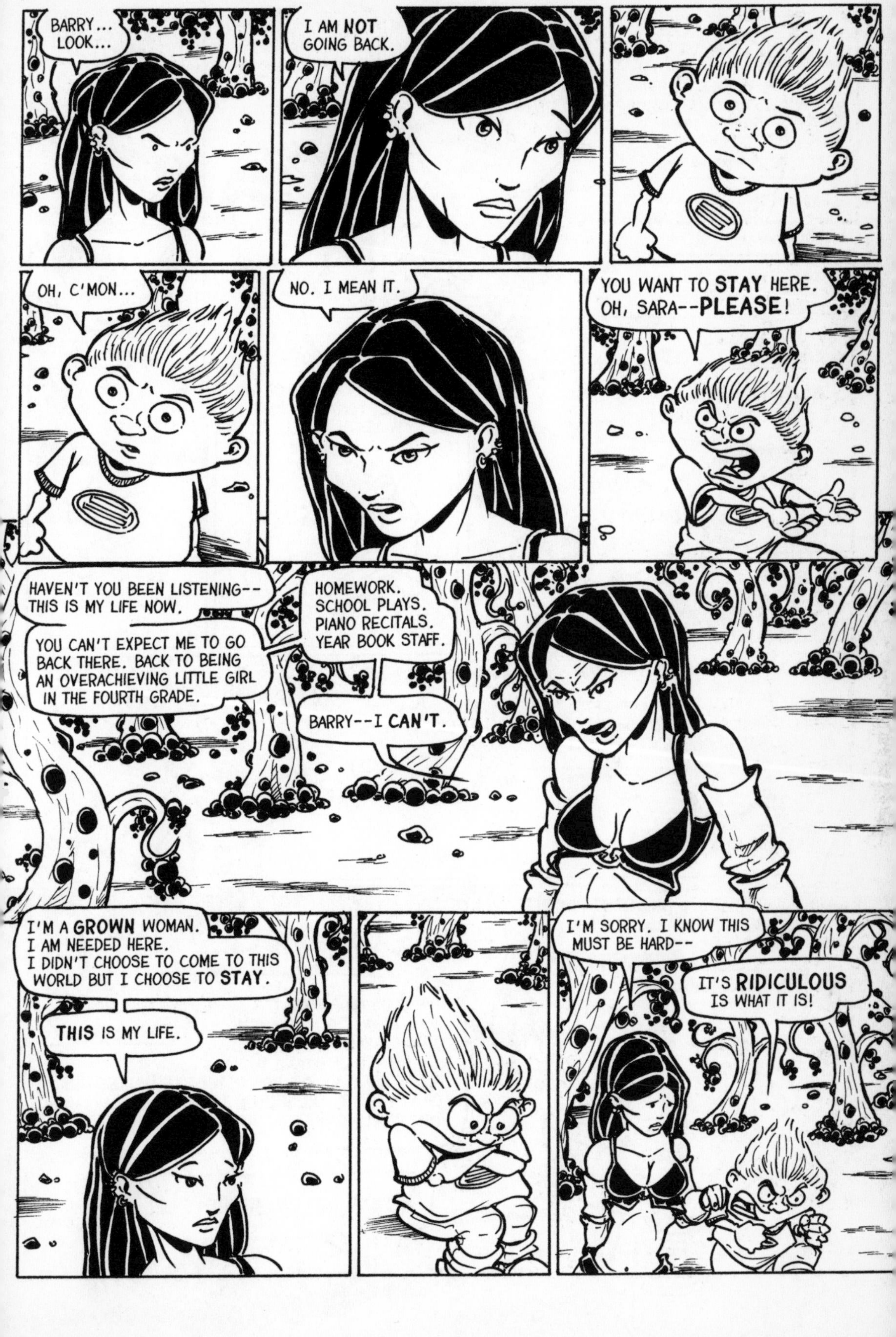
BARRY... LOOK...
I AM NOT GOING BACK.
OH, C'MON...
NO. I MEAN IT.
YOU WANT TO STAY HERE. OH, SARA--PLEASE!
HAVEN'T YOU BEEN LISTENING-- THIS IS MY LIFE NOW.
YOU CAN'T EXPECT ME TO GO BACK THERE. BACK TO BEING AN OVERACHIEVING LITTLE GIRL IN THE FOURTH GRADE.
HOMEWORK. SCHOOL PLAYS. PIANO RECITALS. YEAR BOOK STAFF.
BARRY--I CAN'T.
I'M A GROWN WOMAN. I AM NEEDED HERE. I DIDN'T CHOOSE TO COME TO THIS WORLD BUT I CHOOSE TO STAY.
THIS IS MY LIFE.
I'M SORRY. I KNOW THIS MUST BE HARD--
IT'S RIDICULOUS IS WHAT IT IS!

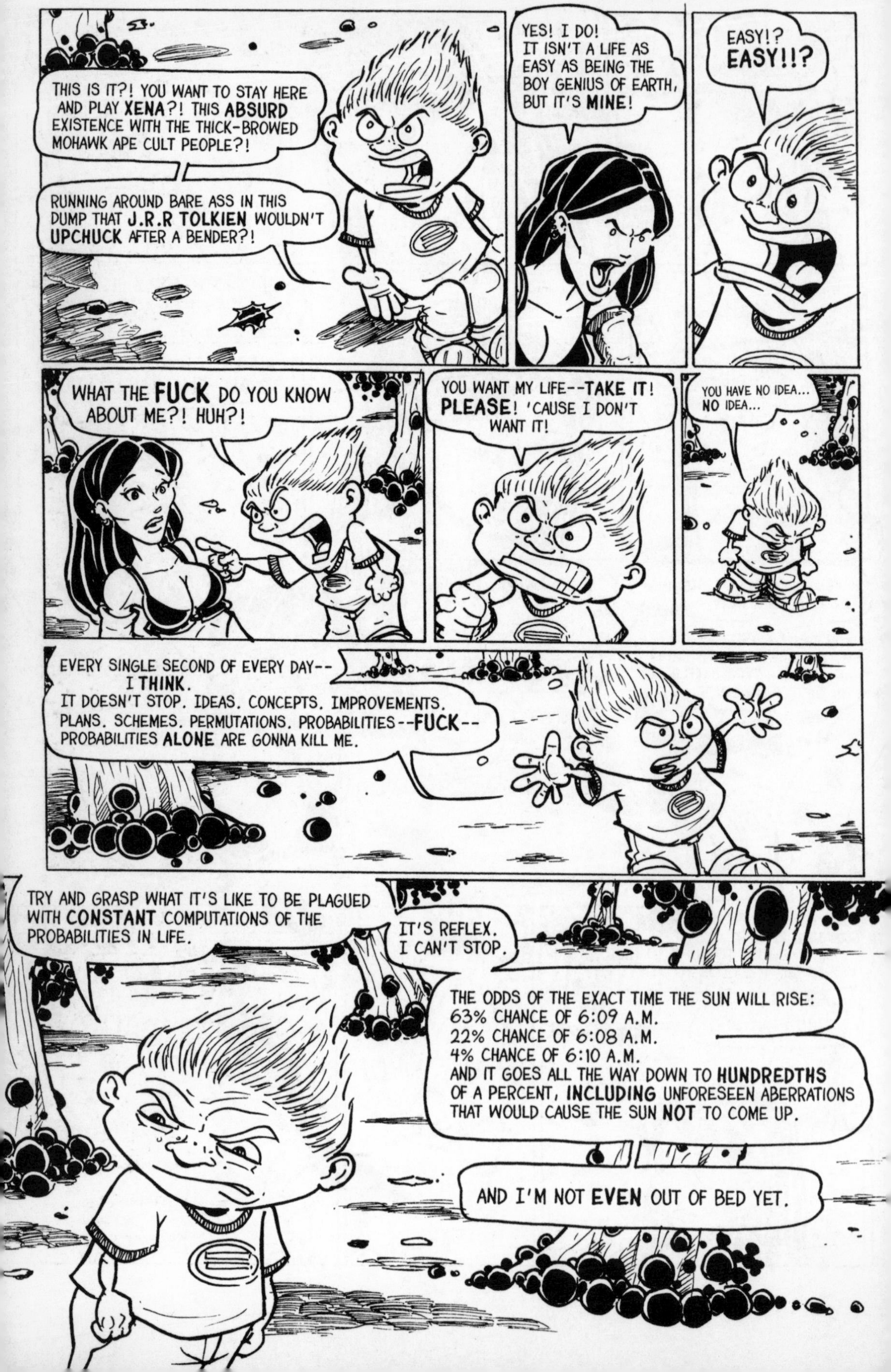

THIS IS IT?! YOU WANT TO STAY HERE AND PLAY XENA?! THIS ABSURD EXISTENCE WITH THE THICK-BROWED MOHAWK APE CULT PEOPLE?!
RUNNING AROUND BARE ASS IN THIS DUMP THAT J.R.R TOLKIEN WOULDN'T UPCHUCK AFTER A BENDER?!
YES! I DO! IT ISN'T A LIFE AS EASY AS BEING THE BOY GENIUS OF EARTH, BUT IT'S MINE!
EASY!? EASY!!?
WHAT THE FUCK DO YOU KNOW ABOUT ME?! HUH?!
YOU WANT MY LIFE--TAKE IT! PLEASE! 'CAUSE I DON'T WANT IT!
YOU HAVE NO IDEA... NO IDEA...
EVERY SINGLE SECOND OF EVERY DAY-- I THINK.
IT DOESN'T STOP. IDEAS. CONCEPTS. IMPROVEMENTS. PLANS. SCHEMES. PERMUTATIONS. PROBABILITIES--FUCK-- PROBABILITIES ALONE ARE GONNA KILL ME.
TRY AND GRASP WHAT IT'S LIKE TO BE PLAGUED WITH CONSTANT COMPUTATIONS OF THE PROBABILITIES IN LIFE.
IT'S REFLEX. I CAN'T STOP.
THE ODDS OF THE EXACT TIME THE SUN WILL RISE: 63% CHANCE OF 6:09 A.M. 22% CHANCE OF 6:08 A.M. 4% CHANCE OF 6:10 A.M. AND IT GOES ALL THE WAY DOWN TO HUNDREDTHS OF A PERCENT, INCLUDING UNFORESEEN ABERRATIONS THAT WOULD CAUSE THE SUN NOT TO COME UP.
AND I'M NOT EVEN OUT OF BED YET.

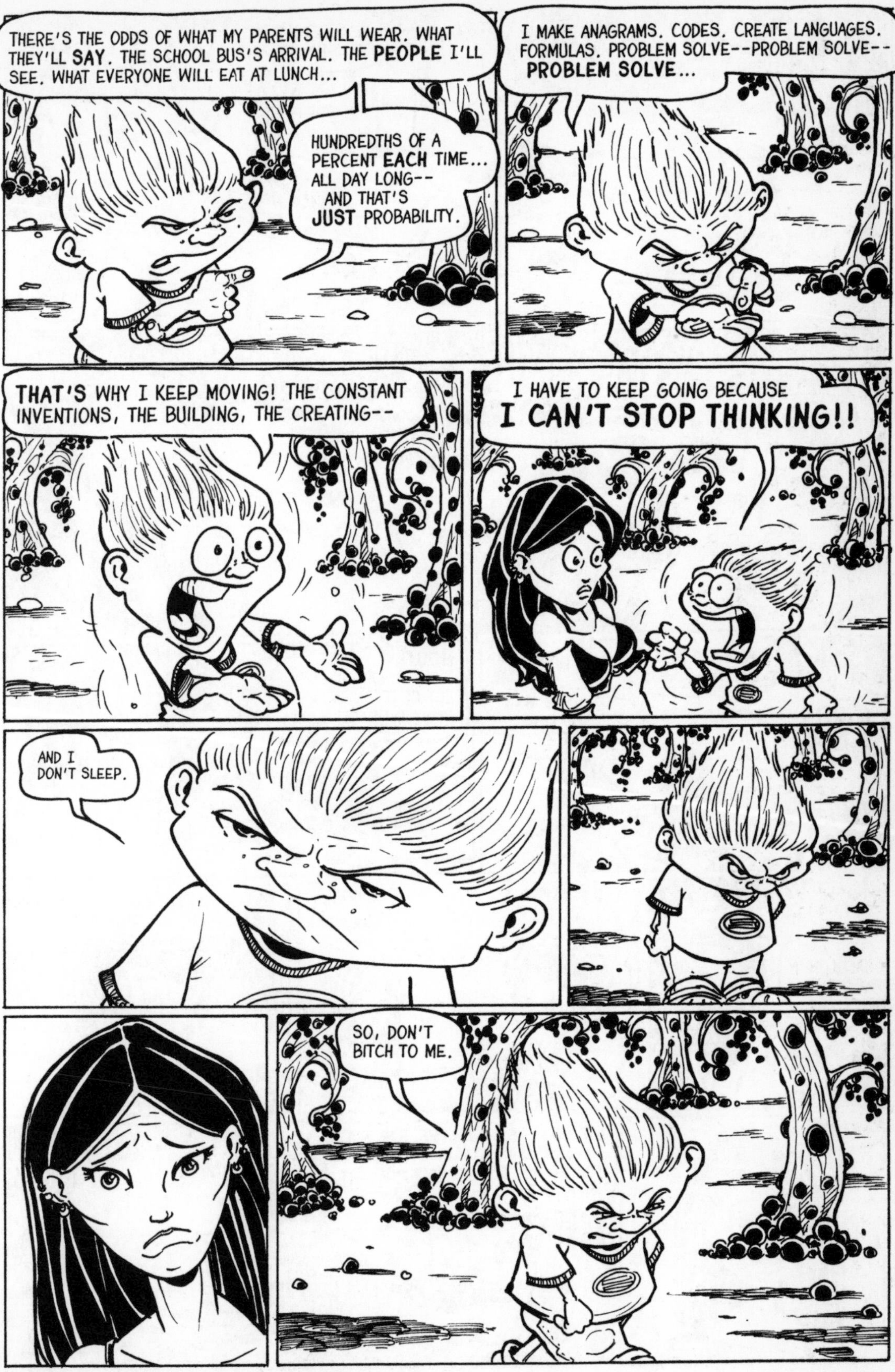
THERE'S THE ODDS OF WHAT MY PARENTS WILL WEAR. WHAT THEY'LL SAY. THE SCHOOL BUS'S ARRIVAL. THE PEOPLE I'LL SEE. WHAT EVERYONE WILL EAT AT LUNCH...
HUNDREDTHS OF A PERCENT EACH TIME... ALL DAY LONG-- AND THAT'S JUST PROBABILITY.
I MAKE ANAGRAMS. CODES. CREATE LANGUAGES. FORMULAS. PROBLEM SOLVE--PROBLEM SOLVE-- PROBLEM SOLVE...
THAT'S WHY I KEEP MOVING! THE CONSTANT INVENTIONS, THE BUILDING, THE CREATING--
I HAVE TO KEEP GOING BECAUSE I CAN'T STOP THINKING!!
AND I DON'T SLEEP.
SO, DON'T BITCH TO ME.

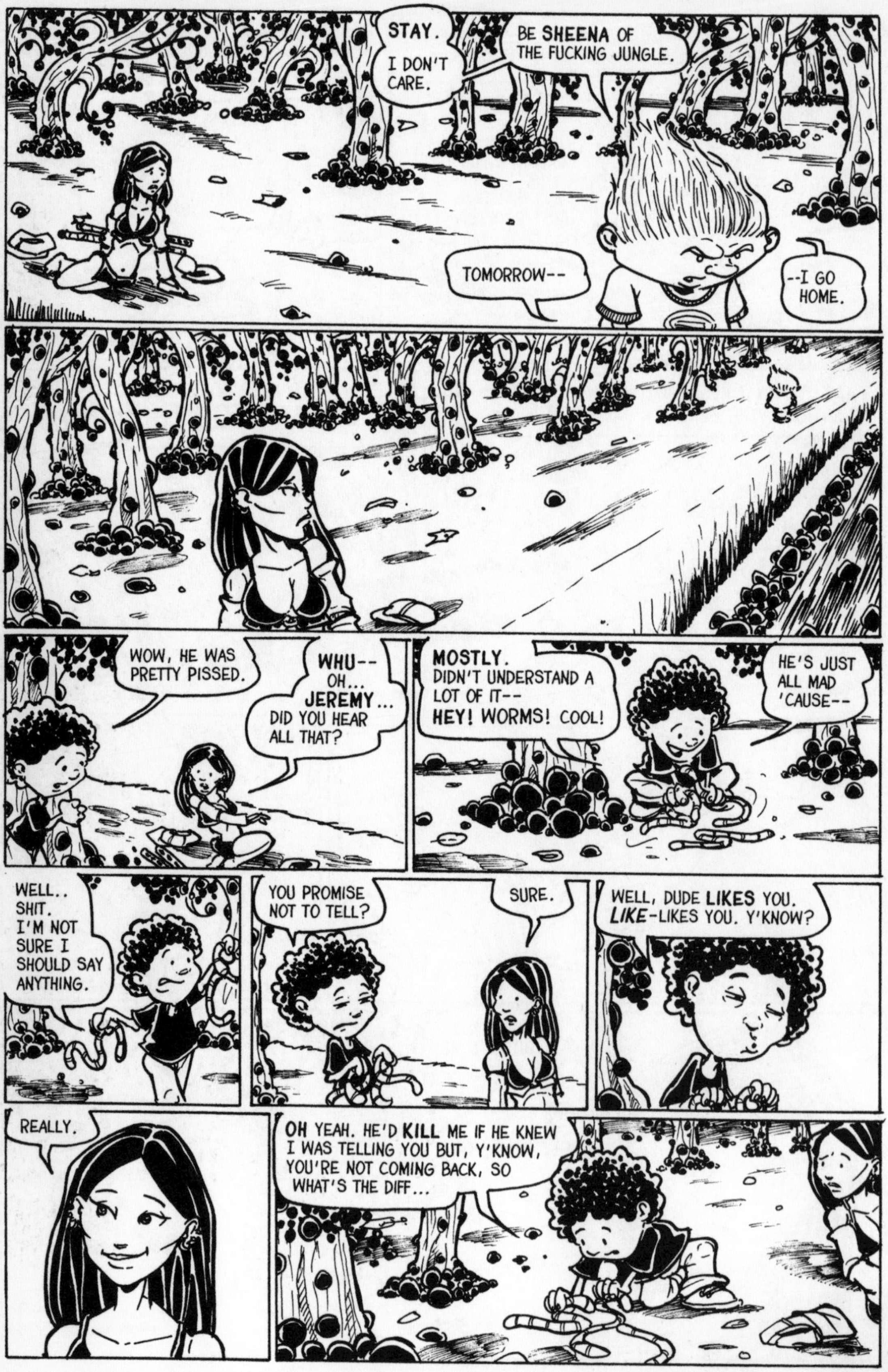
STAY.
I DON'T CARE.
BE SHEENA OF THE FUCKING JUNGLE.
TOMORROW--
--I GO HOME.
WOW, HE WAS PRETTY PISSED.
WHU-- OH... JEREMY... DID YOU HEAR ALL THAT?
MOSTLY. DIDN'T UNDERSTAND A LOT OF IT-- HEY! WORMS! COOL!
HE'S JUST ALL MAD 'CAUSE--
WELL.. SHIT. I'M NOT SURE I SHOULD SAY ANYTHING.
YOU PROMISE NOT TO TELL?
SURE.
WELL, DUDE LIKES YOU. LIKE-LIKES YOU. Y'KNOW?
REALLY.
OH YEAH. HE'D KILL ME IF HE KNEW I WAS TELLING YOU BUT, Y'KNOW, YOU'RE NOT COMING BACK, SO WHAT'S THE DIFF...

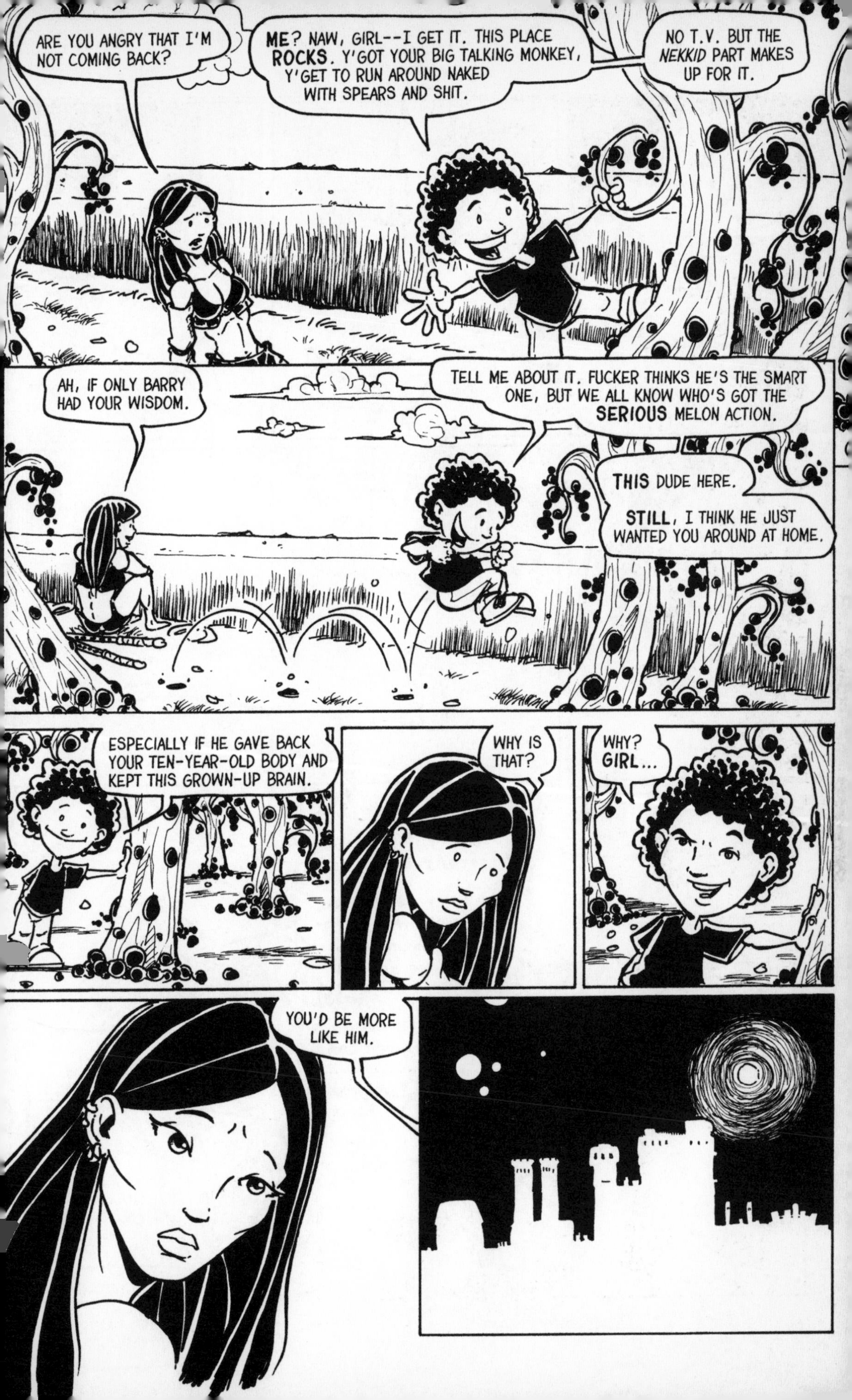
ARE YOU ANGRY THAT I'M NOT COMING BACK?
ME? NAW, GIRL--I GET IT. THIS PLACE ROCKS. Y'GOT YOUR BIG TALKING MONKEY, Y'GET TO RUN AROUND NAKED WITH SPEARS AND SHIT.
NO T.V. BUT THE NEKKID PART MAKES UP FOR IT.
AH, IF ONLY BARRY HAD YOUR WISDOM.
TELL ME ABOUT IT. FUCKER THINKS HE'S THE SMART ONE, BUT WE ALL KNOW WHO'S GOT THE SERIOUS MELON ACTION.
THIS DUDE HERE.
STILL, I THINK HE JUST WANTED YOU AROUND AT HOME.
ESPECIALLY IF HE GAVE BACK YOUR TEN-YEAR-OLD BODY AND KEPT THIS GROWN-UP BRAIN.
WHY IS THAT?
WHY? GIRL...
YOU'D BE MORE LIKE HIM.

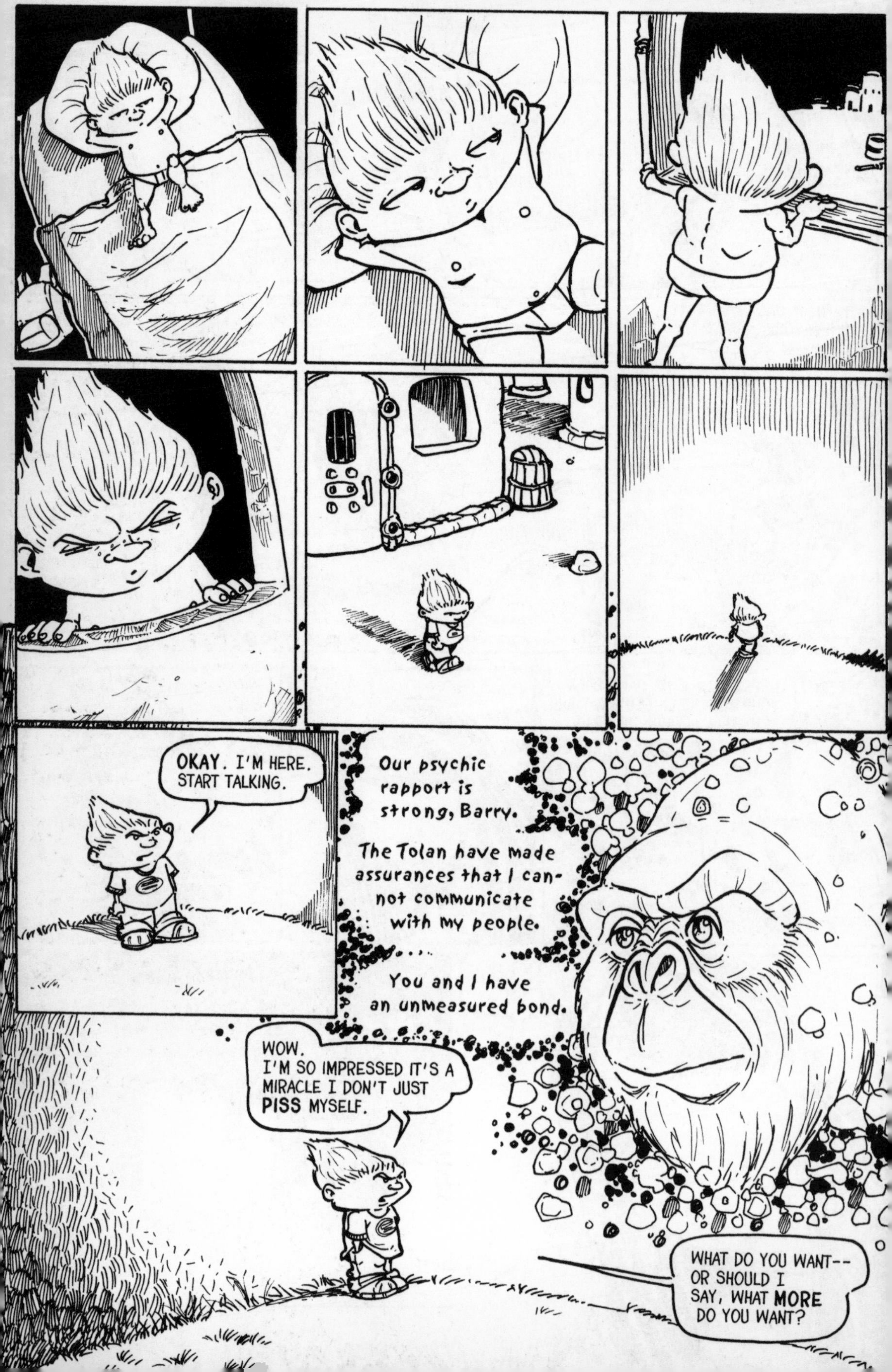
OKAY. I'M HERE. START TALKING.
Our psychic rapport is strong, Barry.
The Tolan have made assurances that I cannot communicate with my people.
You and I have an unmeasured bond.
WOW. I'M SO IMPRESSED IT'S A MIRACLE I DON'T JUST PISS MYSELF.
WHAT DO YOU WANT-- OR SHOULD I SAY, WHAT MORE DO YOU WANT?

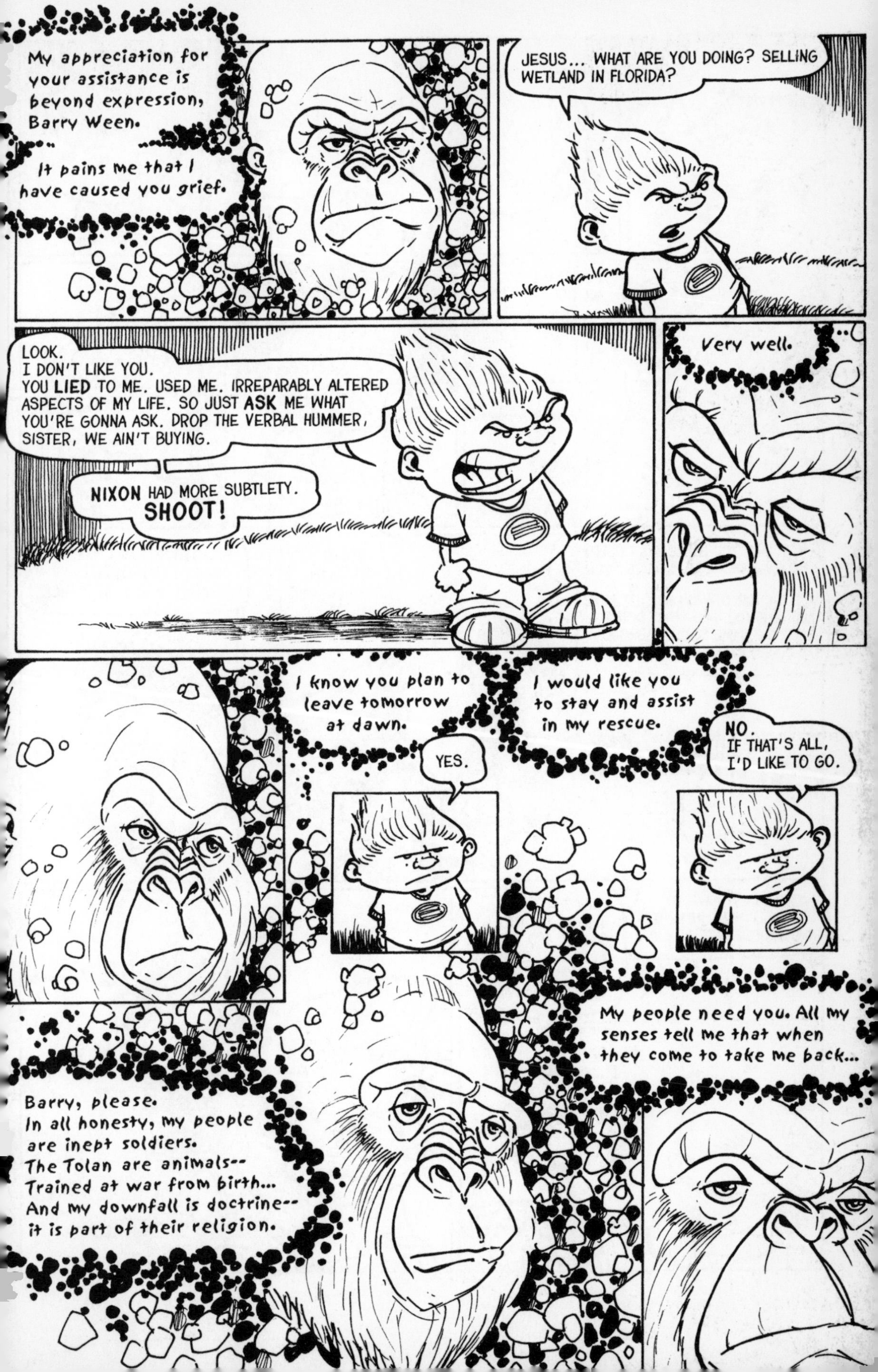
My appreciation for your assistance is beyond expression, Barry Ween.
It pains me that I have caused you grief.
JESUS... WHAT ARE YOU DOING? SELLING WETLAND IN FLORIDA?
LOOK.
I DON'T LIKE YOU.
YOU LIED TO ME. USED ME. IRREPARABLY ALTERED ASPECTS OF MY LIFE. SO JUST ASK ME WHAT YOU'RE GONNA ASK. DROP THE VERBAL HUMMER, SISTER, WE AIN'T BUYING.
NIXON HAD MORE SUBTLETY. SHOOT!
Very well.
I know you plan to leave tomorrow at dawn.
YES.
I would like you to stay and assist in my rescue.
NO.
IF THAT'S ALL, I'D LIKE TO GO.
My people need you. All my senses tell me that when they come to take me back...
Barry, please.
In all honesty, my people are inept soldiers.
The Tolan are animals--
Trained at war from birth...
And my downfall is doctrine--
it is part of their religion.

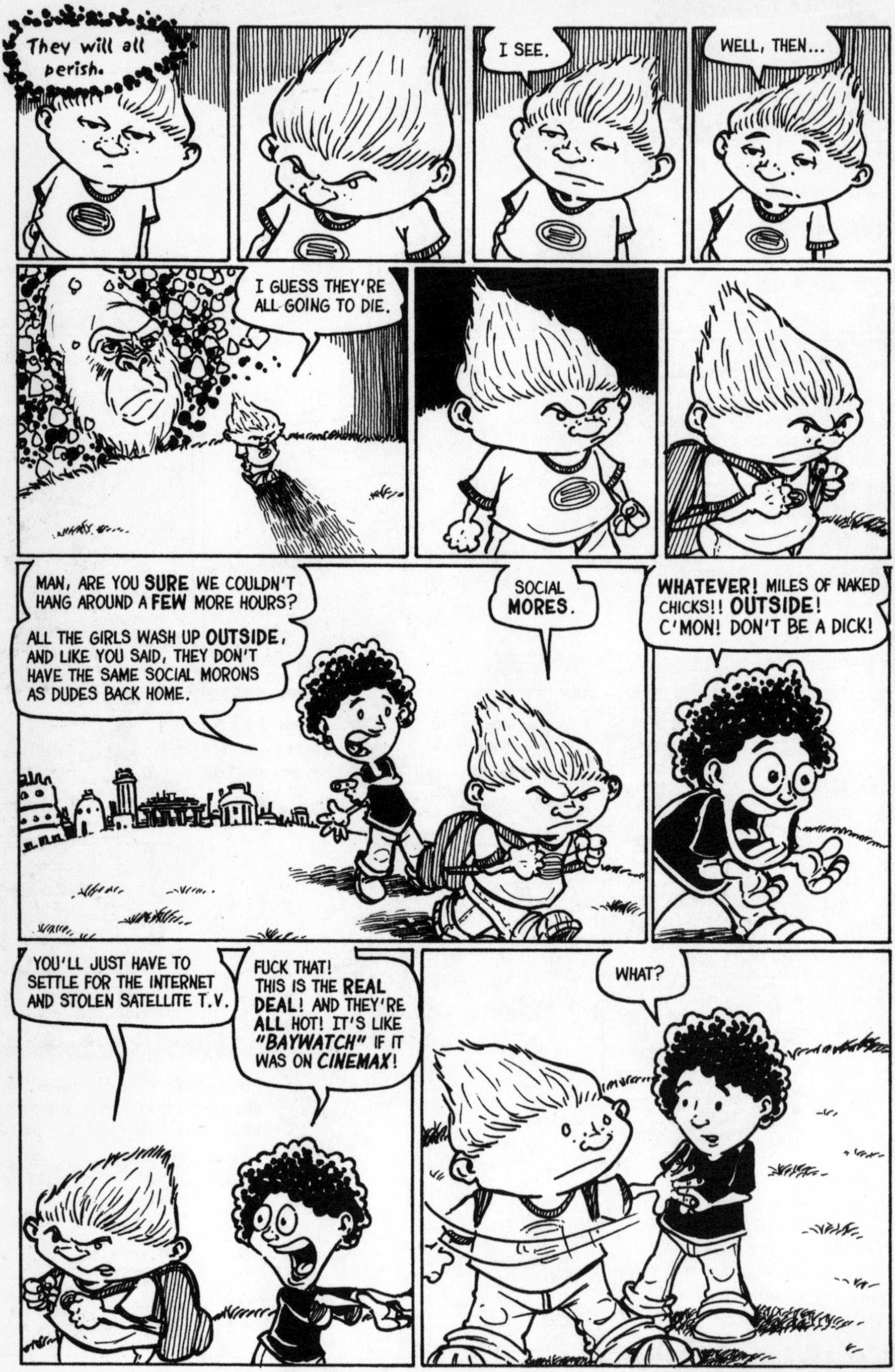
They will all perish.
I SEE.
WELL, THEN...
I GUESS THEY'RE ALL GOING TO DIE.
MAN, ARE YOU SURE WE COULDN'T HANG AROUND A FEW MORE HOURS?
ALL THE GIRLS WASH UP OUTSIDE, AND LIKE YOU SAID, THEY DON'T HAVE THE SAME SOCIAL MORONS AS DUDES BACK HOME.
SOCIAL MORES.
WHATEVER! MILES OF NAKED CHICKS!! OUTSIDE! C'MON! DON'T BE A DICK!
YOU'LL JUST HAVE TO SETTLE FOR THE INTERNET AND STOLEN SATELLITE T.V.
FUCK THAT! THIS IS THE REAL DEAL! AND THEY'RE ALL HOT! IT'S LIKE "BAYWATCH" IF IT WAS ON CINEMAX!
WHAT?

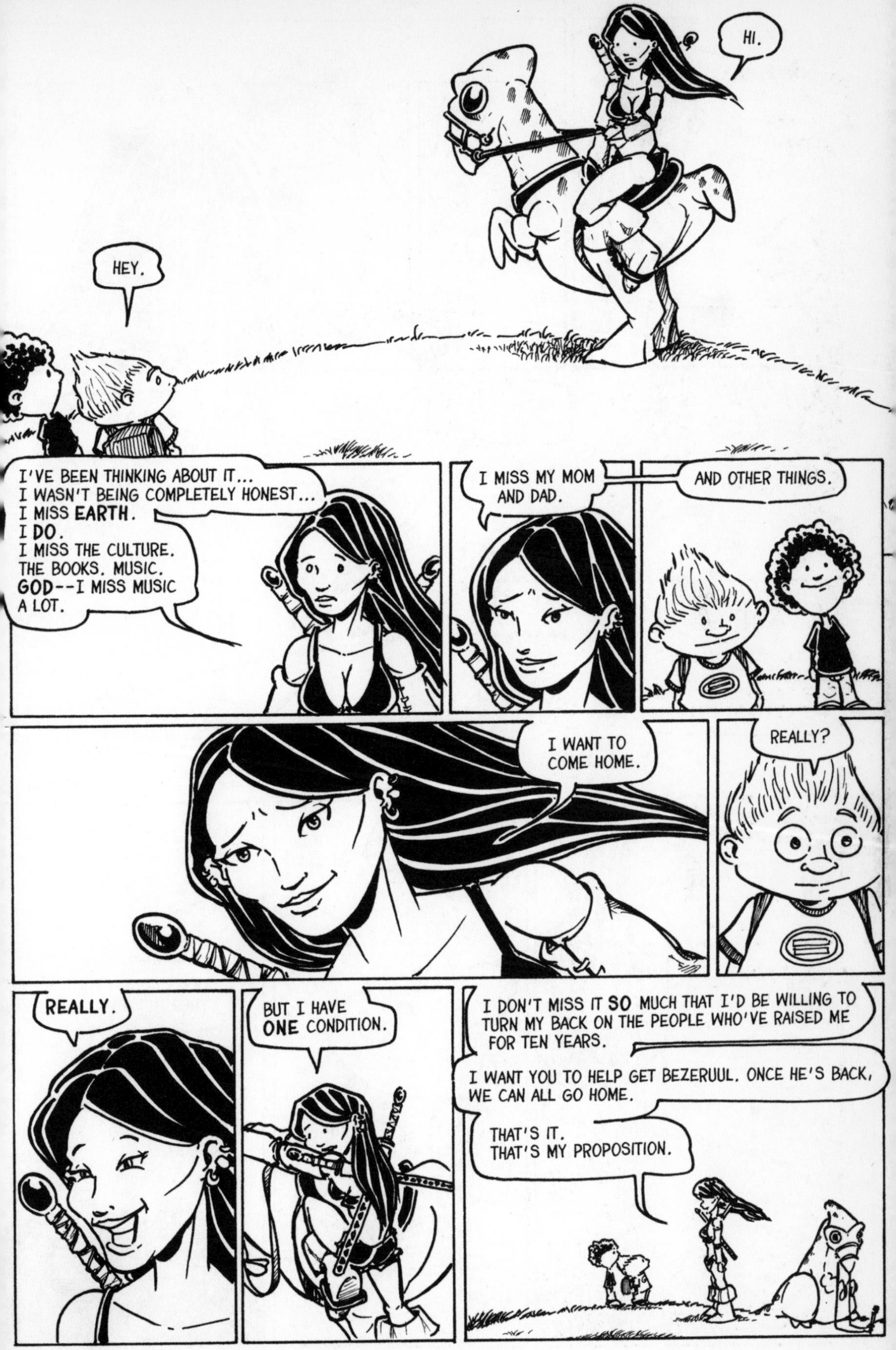
HI.
HEY.
I'VE BEEN THINKING ABOUT IT... I WASN'T BEING COMPLETELY HONEST...
I MISS EARTH. I DO. I MISS THE CULTURE. THE BOOKS. MUSIC. GOD--I MISS MUSIC A LOT.
I MISS MY MOM AND DAD.
AND OTHER THINGS.
I WANT TO COME HOME.
REALLY?
REALLY.
BUT I HAVE ONE CONDITION.
I DON'T MISS IT SO MUCH THAT I'D BE WILLING TO TURN MY BACK ON THE PEOPLE WHO'VE RAISED ME FOR TEN YEARS.
I WANT YOU TO HELP GET BEZERUUL. ONCE HE'S BACK, WE CAN ALL GO HOME.
THAT'S IT. THAT'S MY PROPOSITION.

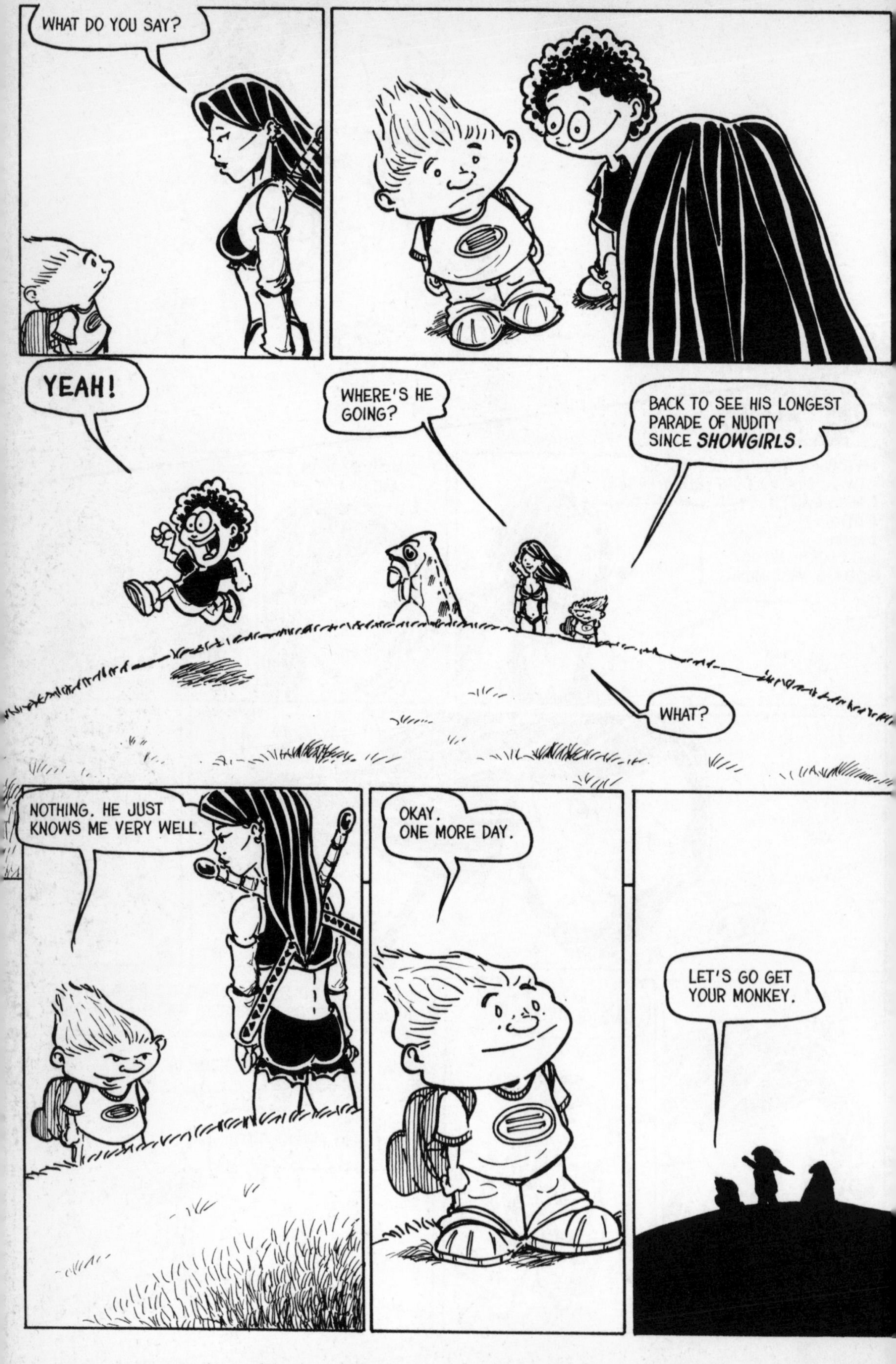
WHAT DO YOU SAY?
YEAH!
WHERE'S HE GOING?
BACK TO SEE HIS LONGEST PARADE OF NUDITY SINCE SHOWGIRLS.
WHAT?
NOTHING. HE JUST KNOWS ME VERY WELL.
OKAY. ONE MORE DAY.
LET'S GO GET YOUR MONKEY.

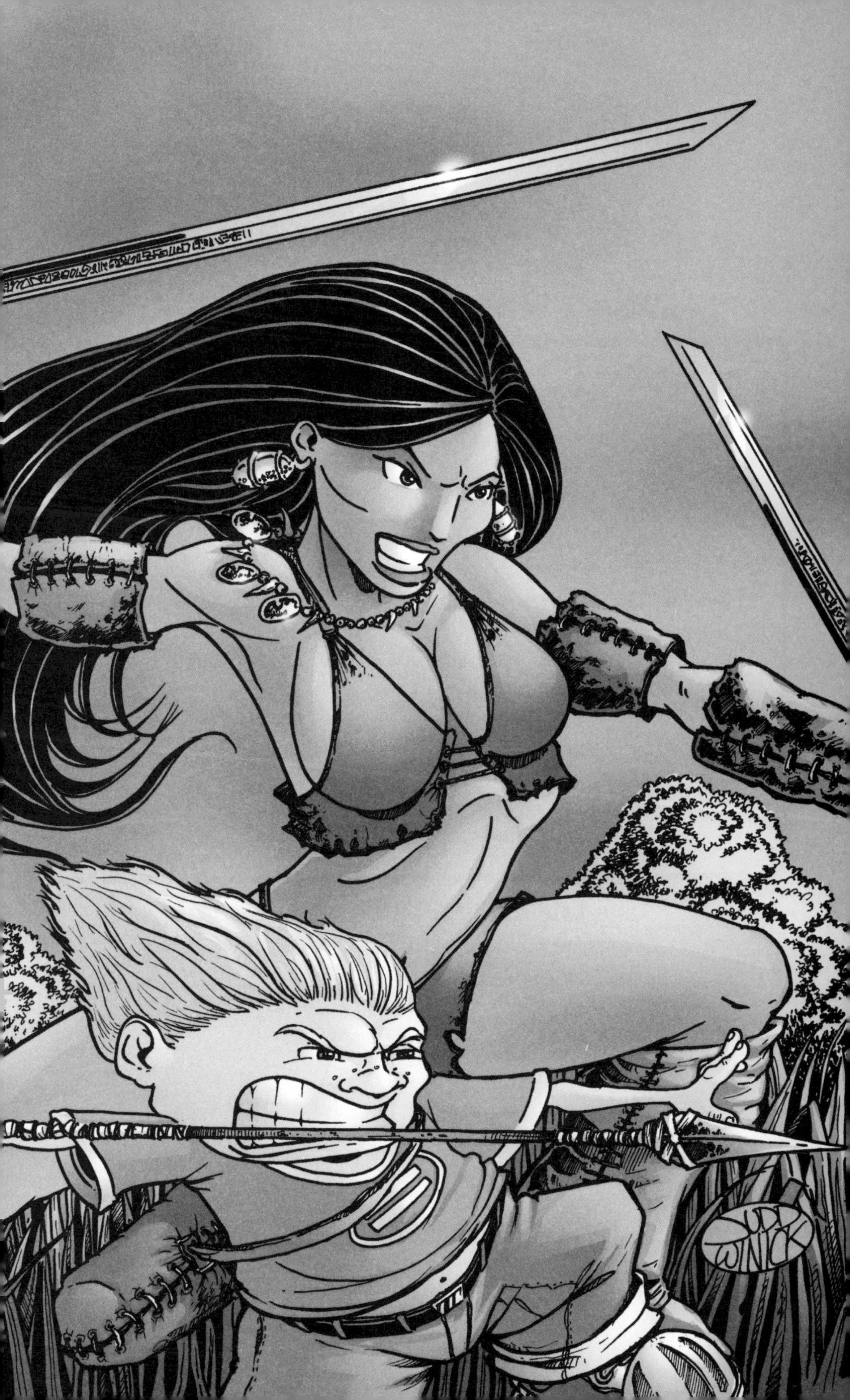

# "The Fastest Runner Who's Not Allowed to Win"

"The Tale of the Great Ape—part three"

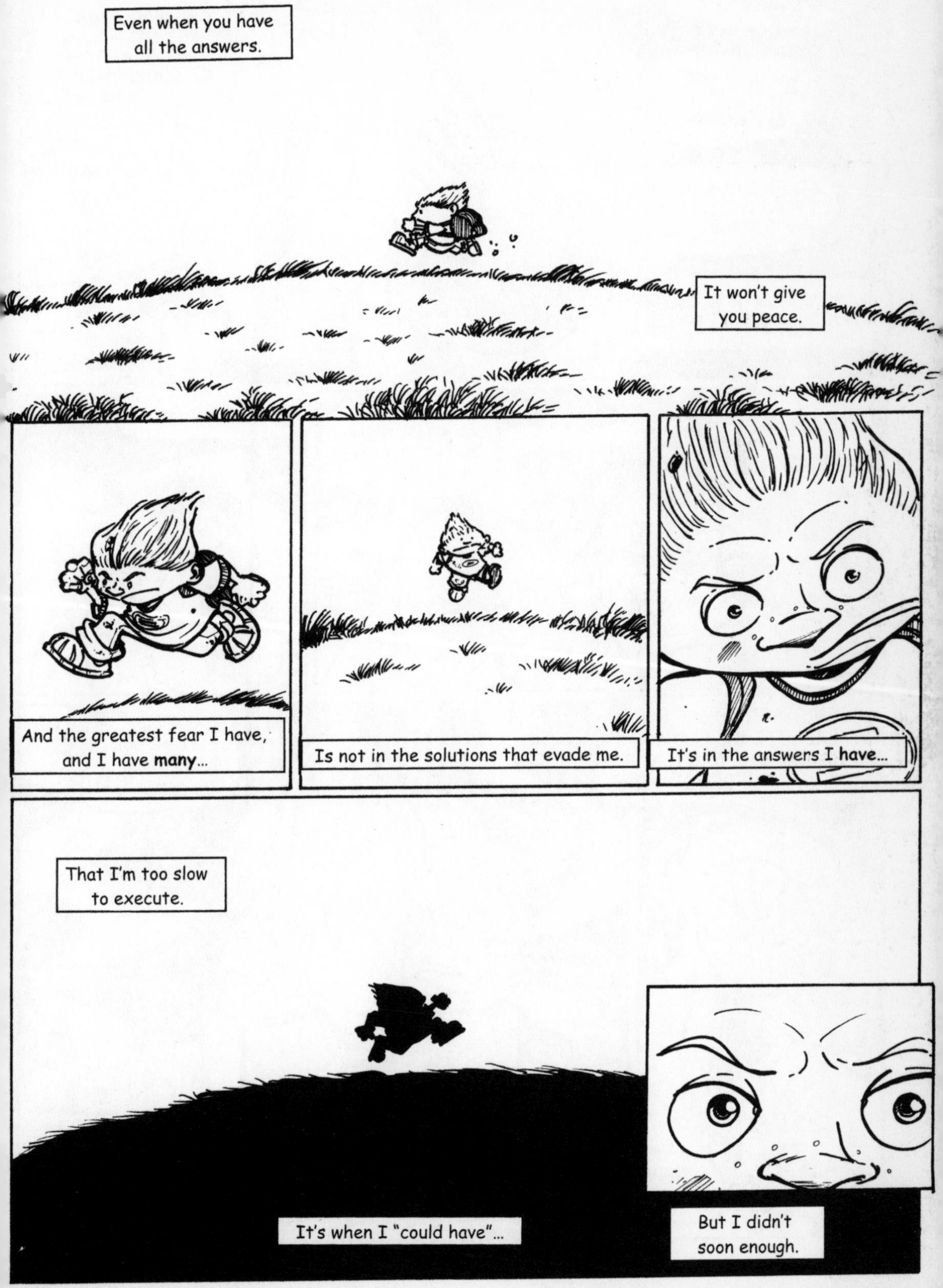
Even when you have all the answers.
It won't give you peace.
And the greatest fear I have, and I have **many**...
Is not in the solutions that evade me.
It's in the answers I **have**...
That I'm too slow to execute.
It's when I "could have"...
But I didn't soon enough.

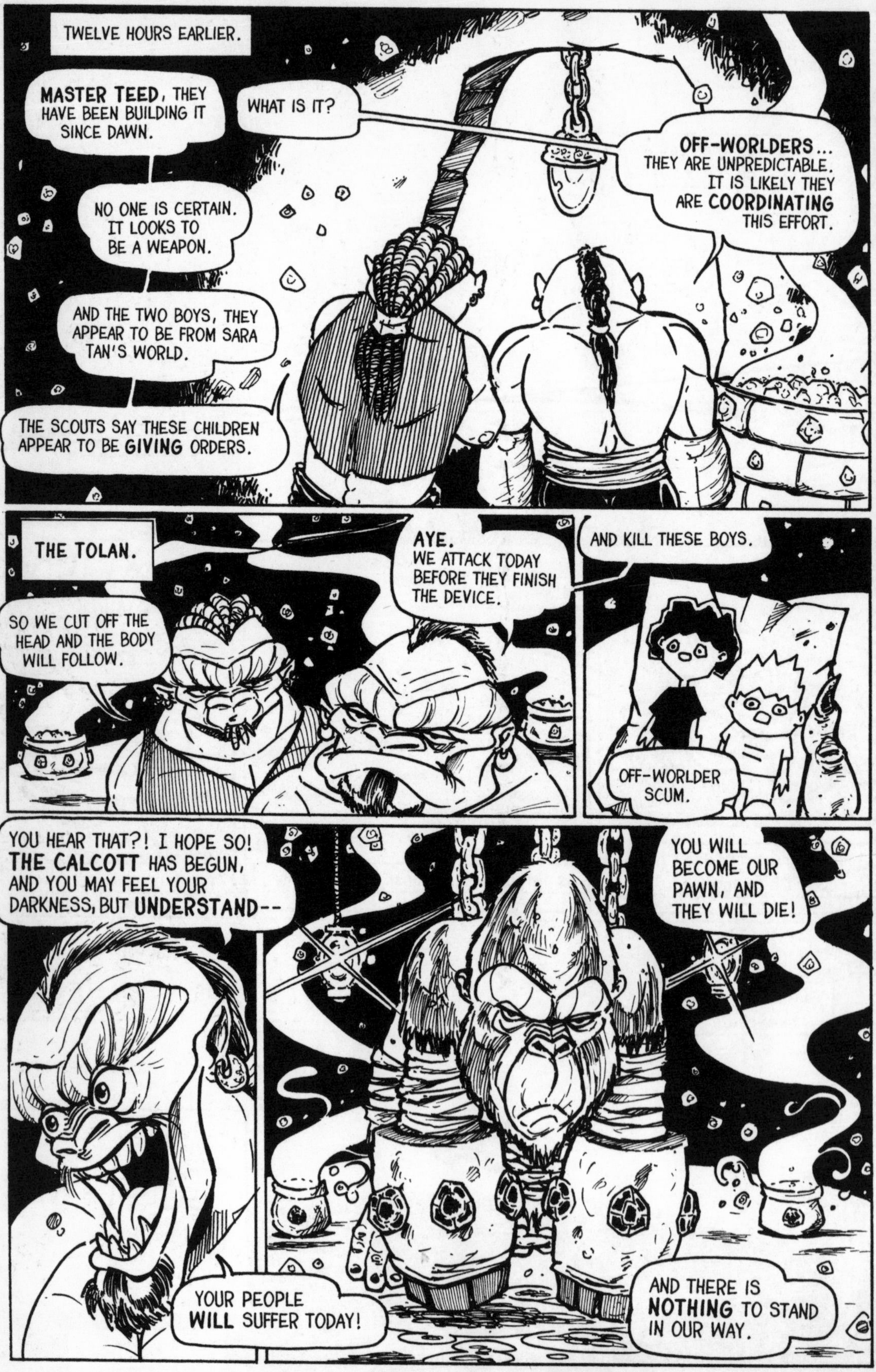
TWELVE HOURS EARLIER.
MASTER TEED, THEY HAVE BEEN BUILDING IT SINCE DAWN.
WHAT IS IT?
NO ONE IS CERTAIN. IT LOOKS TO BE A WEAPON.
AND THE TWO BOYS, THEY APPEAR TO BE FROM SARA TAN'S WORLD.
THE SCOUTS SAY THESE CHILDREN APPEAR TO BE GIVING ORDERS.
OFF-WORLDERS... THEY ARE UNPREDICTABLE. IT IS LIKELY THEY ARE COORDINATING THIS EFFORT.
THE TOLAN.
SO WE CUT OFF THE HEAD AND THE BODY WILL FOLLOW.
AYE. WE ATTACK TODAY BEFORE THEY FINISH THE DEVICE.
AND KILL THESE BOYS.
OFF-WORLDER SCUM.
YOU HEAR THAT?! I HOPE SO! THE CALCOTT HAS BEGUN, AND YOU MAY FEEL YOUR DARKNESS, BUT UNDERSTAND--
YOUR PEOPLE WILL SUFFER TODAY!
YOU WILL BECOME OUR PAWN, AND THEY WILL DIE!
AND THERE IS NOTHING TO STAND IN OUR WAY.

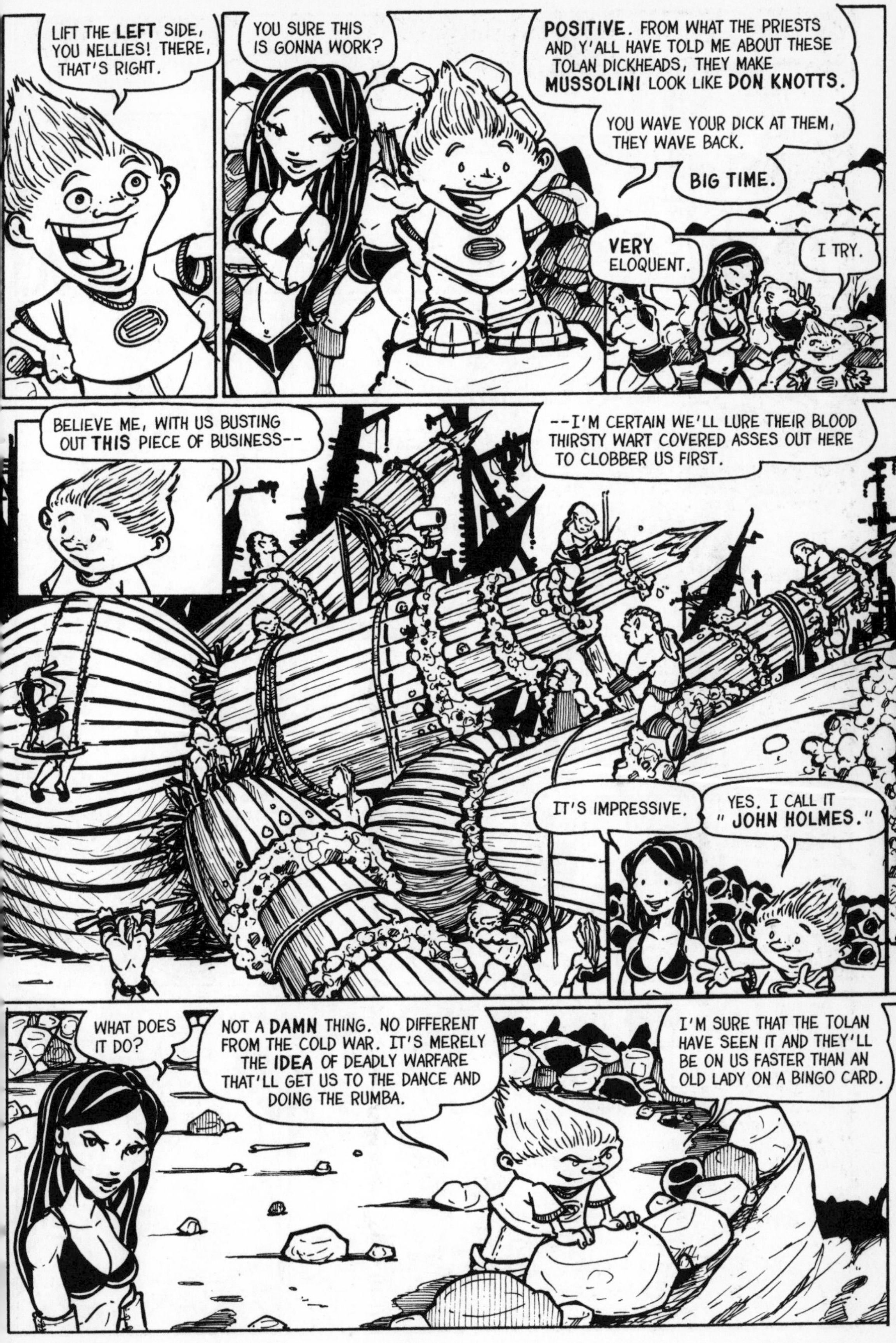
LIFT THE LEFT SIDE, YOU NELLIES! THERE, THAT'S RIGHT.
YOU SURE THIS IS GONNA WORK?
POSITIVE. FROM WHAT THE PRIESTS AND Y'ALL HAVE TOLD ME ABOUT THESE TOLAN DICKHEADS, THEY MAKE MUSSOLINI LOOK LIKE DON KNOTTS.
YOU WAVE YOUR DICK AT THEM, THEY WAVE BACK.
BIG TIME.
VERY ELOQUENT.
I TRY.
BELIEVE ME, WITH US BUSTING OUT THIS PIECE OF BUSINESS--
--I'M CERTAIN WE'LL LURE THEIR BLOOD THIRSTY WART COVERED ASSES OUT HERE TO CLOBBER US FIRST.
IT'S IMPRESSIVE.
YES. I CALL IT "JOHN HOLMES."
WHAT DOES IT DO?
NOT A DAMN THING. NO DIFFERENT FROM THE COLD WAR. IT'S MERELY THE IDEA OF DEADLY WARFARE THAT'LL GET US TO THE DANCE AND DOING THE RUMBA.
I'M SURE THAT THE TOLAN HAVE SEEN IT AND THEY'LL BE ON US FASTER THAN AN OLD LADY ON A BINGO CARD.

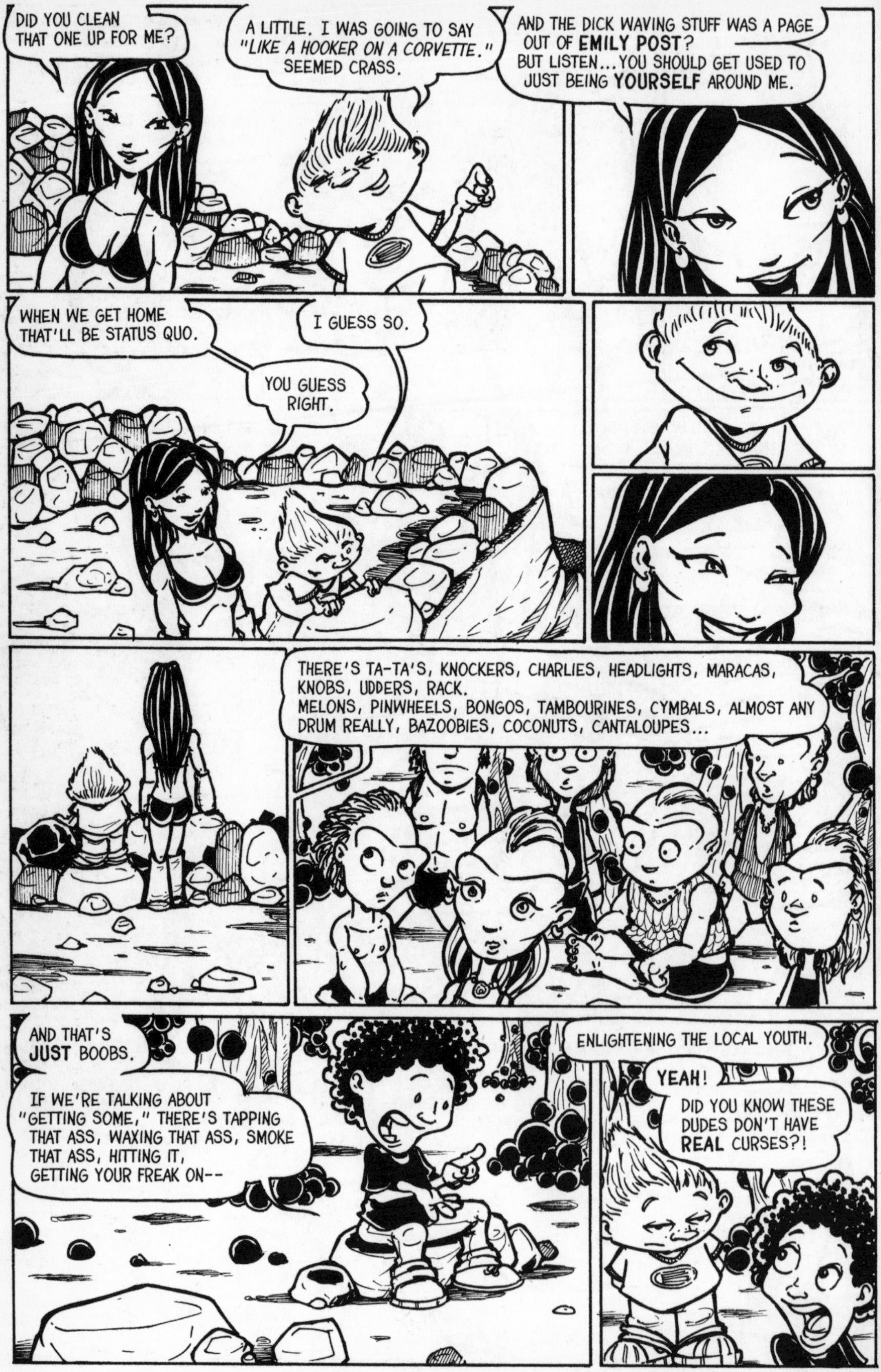
DID YOU CLEAN THAT ONE UP FOR ME?
A LITTLE. I WAS GOING TO SAY "LIKE A HOOKER ON A CORVETTE." SEEMED CRASS.
AND THE DICK WAVING STUFF WAS A PAGE OUT OF EMILY POST? BUT LISTEN... YOU SHOULD GET USED TO JUST BEING YOURSELF AROUND ME.
WHEN WE GET HOME THAT'LL BE STATUS QUO.
I GUESS SO.
YOU GUESS RIGHT.
THERE'S TA-TA'S, KNOCKERS, CHARLIES, HEADLIGHTS, MARACAS, KNOBS, UDDERS, RACK. MELONS, PINWHEELS, BONGOS, TAMBOURINES, CYMBALS, ALMOST ANY DRUM REALLY, BAZOOBIES, COCONUTS, CANTALOUPES...
AND THAT'S JUST BOOBS.
IF WE'RE TALKING ABOUT "GETTING SOME," THERE'S TAPPING THAT ASS, WAXING THAT ASS, SMOKE THAT ASS, HITTING IT, GETTING YOUR FREAK ON--
ENLIGHTENING THE LOCAL YOUTH.
YEAH!
DID YOU KNOW THESE DUDES DON'T HAVE REAL CURSES?!

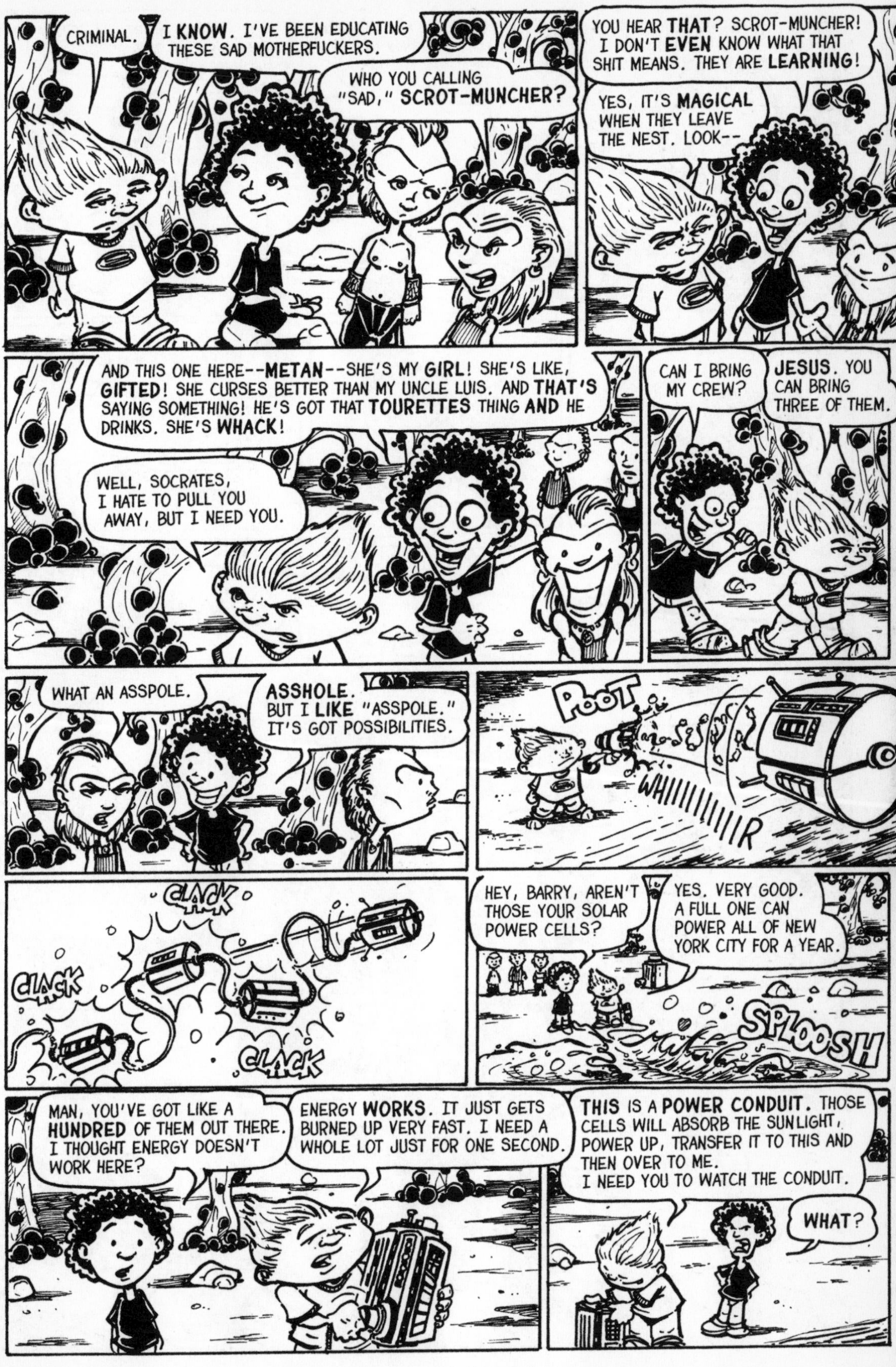
CRIMINAL.
I KNOW. I'VE BEEN EDUCATING THESE SAD MOTHERFUCKERS.
WHO YOU CALLING "SAD," SCROT-MUNCHER?
YOU HEAR THAT? SCROT-MUNCHER! I DON'T EVEN KNOW WHAT THAT SHIT MEANS. THEY ARE LEARNING!
YES, IT'S MAGICAL WHEN THEY LEAVE THE NEST. LOOK--
AND THIS ONE HERE--METAN--SHE'S MY GIRL! SHE'S LIKE, GIFTED! SHE CURSES BETTER THAN MY UNCLE LUIS. AND THAT'S SAYING SOMETHING! HE'S GOT THAT TOURETTES THING AND HE DRINKS. SHE'S WHACK!
WELL, SOCRATES, I HATE TO PULL YOU AWAY, BUT I NEED YOU.
CAN I BRING MY CREW?
JESUS. YOU CAN BRING THREE OF THEM.
WHAT AN ASSPOLE.
ASSHOLE. BUT I LIKE "ASSPOLE." IT'S GOT POSSIBILITIES.
POOT
WHIIIIIIIIIR
CLACK
CLACK
CLACK
HEY, BARRY, AREN'T THOSE YOUR SOLAR POWER CELLS?
YES. VERY GOOD. A FULL ONE CAN POWER ALL OF NEW YORK CITY FOR A YEAR.
SPLOOSH
MAN, YOU'VE GOT LIKE A HUNDRED OF THEM OUT THERE. I THOUGHT ENERGY DOESN'T WORK HERE?
ENERGY WORKS. IT JUST GETS BURNED UP VERY FAST. I NEED A WHOLE LOT JUST FOR ONE SECOND.
THIS IS A POWER CONDUIT. THOSE CELLS WILL ABSORB THE SUNLIGHT, POWER UP, TRANSFER IT TO THIS AND THEN OVER TO ME. I NEED YOU TO WATCH THE CONDUIT.
WHAT?

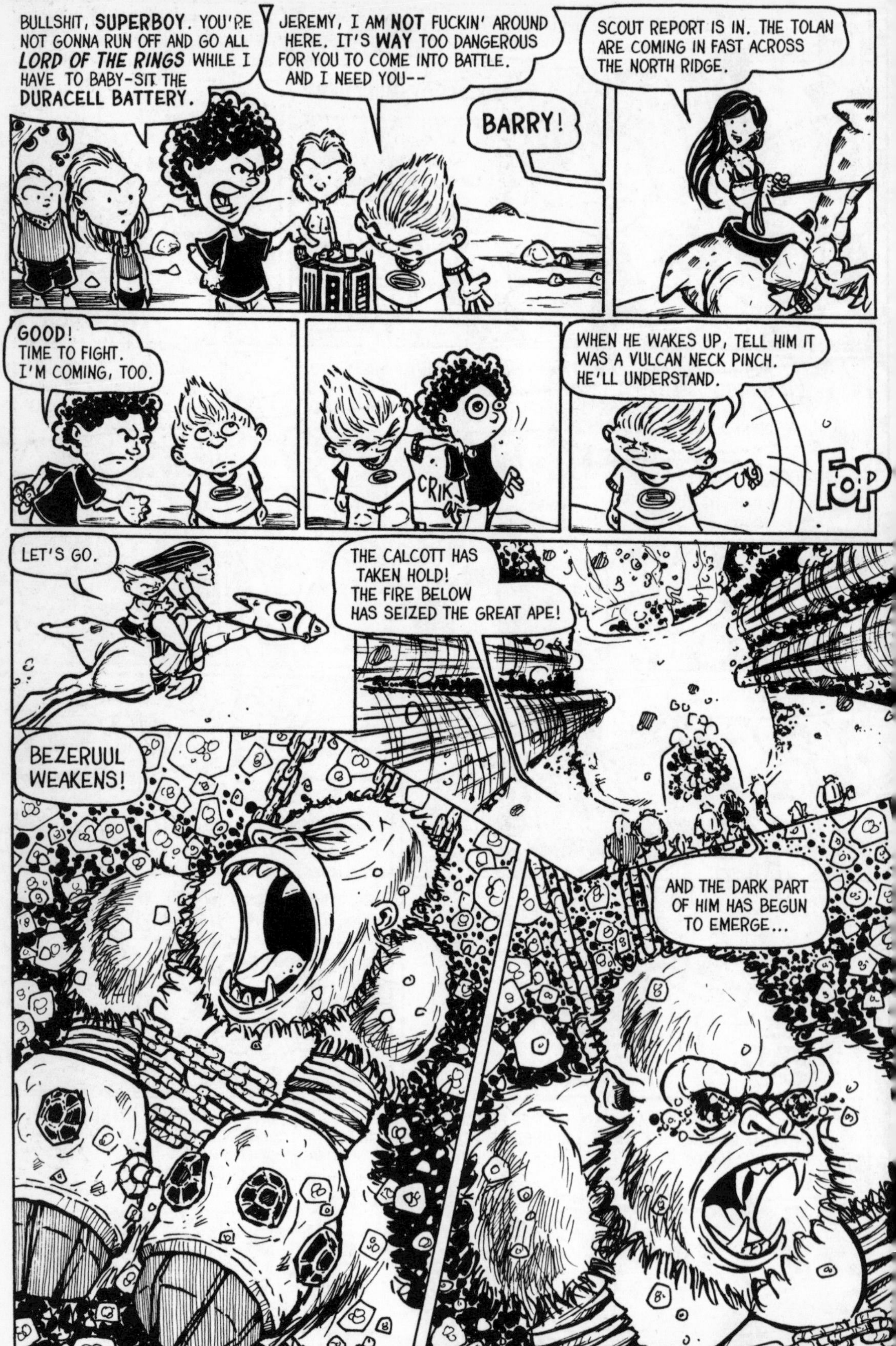
BULLSHIT, SUPERBOY. YOU'RE NOT GONNA RUN OFF AND GO ALL LORD OF THE RINGS WHILE I HAVE TO BABY-SIT THE DURACELL BATTERY.
JEREMY, I AM NOT FUCKIN' AROUND HERE. IT'S WAY TOO DANGEROUS FOR YOU TO COME INTO BATTLE. AND I NEED YOU--
BARRY!
SCOUT REPORT IS IN. THE TOLAN ARE COMING IN FAST ACROSS THE NORTH RIDGE.
GOOD! TIME TO FIGHT. I'M COMING, TOO.
CRIK
WHEN HE WAKES UP, TELL HIM IT WAS A VULCAN NECK PINCH. HE'LL UNDERSTAND.
FOP
LET'S GO.
THE CALCOTT HAS TAKEN HOLD! THE FIRE BELOW HAS SEIZED THE GREAT APE!
BEZERUUL WEAKENS!
AND THE DARK PART OF HIM HAS BEGUN TO EMERGE...

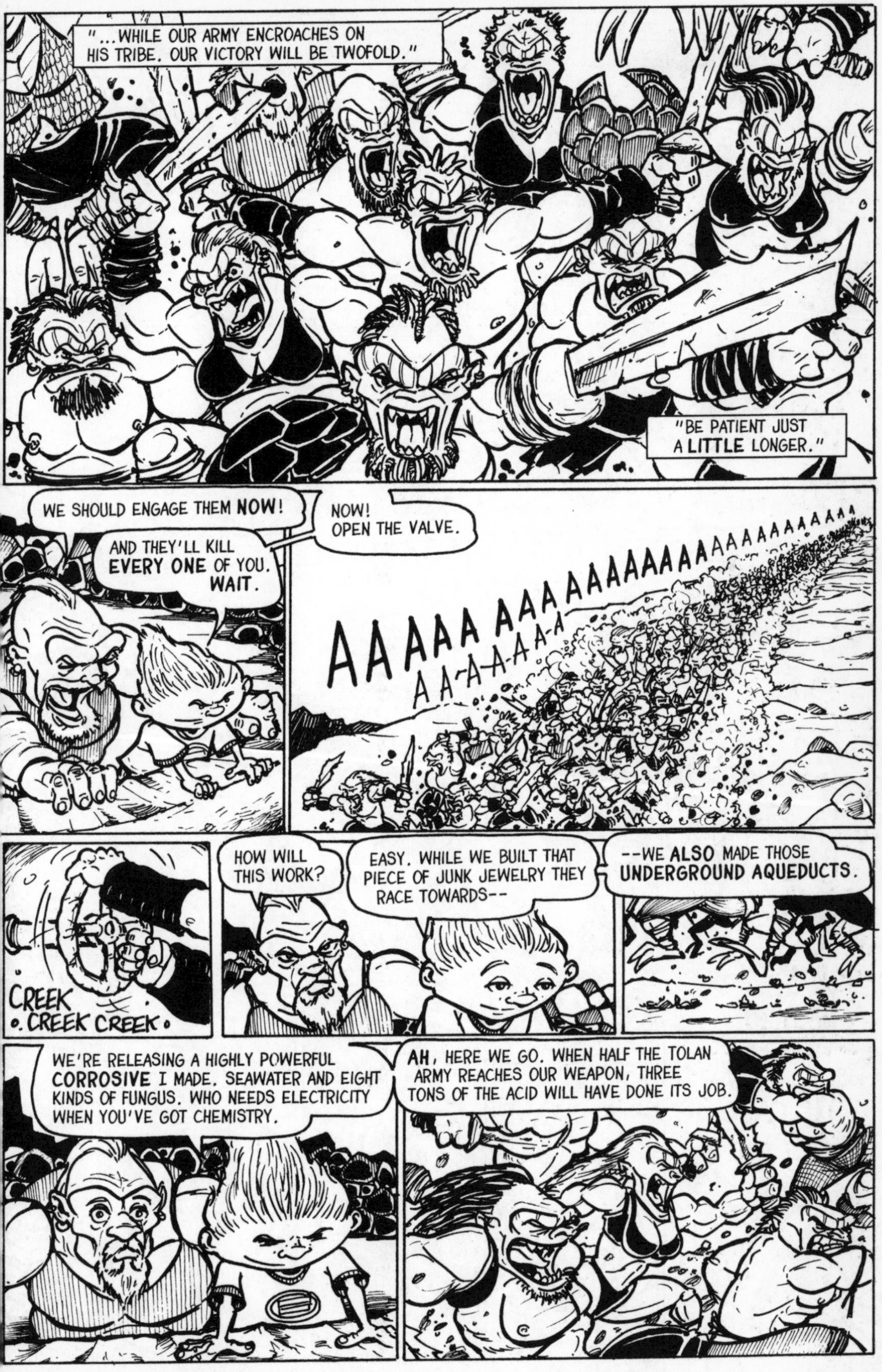
"...WHILE OUR ARMY ENCROACHES ON HIS TRIBE. OUR VICTORY WILL BE TWOFOLD."
"BE PATIENT JUST A LITTLE LONGER."
WE SHOULD ENGAGE THEM NOW!
AND THEY'LL KILL EVERY ONE OF YOU. WAIT.
NOW! OPEN THE VALVE.
AAAAAAAAAAAAAAAAAAAAAAAAAAA
AA-A-A-A-A-A
CREEK CREEK CREEK
HOW WILL THIS WORK?
EASY. WHILE WE BUILT THAT PIECE OF JUNK JEWELRY THEY RACE TOWARDS--
--WE ALSO MADE THOSE UNDERGROUND AQUEDUCTS.
WE'RE RELEASING A HIGHLY POWERFUL CORROSIVE I MADE. SEAWATER AND EIGHT KINDS OF FUNGUS. WHO NEEDS ELECTRICITY WHEN YOU'VE GOT CHEMISTRY.
AH, HERE WE GO. WHEN HALF THE TOLAN ARMY REACHES OUR WEAPON, THREE TONS OF THE ACID WILL HAVE DONE ITS JOB.

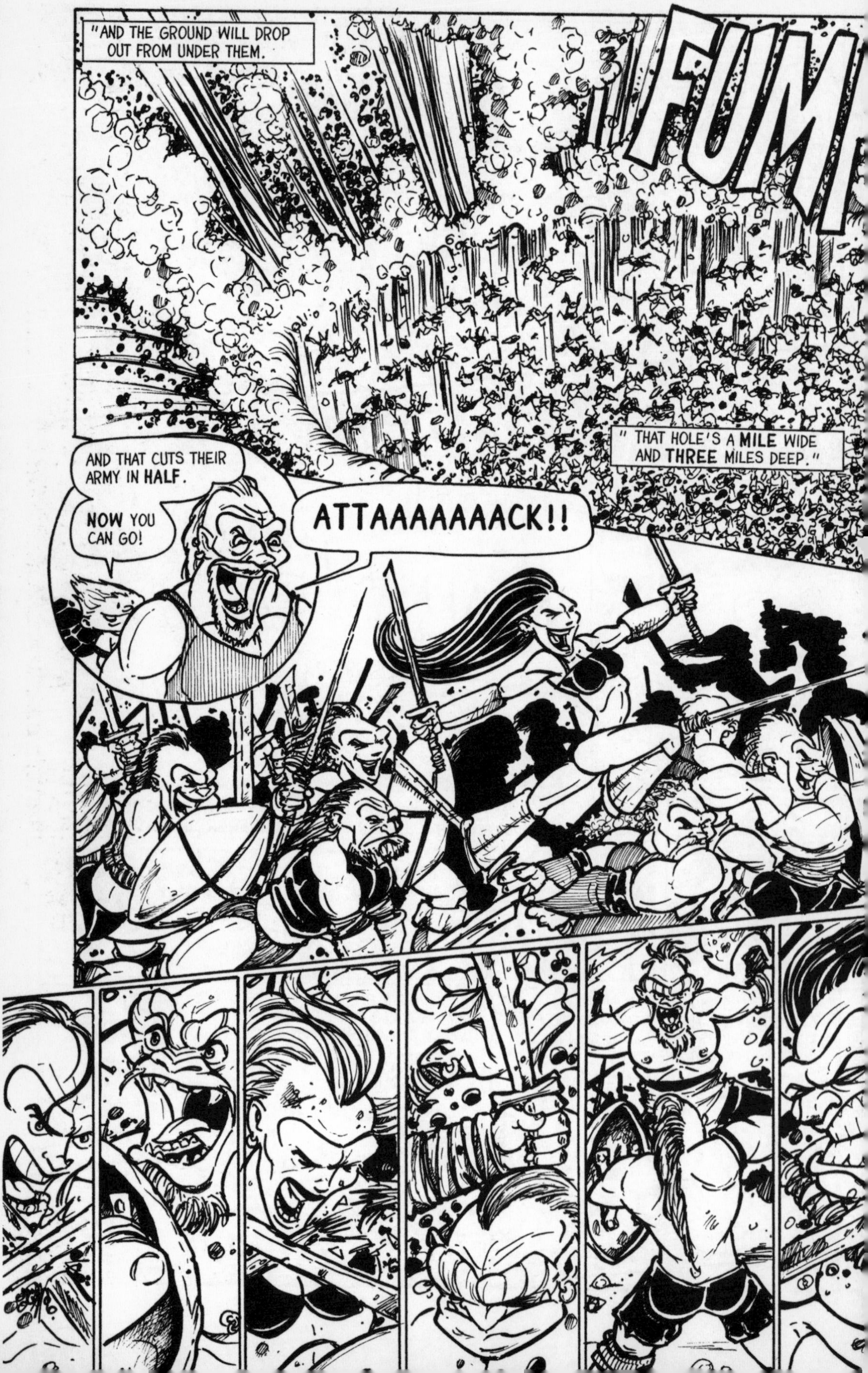
"AND THE GROUND WILL DROP OUT FROM UNDER THEM.
FUM
" THAT HOLE'S A MILE WIDE AND THREE MILES DEEP."
AND THAT CUTS THEIR ARMY IN HALF.
NOW YOU CAN GO!
ATTAAAAAAACK!!

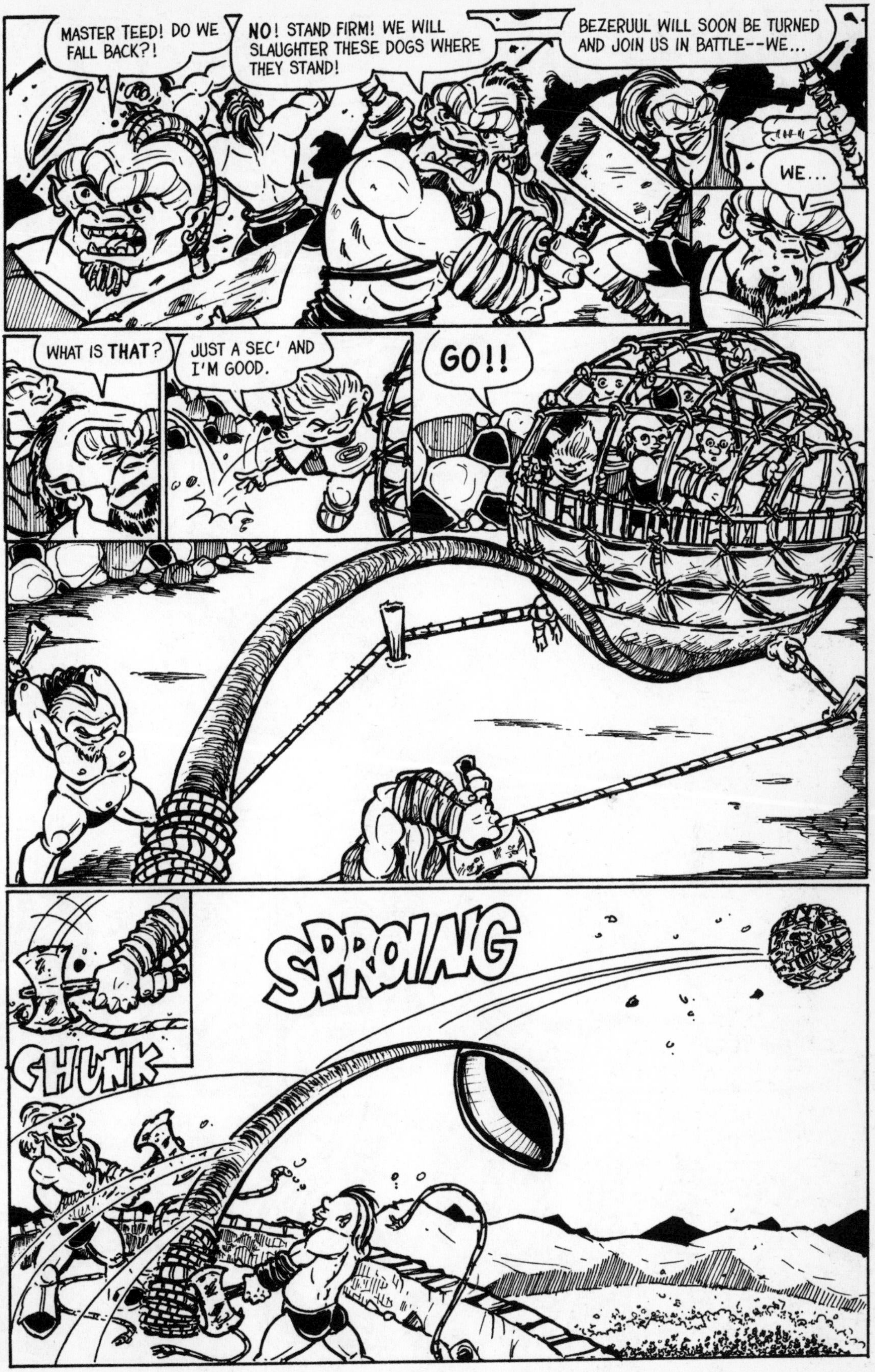
MASTER TEED! DO WE FALL BACK?!
NO! STAND FIRM! WE WILL SLAUGHTER THESE DOGS WHERE THEY STAND!
BEZERUUL WILL SOON BE TURNED AND JOIN US IN BATTLE--WE...
WE...
WHAT IS THAT?
JUST A SEC' AND I'M GOOD.
GO!!
CHUNK
SPROING

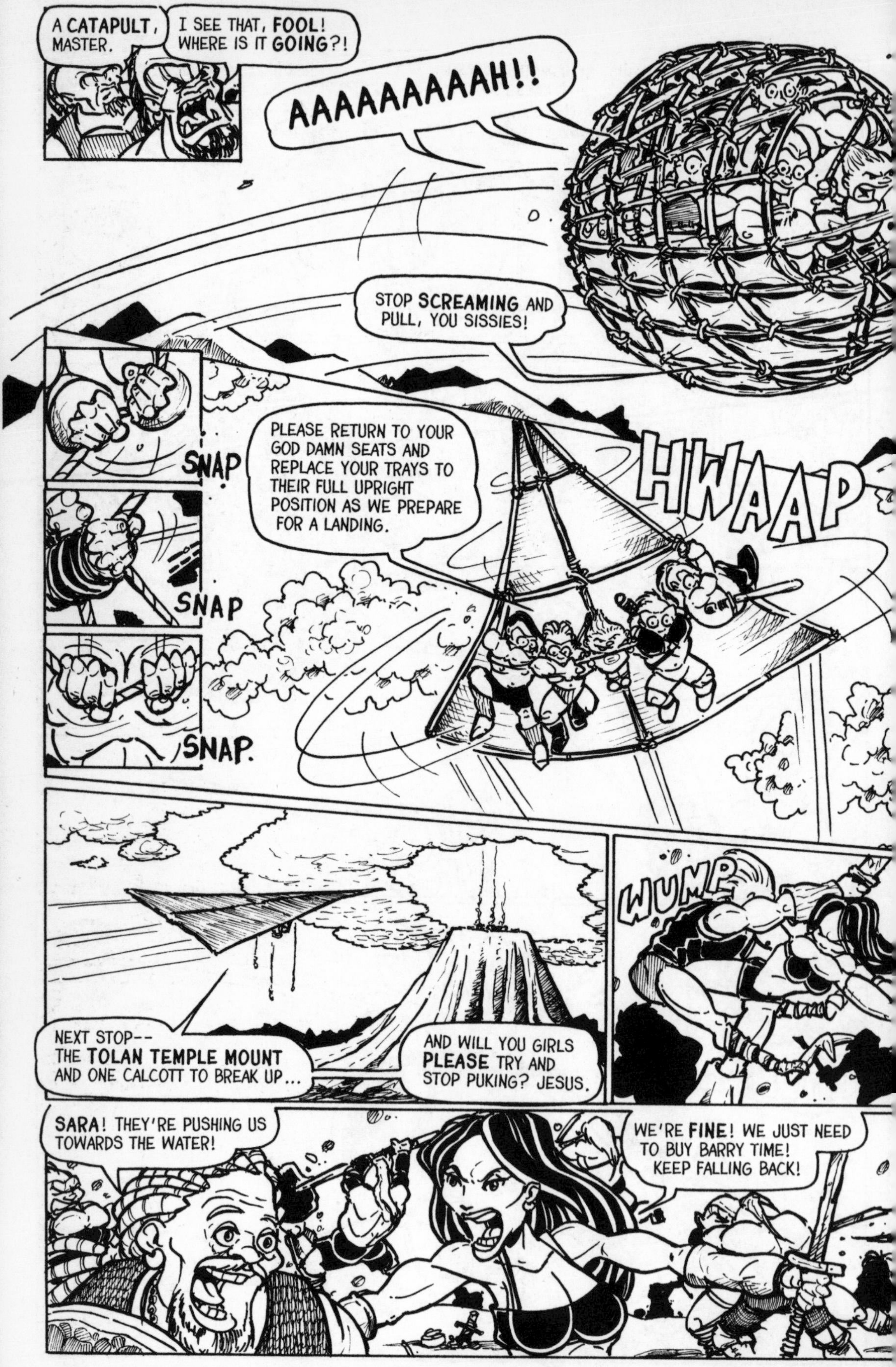
A CATAPULT, MASTER.
I SEE THAT, FOOL! WHERE IS IT GOING?!
AAAAAAAAAH!!
STOP SCREAMING AND PULL, YOU SISSIES!
SNAP
SNAP
SNAP.
PLEASE RETURN TO YOUR GOD DAMN SEATS AND REPLACE YOUR TRAYS TO THEIR FULL UPRIGHT POSITION AS WE PREPARE FOR A LANDING.
HWAAP
NEXT STOP-- THE TOLAN TEMPLE MOUNT AND ONE CALCOTT TO BREAK UP...
AND WILL YOU GIRLS PLEASE TRY AND STOP PUKING? JESUS.
WUMP
SARA! THEY'RE PUSHING US TOWARDS THE WATER!
WE'RE FINE! WE JUST NEED TO BUY BARRY TIME! KEEP FALLING BACK!

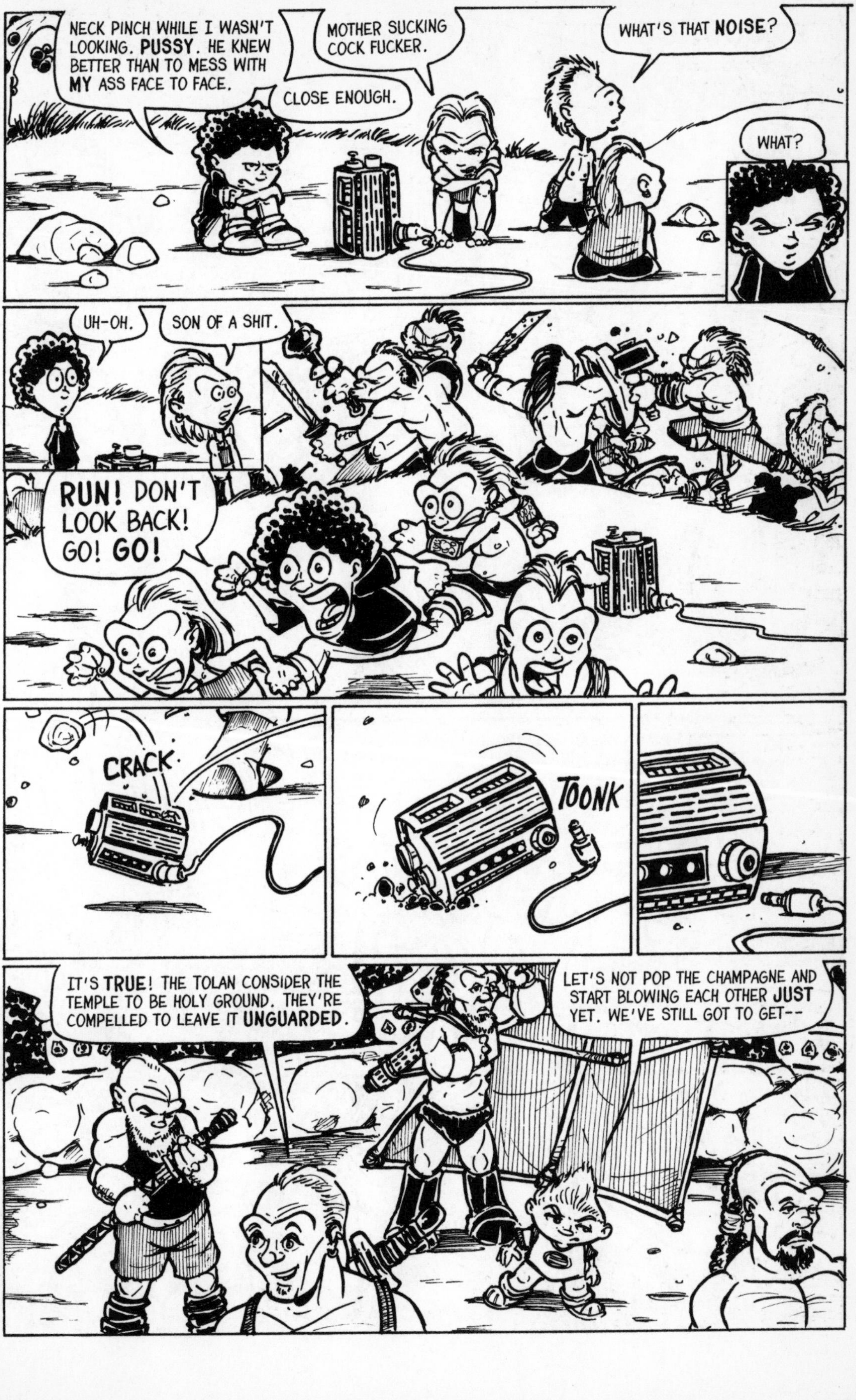

NECK PINCH WHILE I WASN'T LOOKING. PUSSY. HE KNEW BETTER THAN TO MESS WITH MY ASS FACE TO FACE.
CLOSE ENOUGH.
MOTHER SUCKING COCK FUCKER.
WHAT'S THAT NOISE?
WHAT?
UH-OH.
SON OF A SHIT.
RUN! DON'T LOOK BACK! GO! GO!
CRACK
TOONK
IT'S TRUE! THE TOLAN CONSIDER THE TEMPLE TO BE HOLY GROUND. THEY'RE COMPELLED TO LEAVE IT UNGUARDED.
LET'S NOT POP THE CHAMPAGNE AND START BLOWING EACH OTHER JUST YET. WE'VE STILL GOT TO GET--

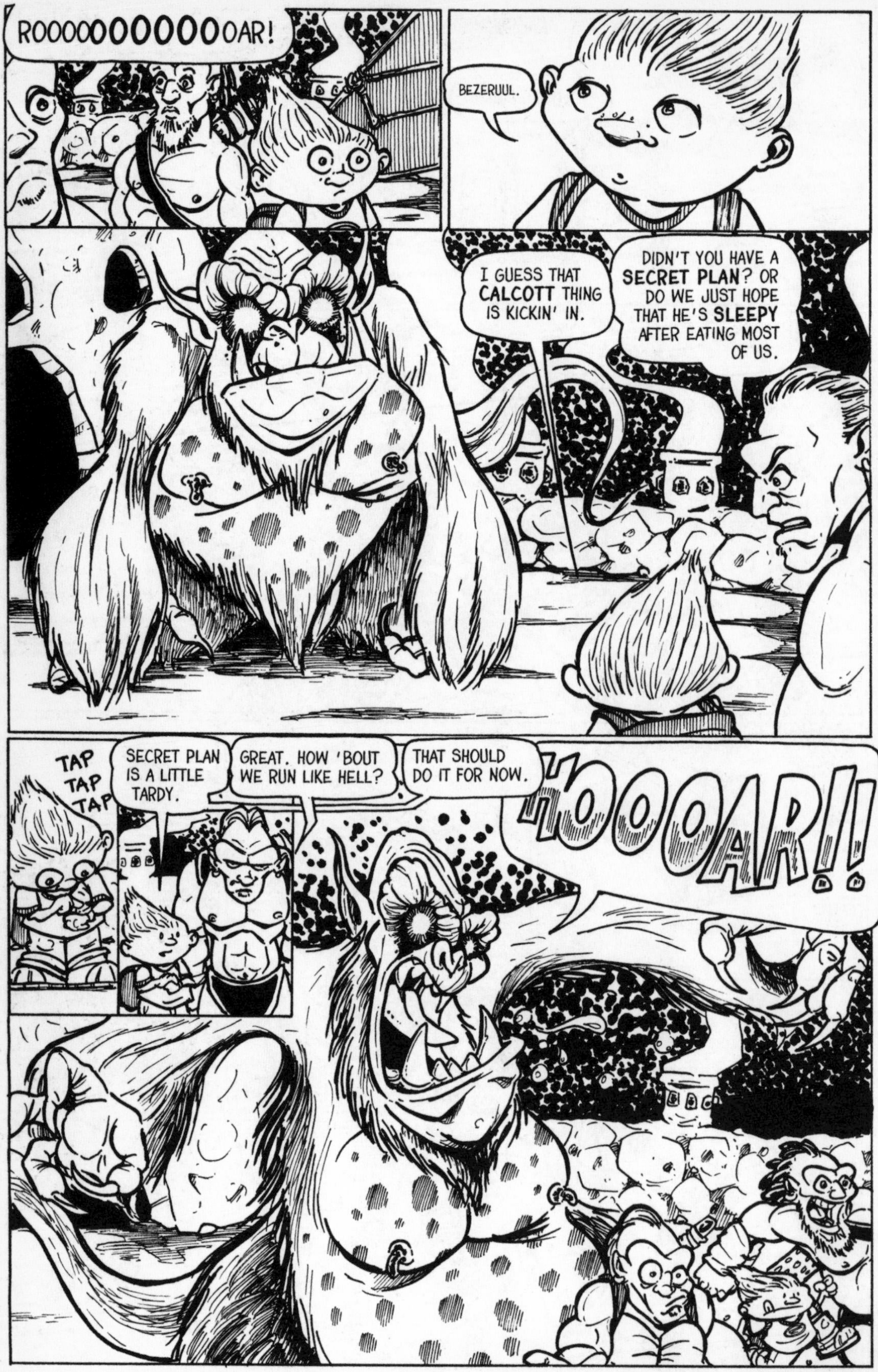
ROOOOOOOOOOOOAR!
BEZERUUL.
I GUESS THAT CALCOTT THING IS KICKIN' IN.
DIDN'T YOU HAVE A SECRET PLAN? OR DO WE JUST HOPE THAT HE'S SLEEPY AFTER EATING MOST OF US.
TAP TAP TAP
SECRET PLAN IS A LITTLE TARDY.
GREAT. HOW 'BOUT WE RUN LIKE HELL?
THAT SHOULD DO IT FOR NOW.
HOOOAR!!

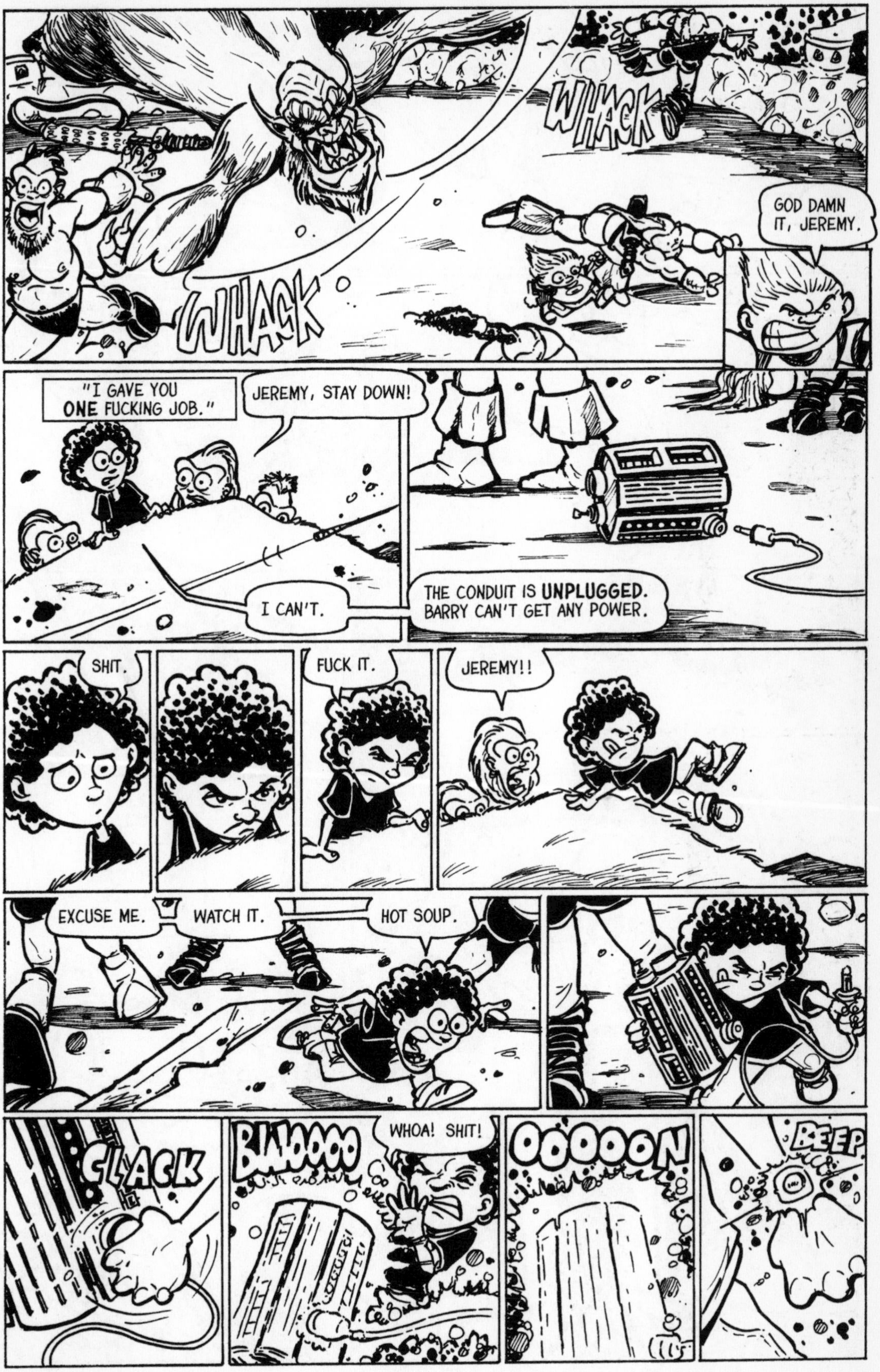
WHACK
WHACK
GOD DAMN IT, JEREMY.
"I GAVE YOU ONE FUCKING JOB."
JEREMY, STAY DOWN!
I CAN'T.
THE CONDUIT IS UNPLUGGED. BARRY CAN'T GET ANY POWER.
SHIT.
FUCK IT.
JEREMY!!
EXCUSE ME.
WATCH IT.
HOT SOUP.
CLACK
BWOOOO
WHOA! SHIT!
OOOOON
BEEP

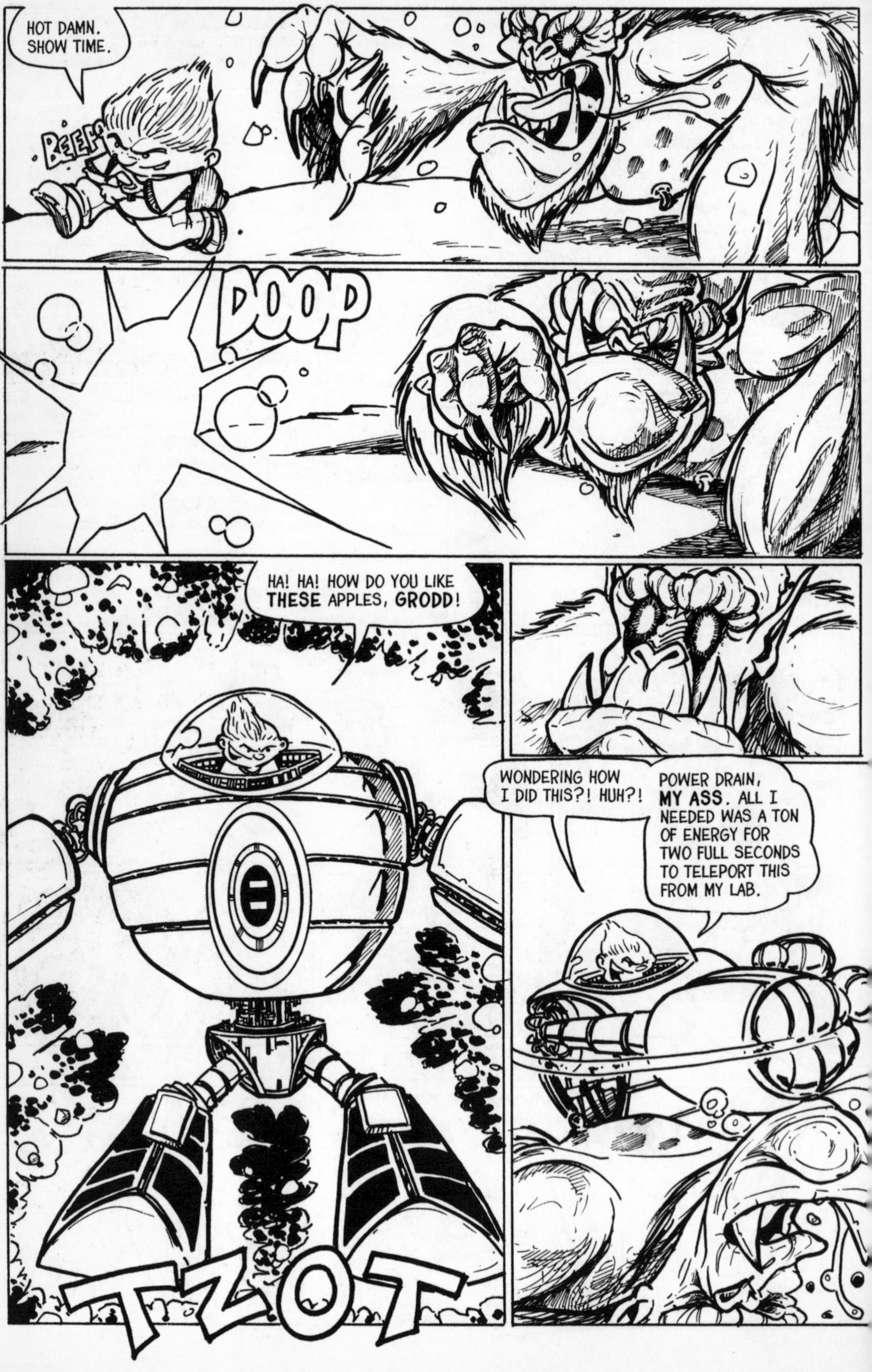
HOT DAMN. SHOW TIME.
BEEP
DOOP
HA! HA! HOW DO YOU LIKE THESE APPLES, GRODD!
TZOT
WONDERING HOW I DID THIS?! HUH?!
POWER DRAIN, MY ASS. ALL I NEEDED WAS A TON OF ENERGY FOR TWO FULL SECONDS TO TELEPORT THIS FROM MY LAB.

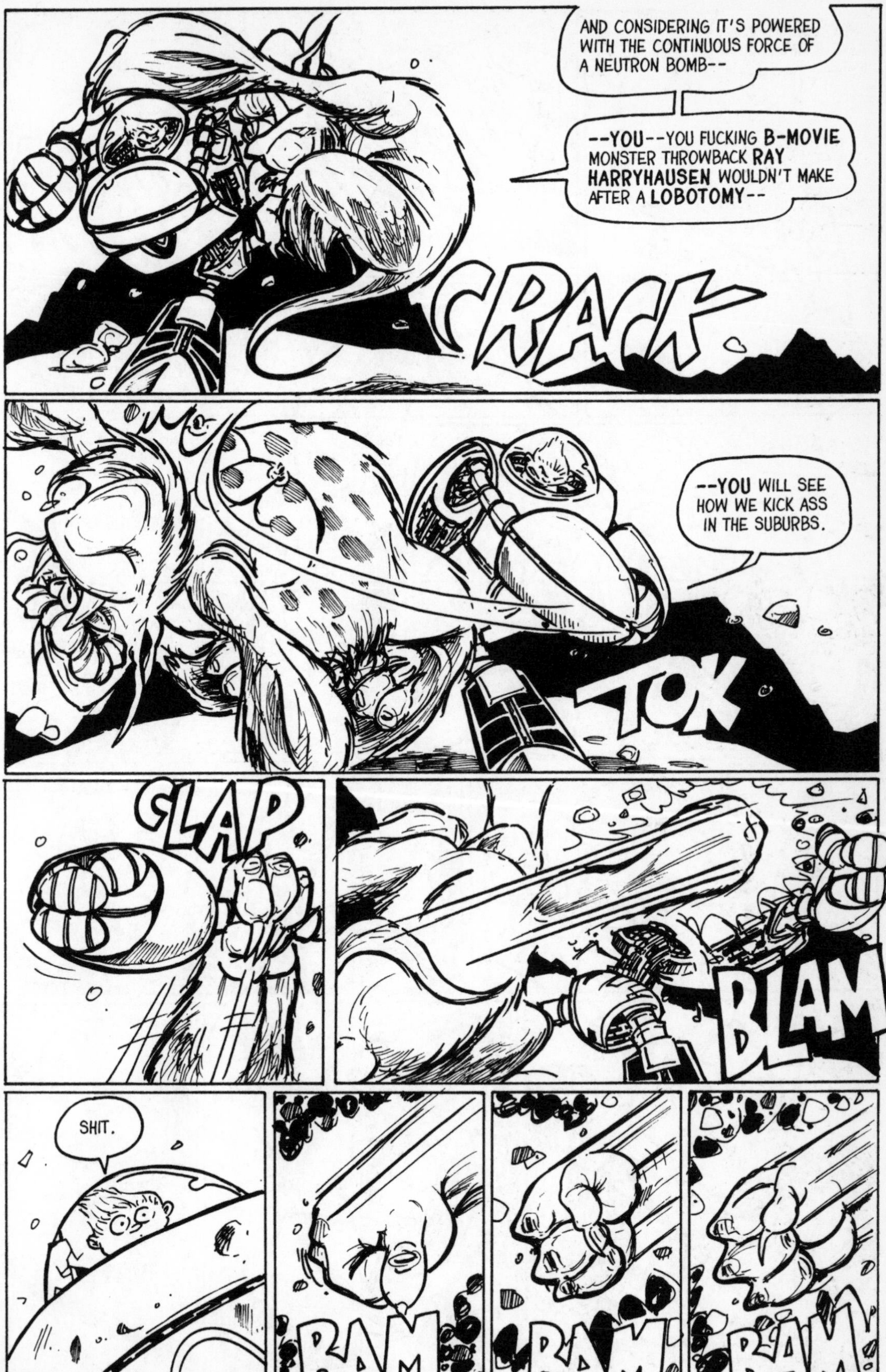
AND CONSIDERING IT'S POWERED WITH THE CONTINUOUS FORCE OF A NEUTRON BOMB--
--YOU--YOU FUCKING B-MOVIE MONSTER THROWBACK RAY HARRYHAUSEN WOULDN'T MAKE AFTER A LOBOTOMY--
CRACK
--YOU WILL SEE HOW WE KICK ASS IN THE SUBURBS.
TOK
CLAP
BLAM
SHIT.
BAM
BAM!
BAM!

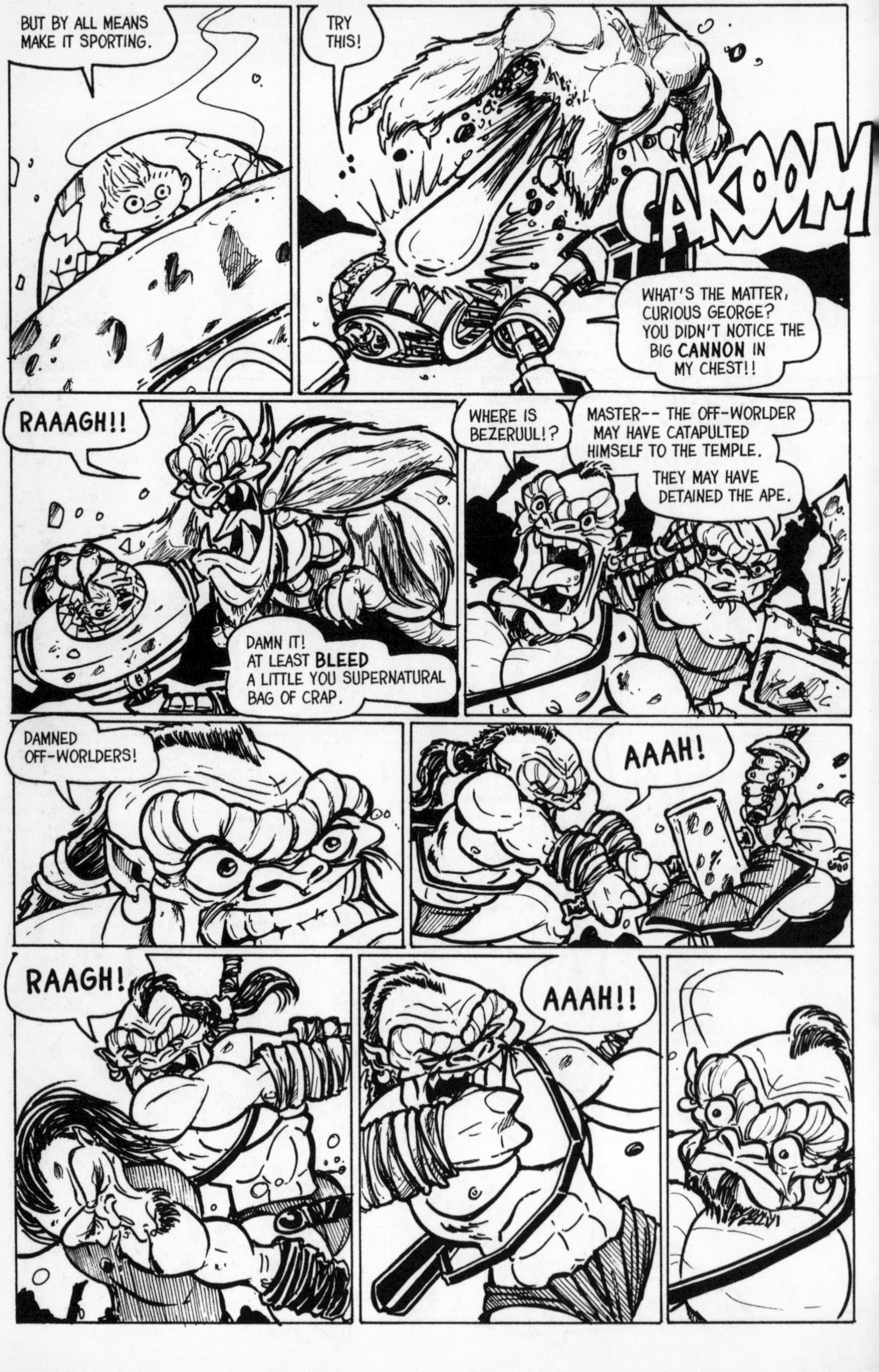
BUT BY ALL MEANS MAKE IT SPORTING.
TRY THIS!
CAKOOM
WHAT'S THE MATTER, CURIOUS GEORGE? YOU DIDN'T NOTICE THE BIG CANNON IN MY CHEST!!
RAAAGH!!
DAMN IT! AT LEAST BLEED A LITTLE YOU SUPERNATURAL BAG OF CRAP.
WHERE IS BEZERUUL!?
MASTER-- THE OFF-WORLDER MAY HAVE CATAPULTED HIMSELF TO THE TEMPLE.
THEY MAY HAVE DETAINED THE APE.
DAMNED OFF-WORLDERS!
AAAH!
RAAGH!
AAAH!!

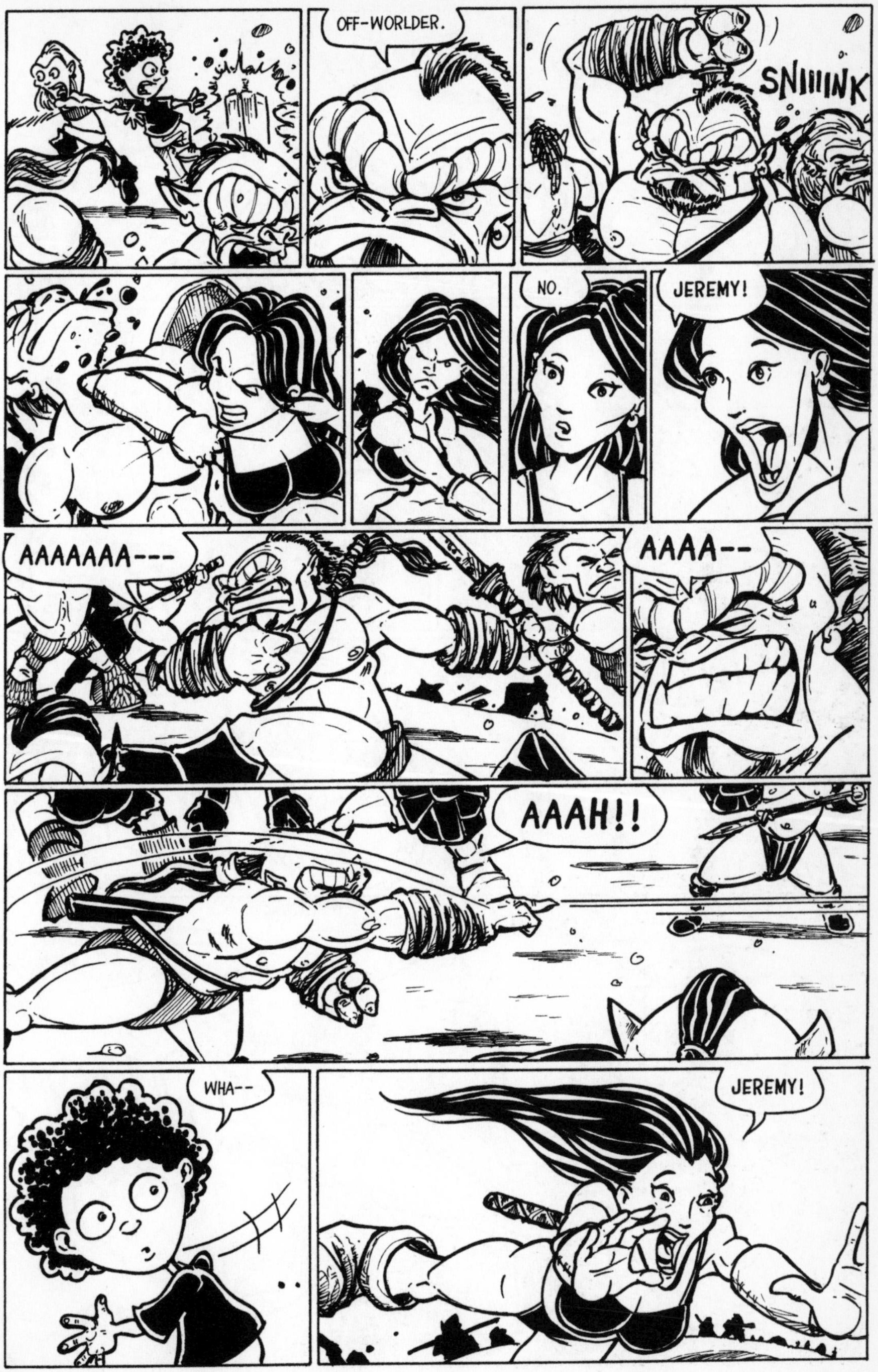
OFF-WORLDER.
SNIIIINK
NO.
JEREMY!
AAAAAAA---
AAAA--
AAAH!!
WHA--
JEREMY!

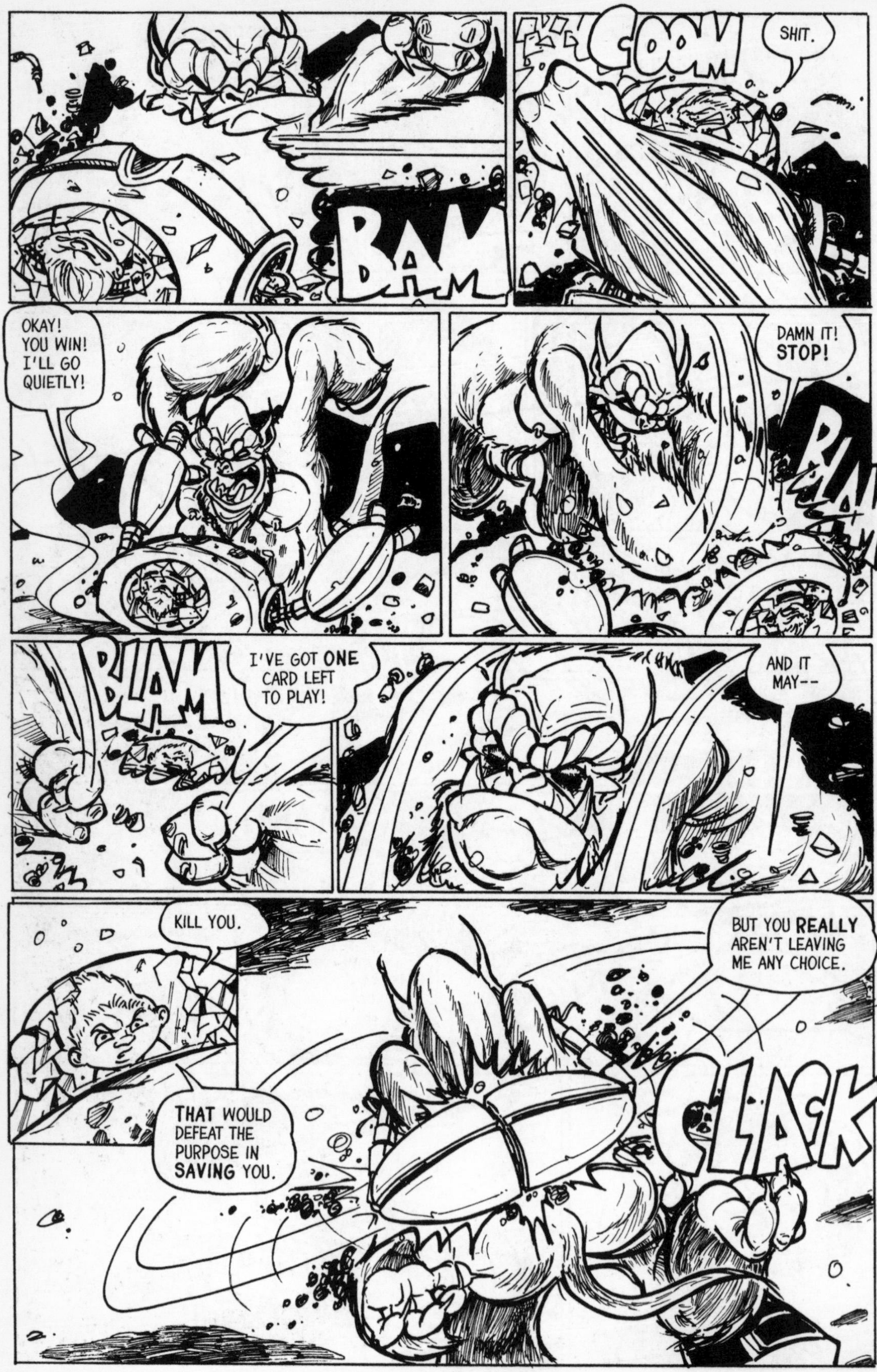
BAM
COOM
SHIT.
OKAY! YOU WIN! I'LL GO QUIETLY!
DAMN IT! STOP!
BLAM
BLAM
I'VE GOT ONE CARD LEFT TO PLAY!
AND IT MAY--
KILL YOU.
BUT YOU REALLY AREN'T LEAVING ME ANY CHOICE.
THAT WOULD DEFEAT THE PURPOSE IN SAVING YOU.
CLACK

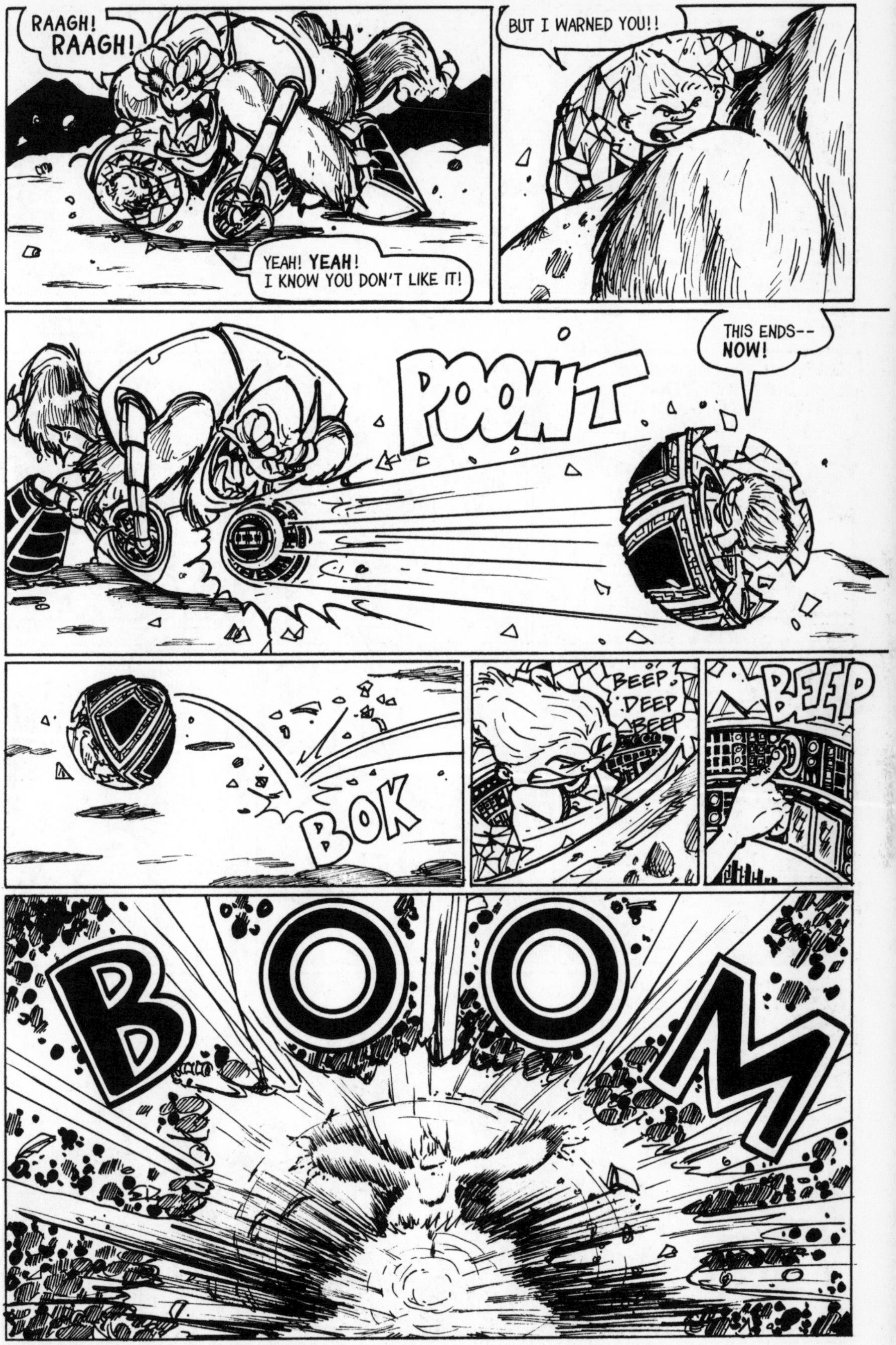
RAAGH! RAAGH!
YEAH! YEAH! I KNOW YOU DON'T LIKE IT!
BUT I WARNED YOU!!
POOWT
THIS ENDS-- NOW!
BOK
BEEP DEEP BEEP
BEEP
BOOM

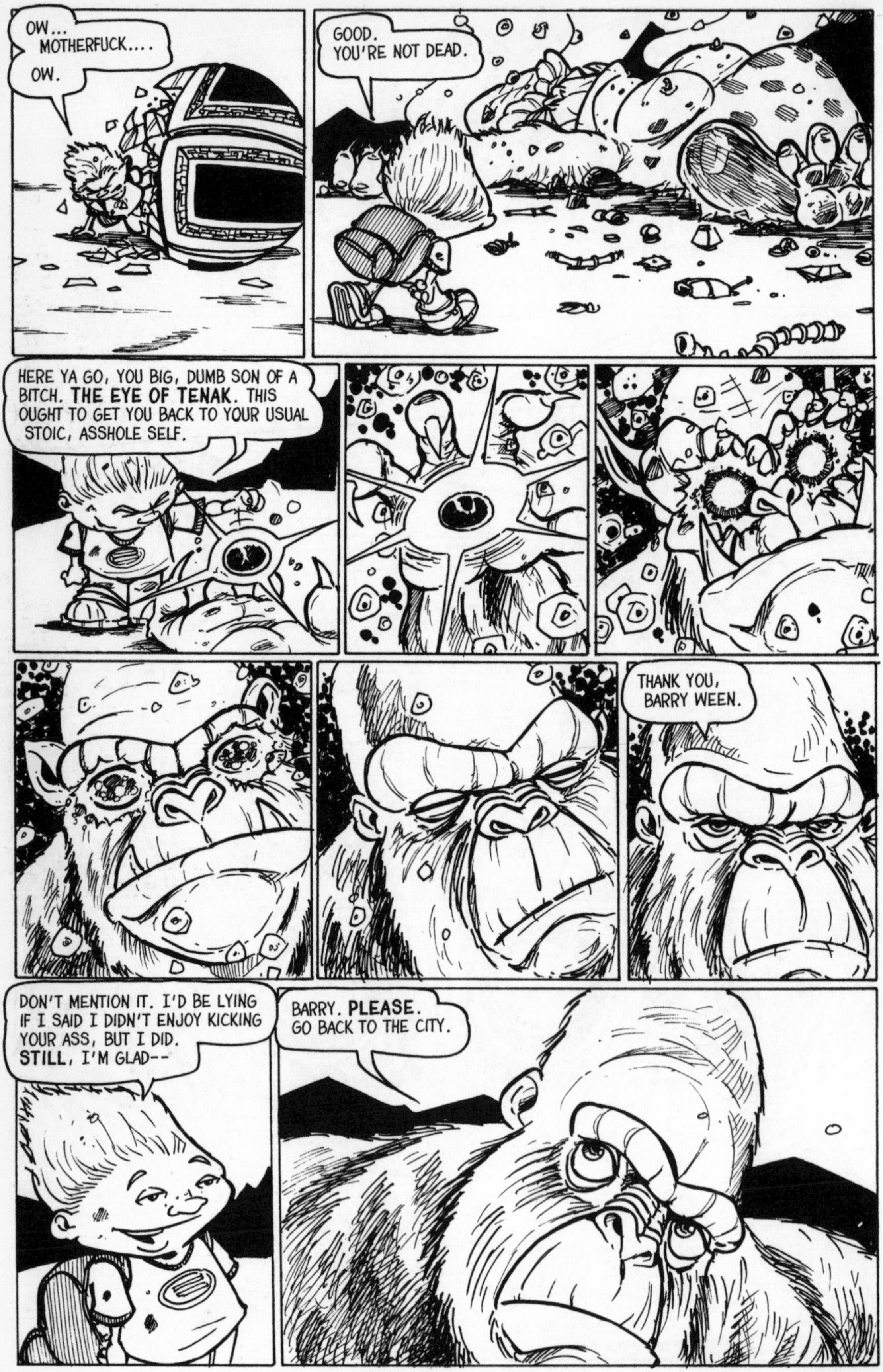
OW...
MOTHERFUCK....
OW.
GOOD.
YOU'RE NOT DEAD.
HERE YA GO, YOU BIG, DUMB SON OF A BITCH. **THE EYE OF TENAK.** THIS OUGHT TO GET YOU BACK TO YOUR USUAL STOIC, ASSHOLE SELF.
THANK YOU, BARRY WEEN.
DON'T MENTION IT. I'D BE LYING IF I SAID I DIDN'T ENJOY KICKING YOUR ASS, BUT I DID. **STILL**, I'M GLAD--
BARRY. **PLEASE.** GO BACK TO THE CITY.

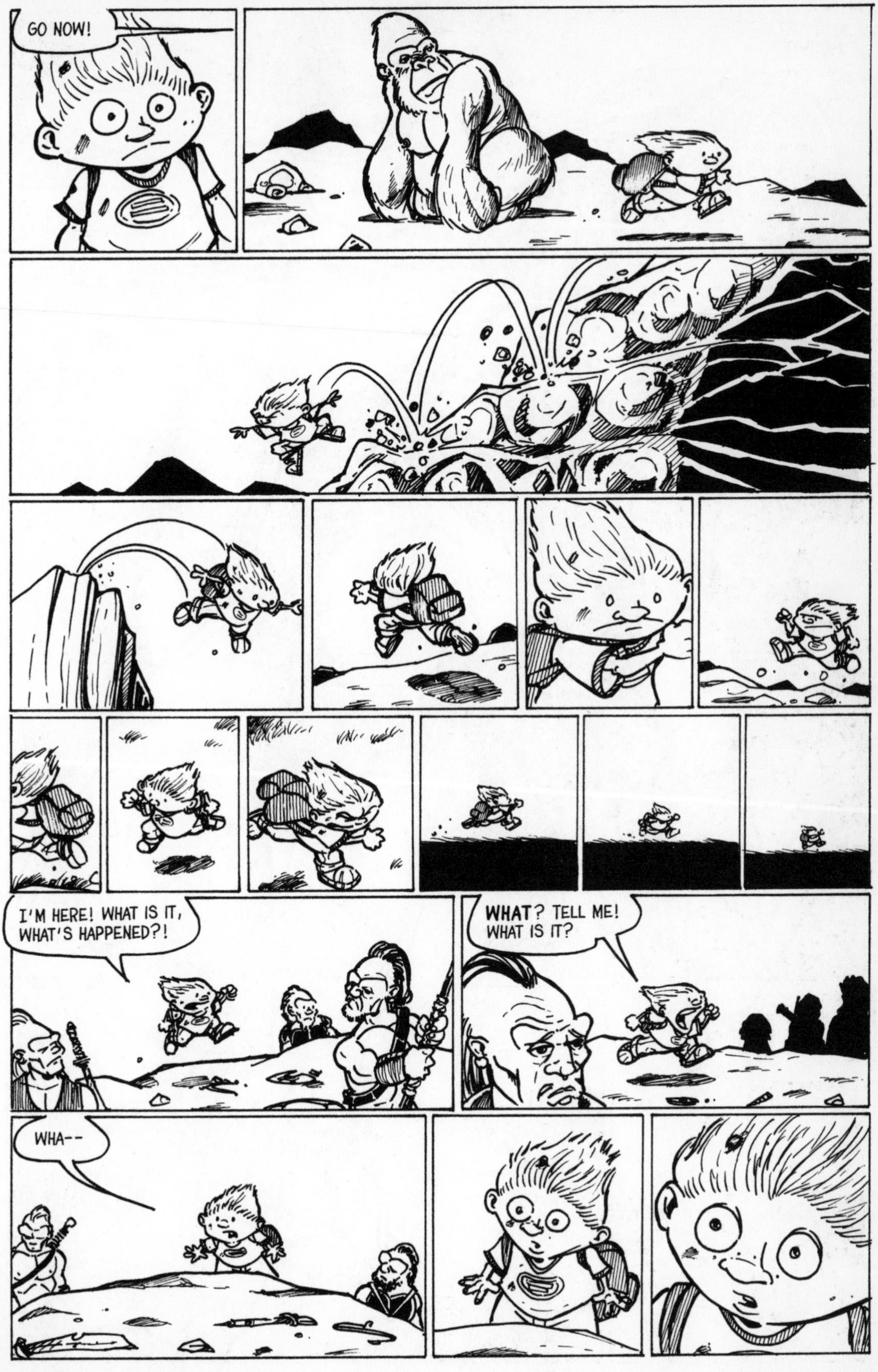
GO NOW!
I'M HERE! WHAT IS IT, WHAT'S HAPPENED?!
WHAT? TELL ME! WHAT IS IT?
WHA--

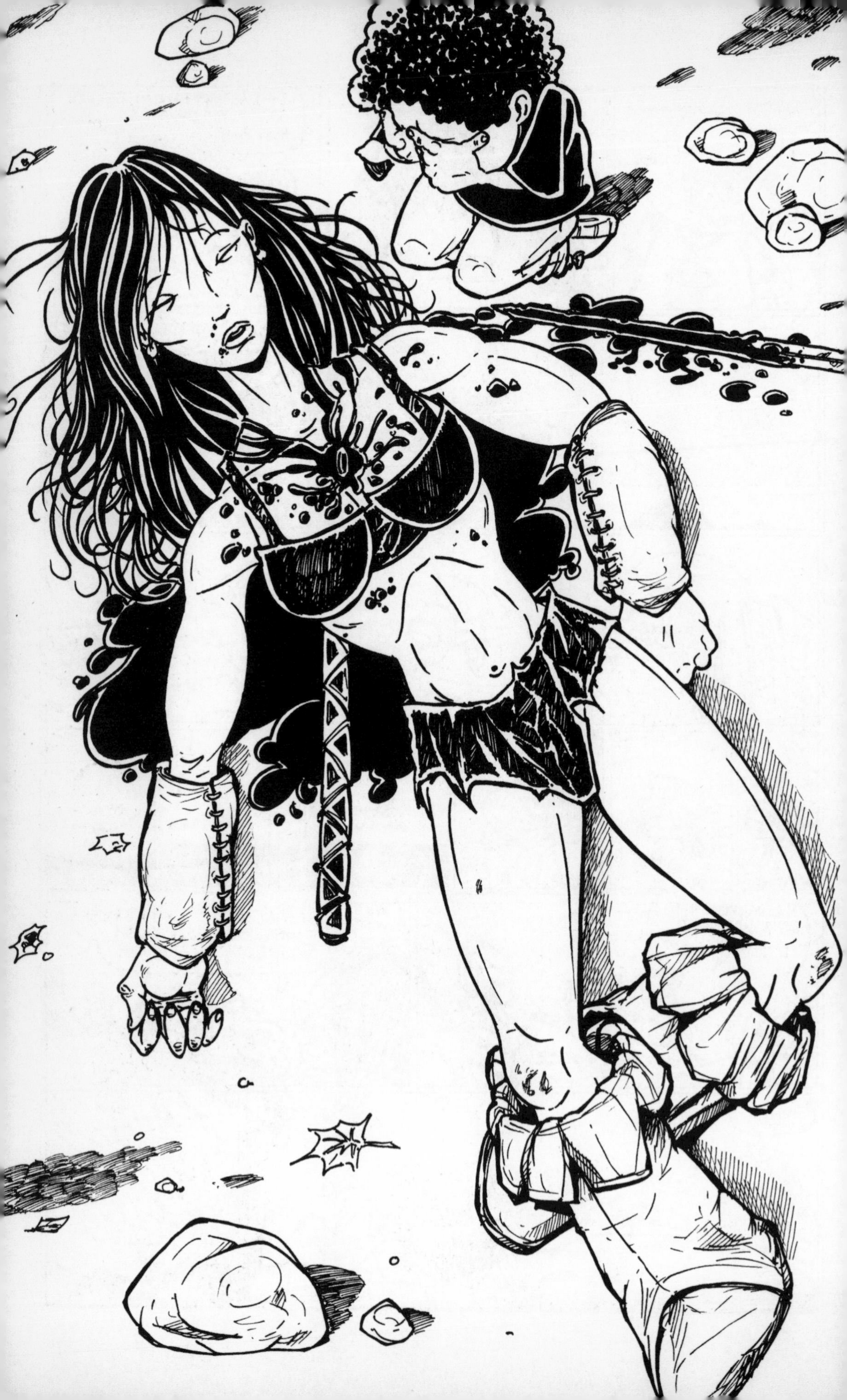

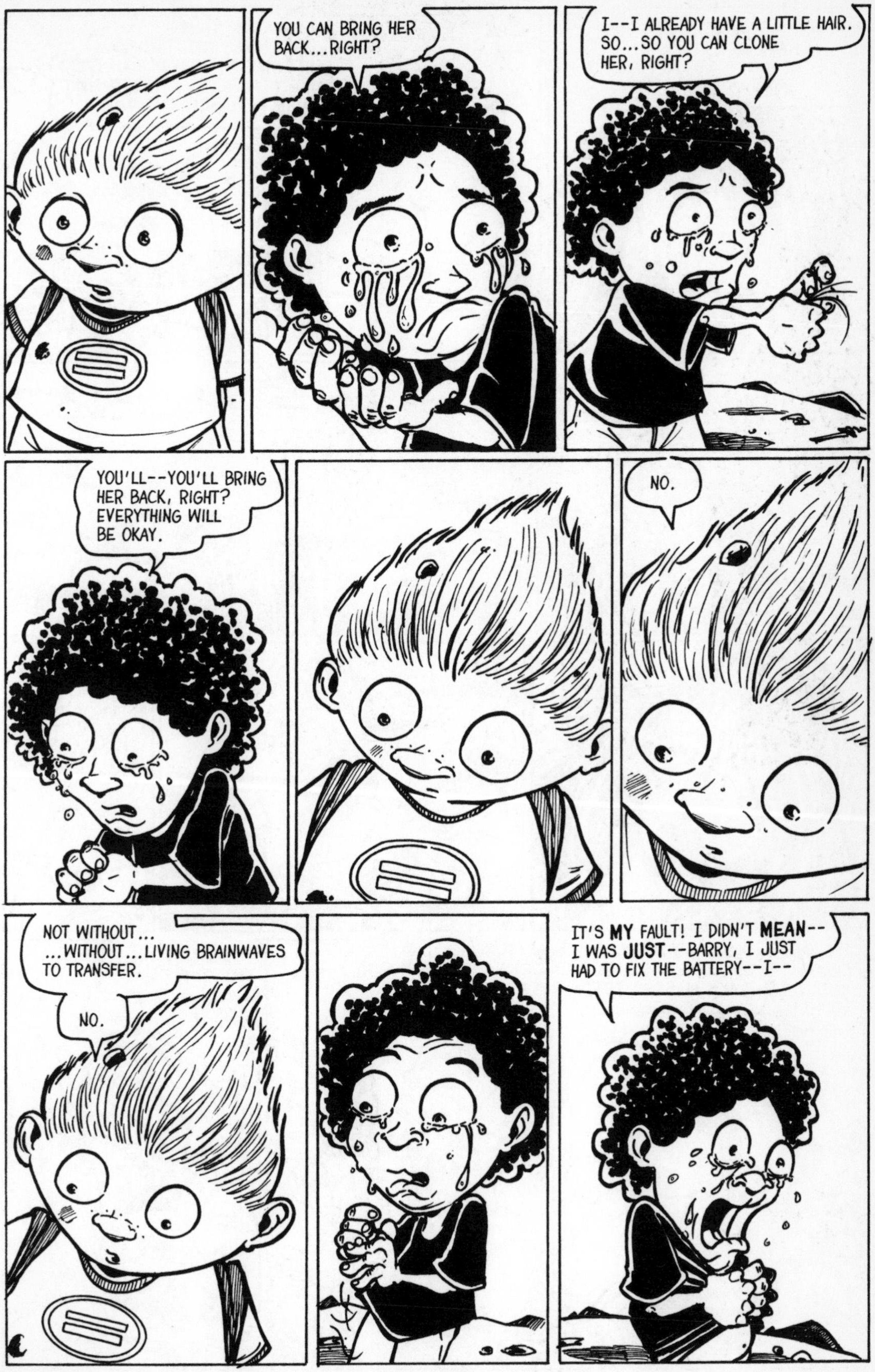
YOU CAN BRING HER BACK...RIGHT?
I--I ALREADY HAVE A LITTLE HAIR. SO...SO YOU CAN CLONE HER, RIGHT?
YOU'LL--YOU'LL BRING HER BACK, RIGHT? EVERYTHING WILL BE OKAY.
NO.
NOT WITHOUT... ...WITHOUT...LIVING BRAINWAVES TO TRANSFER.
NO.
IT'S MY FAULT! I DIDN'T MEAN-- I WAS JUST--BARRY, I JUST HAD TO FIX THE BATTERY--I--

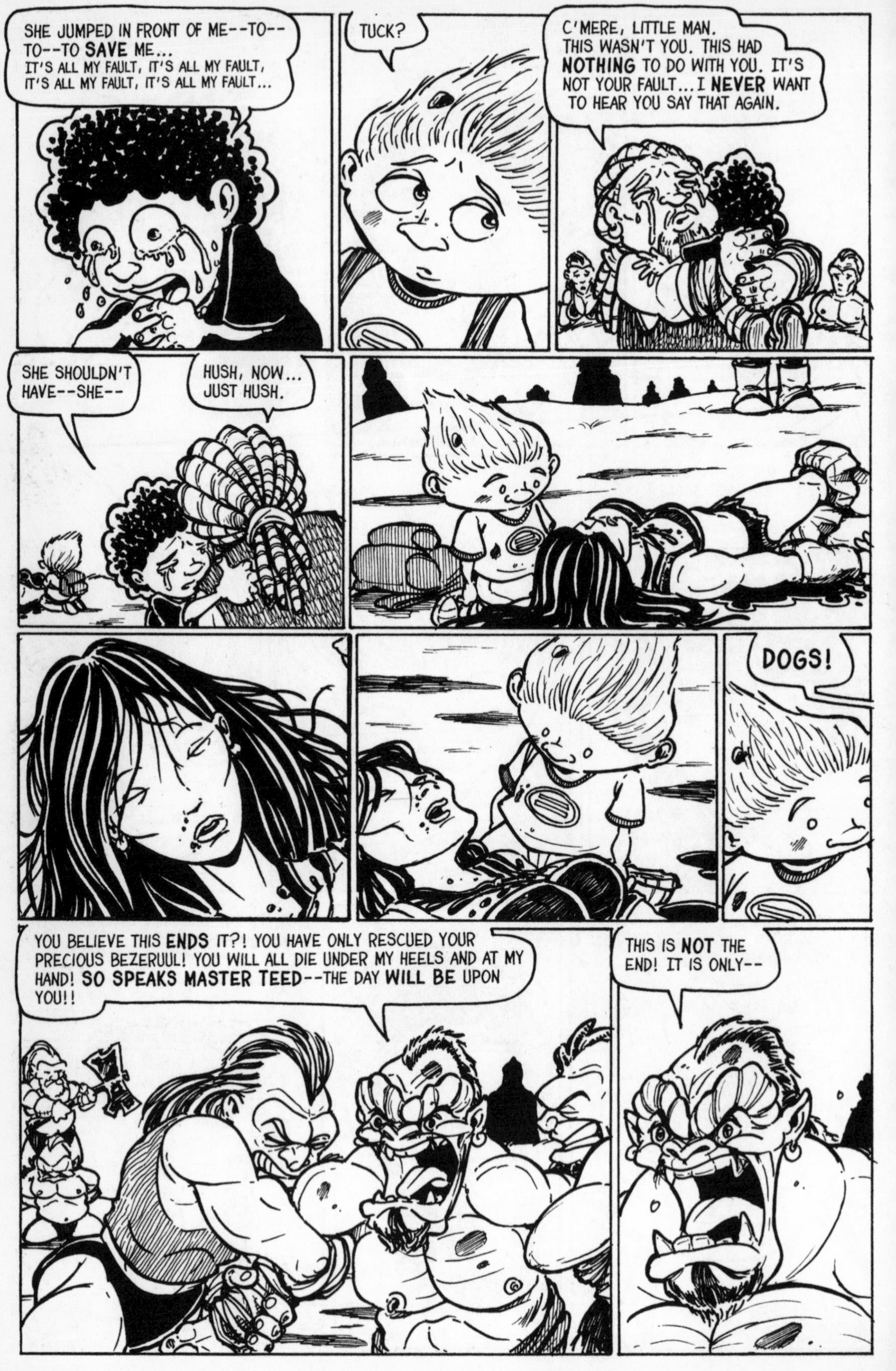
SHE JUMPED IN FRONT OF ME--TO--TO--TO SAVE ME... IT'S ALL MY FAULT, IT'S ALL MY FAULT, IT'S ALL MY FAULT, IT'S ALL MY FAULT...
TUCK?
C'MERE, LITTLE MAN. THIS WASN'T YOU. THIS HAD NOTHING TO DO WITH YOU. IT'S NOT YOUR FAULT... I NEVER WANT TO HEAR YOU SAY THAT AGAIN.
SHE SHOULDN'T HAVE--SHE--
HUSH, NOW... JUST HUSH.
DOGS!
YOU BELIEVE THIS ENDS IT?! YOU HAVE ONLY RESCUED YOUR PRECIOUS BEZERUUL! YOU WILL ALL DIE UNDER MY HEELS AND AT MY HAND! SO SPEAKS MASTER TEED--THE DAY WILL BE UPON YOU!!
THIS IS NOT THE END! IT IS ONLY--

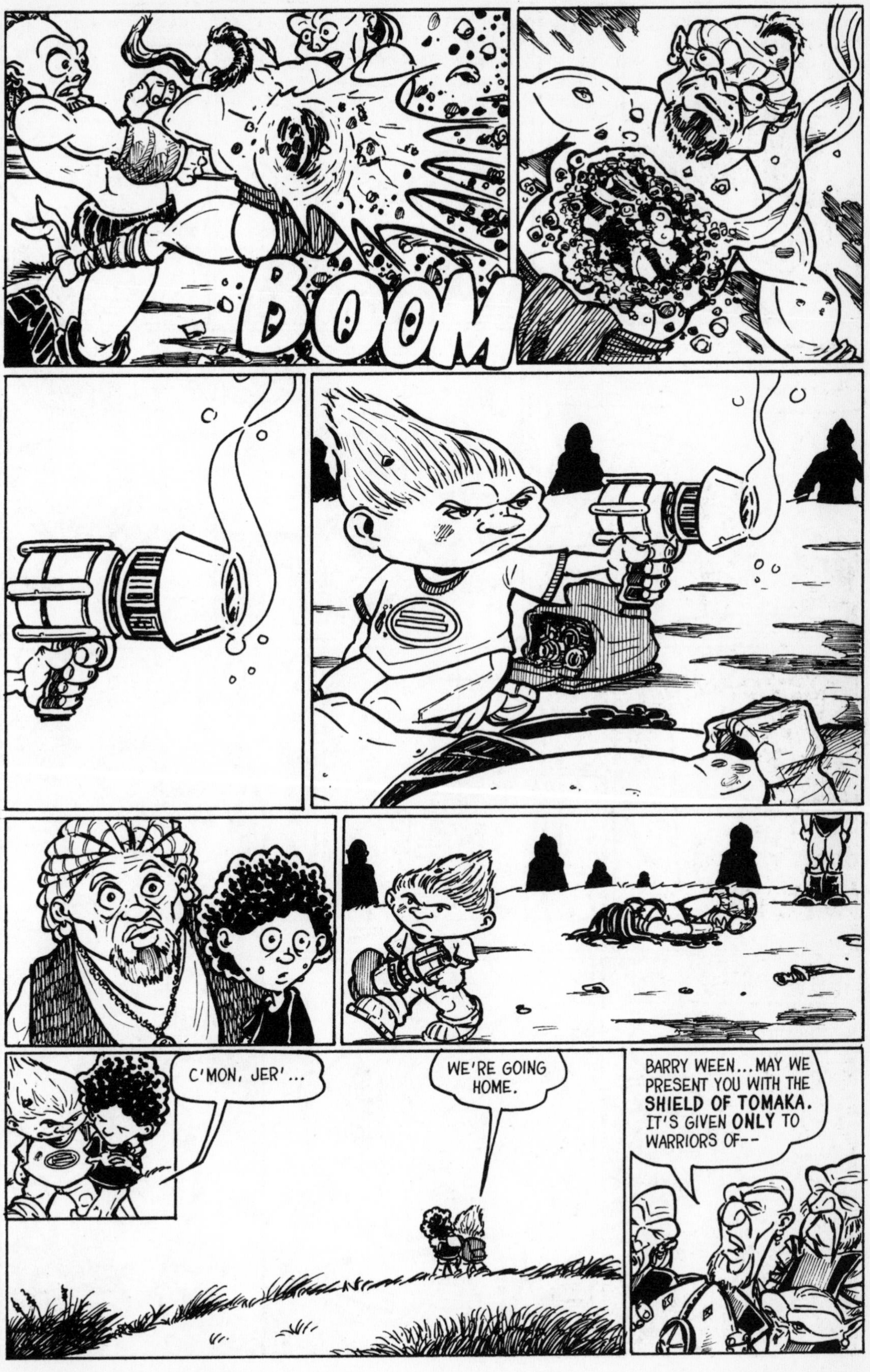
BOOM
C'MON, JER'...
WE'RE GOING HOME.
BARRY WEEN...MAY WE PRESENT YOU WITH THE **SHIELD OF TOMAKA.** IT'S GIVEN **ONLY** TO WARRIORS OF--

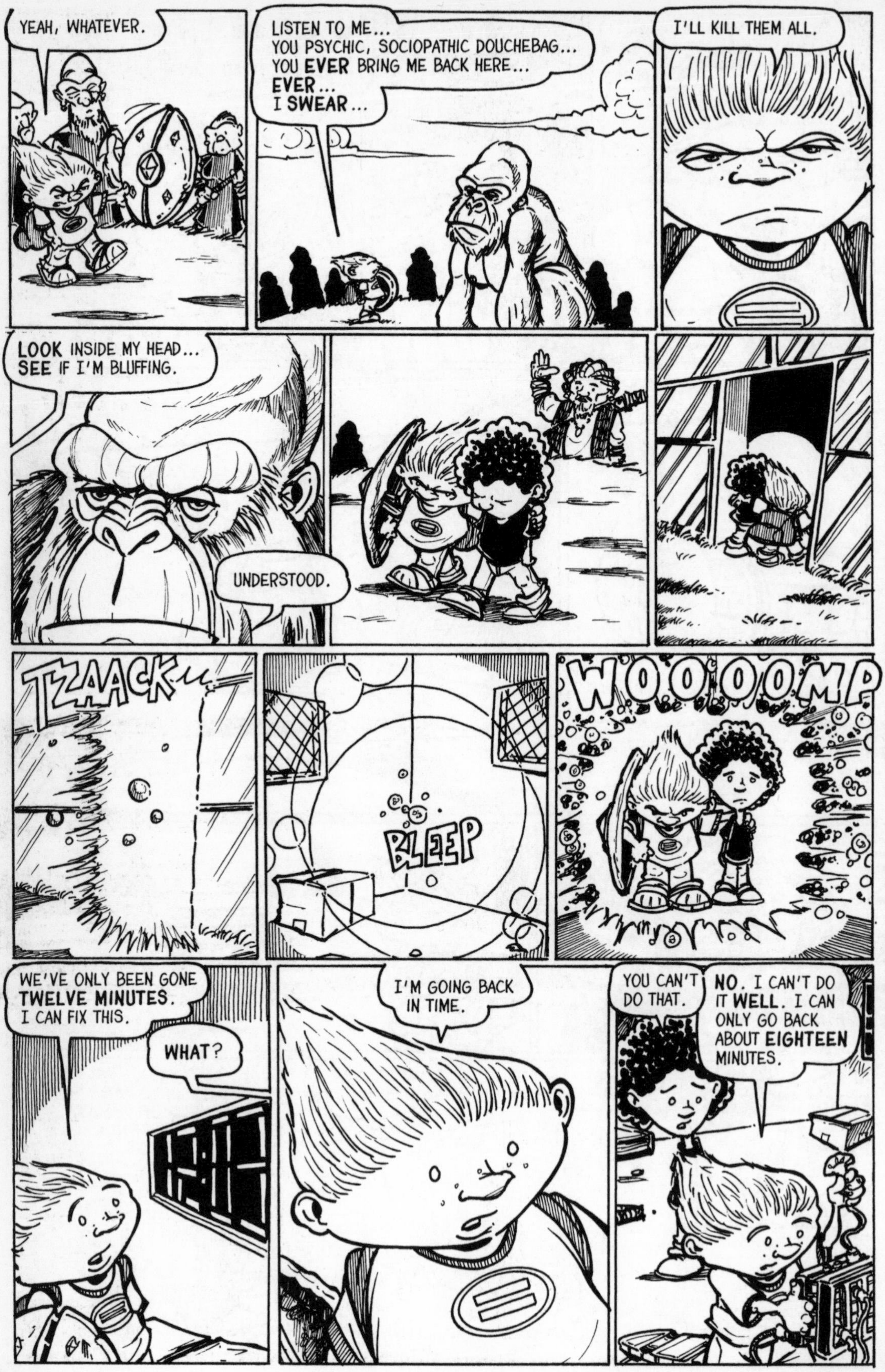

YEAH, WHATEVER.
LISTEN TO ME... YOU PSYCHIC, SOCIOPATHIC DOUCHEBAG... YOU **EVER** BRING ME BACK HERE... **EVER**... I **SWEAR**...
I'LL KILL THEM ALL.
**LOOK** INSIDE MY HEAD... **SEE** IF I'M BLUFFING.
UNDERSTOOD.
TZAACK
BLEEP
WOOOOOMP
WE'VE ONLY BEEN GONE **TWELVE MINUTES**. I CAN FIX THIS.
WHAT?
I'M GOING BACK IN TIME.
YOU CAN'T DO THAT.
**NO**. I CAN'T DO IT **WELL**. I CAN ONLY GO BACK ABOUT **EIGHTEEN** MINUTES.

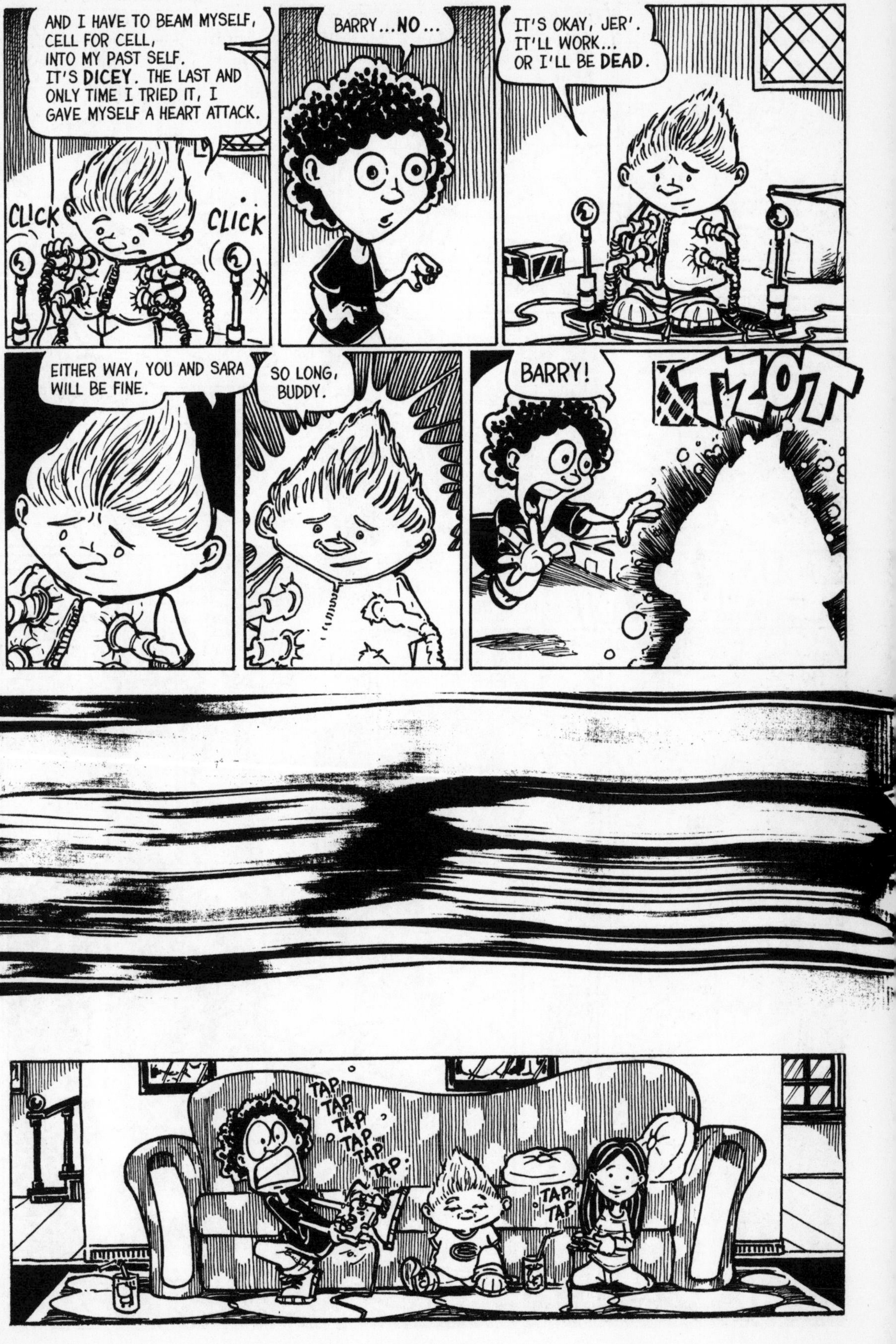
AND I HAVE TO BEAM MYSELF, CELL FOR CELL, INTO MY PAST SELF. IT'S DICEY. THE LAST AND ONLY TIME I TRIED IT, I GAVE MYSELF A HEART ATTACK.
CLICK
CLICK
BARRY...NO...
IT'S OKAY, JER'. IT'LL WORK... OR I'LL BE DEAD.
EITHER WAY, YOU AND SARA WILL BE FINE.
SO LONG, BUDDY.
BARRY!
TZOT
TAP TAP TAP TAP TAP TAP
TAP TAP

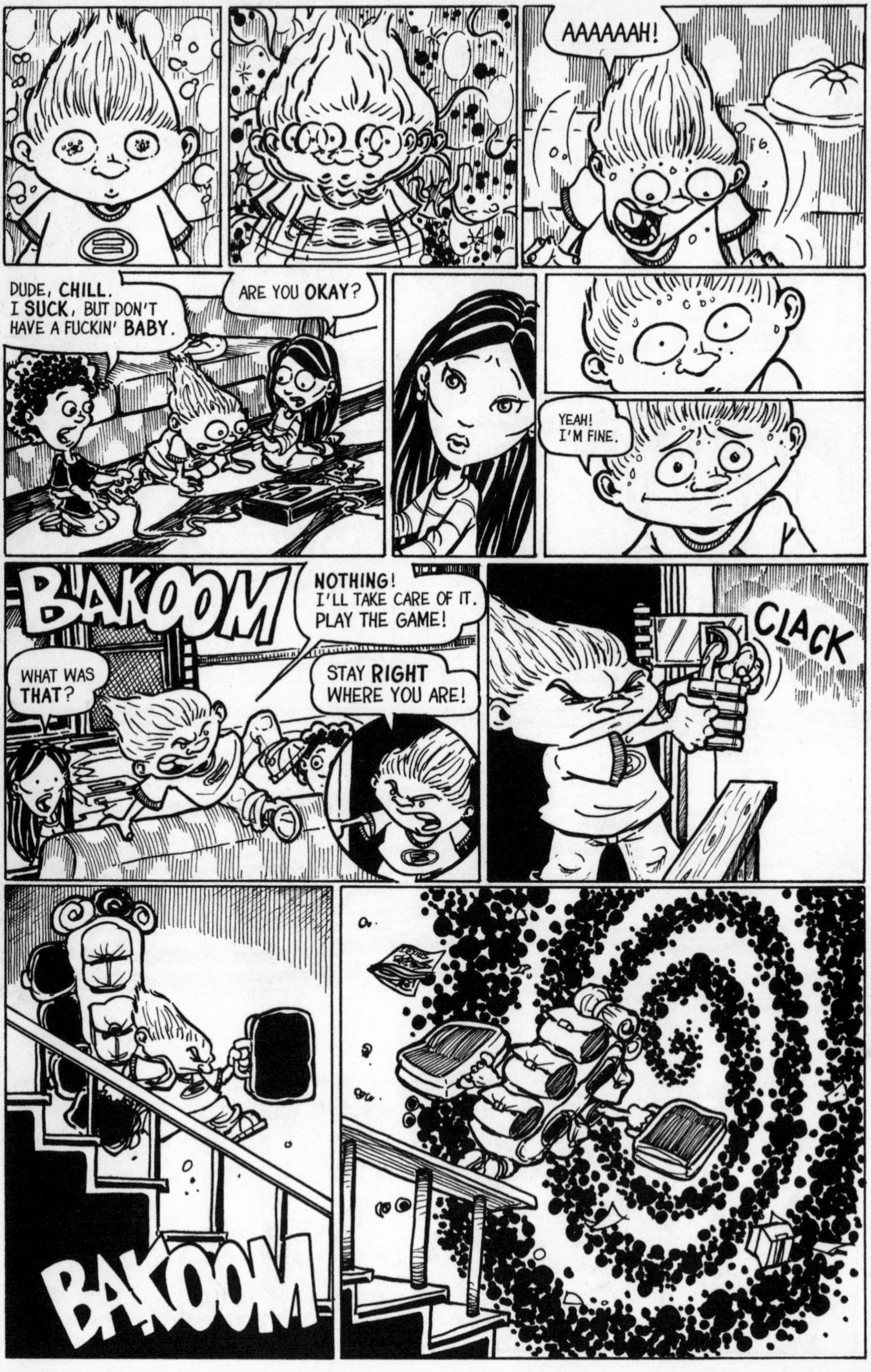
AAAAAAH!
DUDE, CHILL. I SUCK, BUT DON'T HAVE A FUCKIN' BABY.
ARE YOU OKAY?
YEAH! I'M FINE.
BAKOOM
WHAT WAS THAT?
NOTHING! I'LL TAKE CARE OF IT. PLAY THE GAME!
STAY RIGHT WHERE YOU ARE!
CLACK
BAKOOM

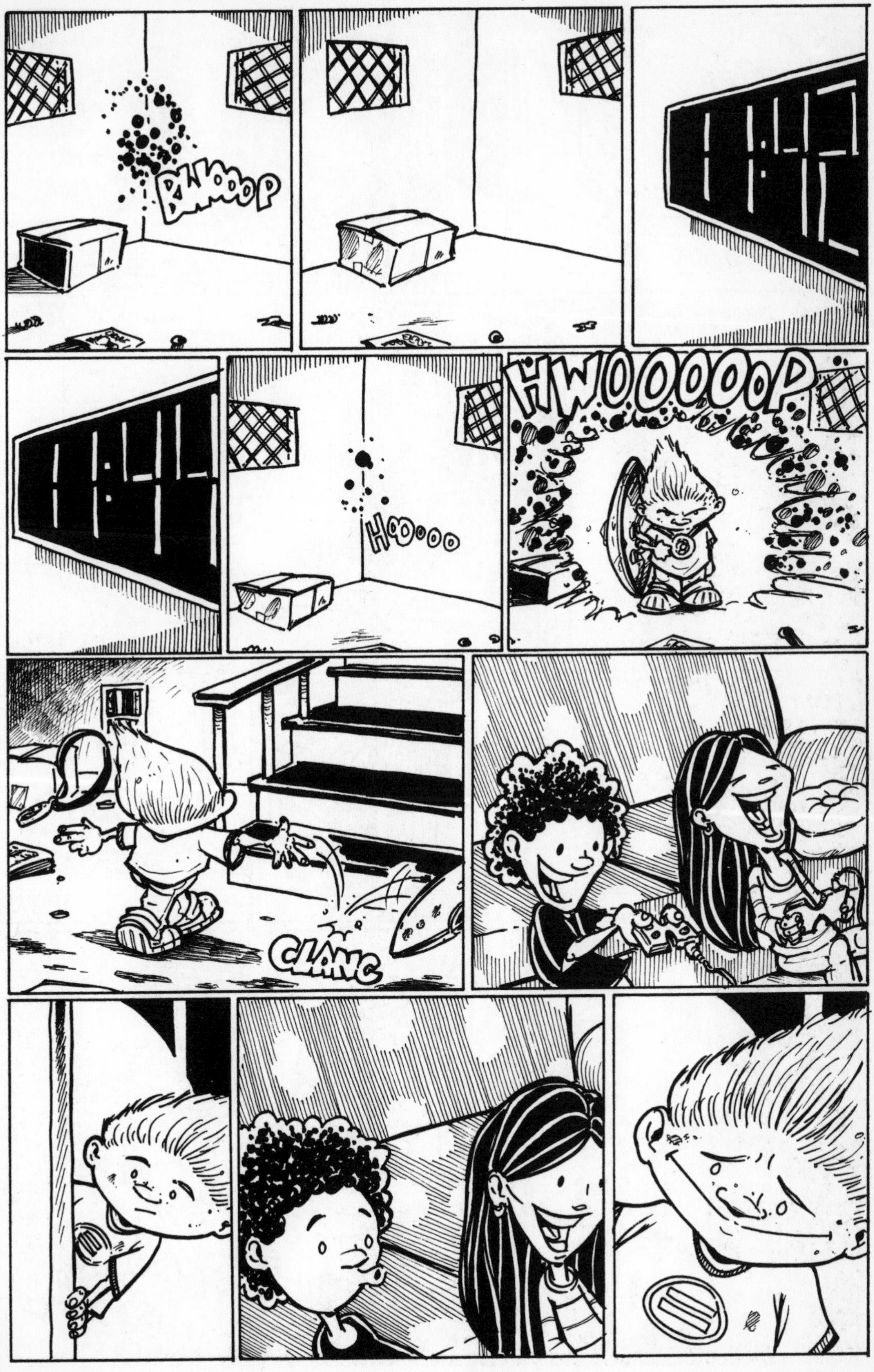
BWOOOP
HWOOOOOP
HOOOOO
CLANG

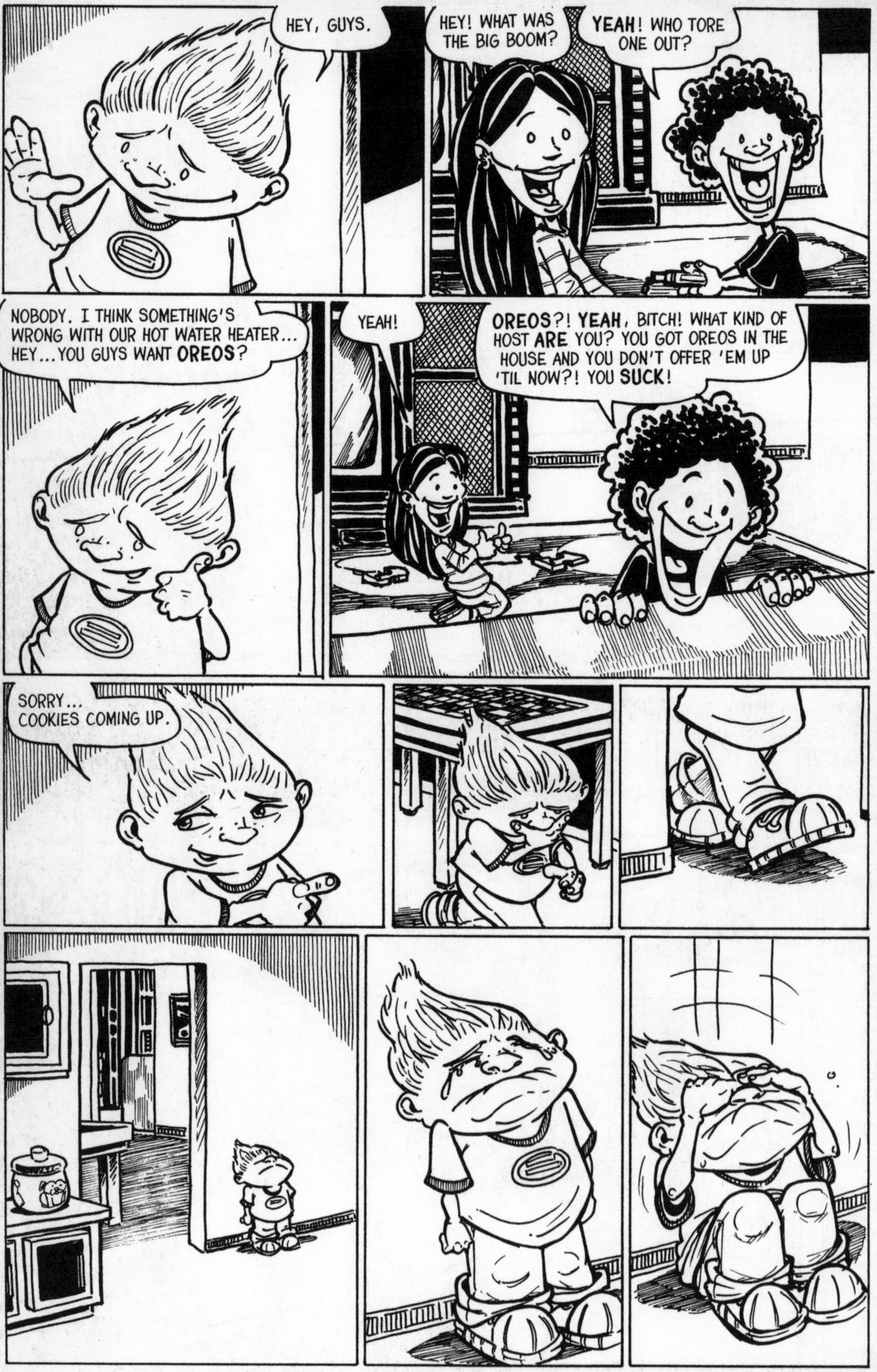
HEY, GUYS.
HEY! WHAT WAS THE BIG BOOM?
YEAH! WHO TORE ONE OUT?
NOBODY. I THINK SOMETHING'S WRONG WITH OUR HOT WATER HEATER... HEY... YOU GUYS WANT OREOS?
YEAH!
OREOS?! YEAH, BITCH! WHAT KIND OF HOST ARE YOU? YOU GOT OREOS IN THE HOUSE AND YOU DON'T OFFER 'EM UP 'TIL NOW?! YOU SUCK!
SORRY... COOKIES COMING UP.

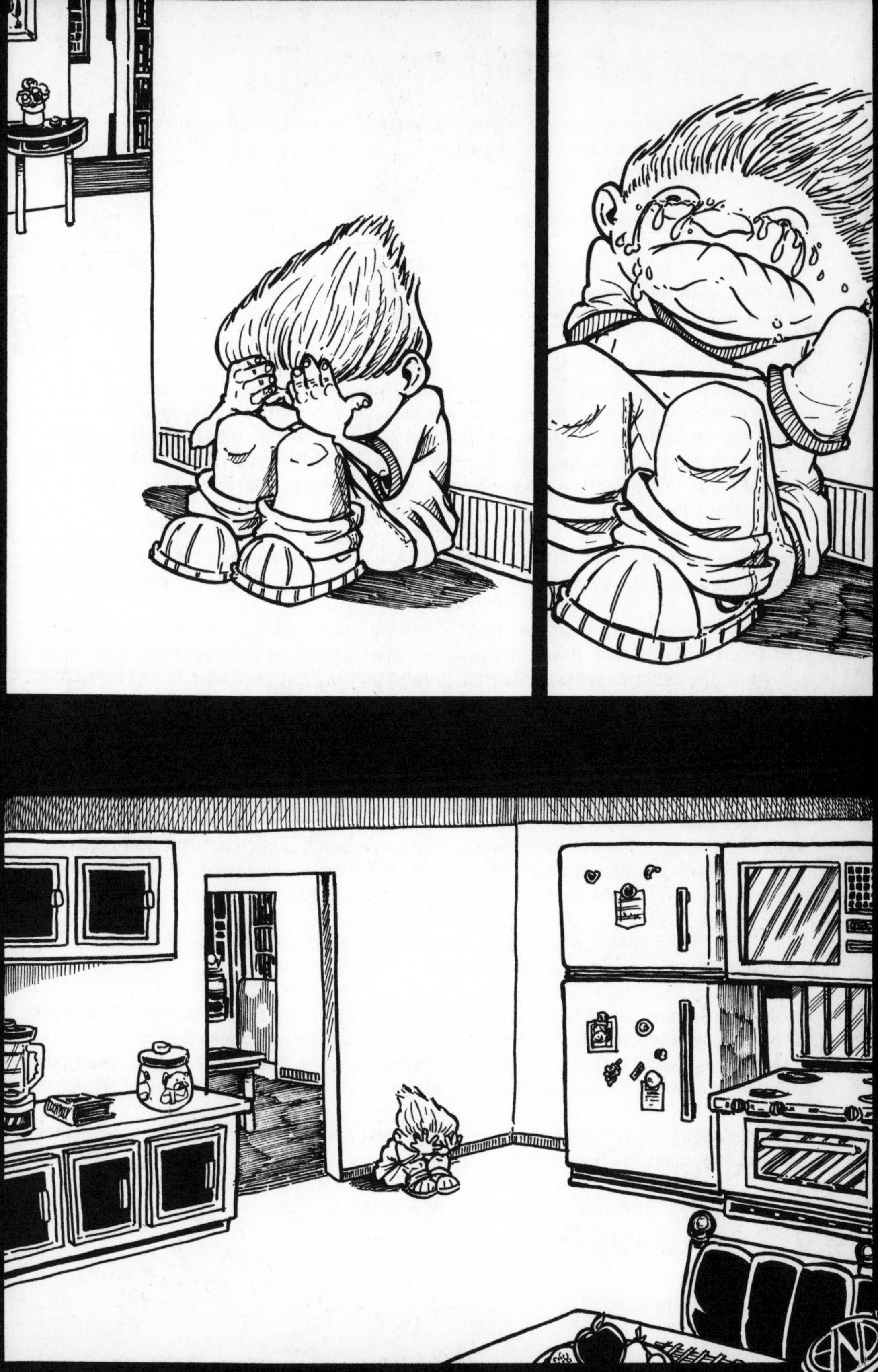
END

# AFTERWORD

It began with crass commercialism. I swear to God. And it all happened in under two minutes. I was kicking around ways to bring in more readers to *Barry Ween* and I hit on: **Monkeys and big breasted bikini women on the covers.**

Do **not** look at me with disappointment.

This is a comic that has found more ways to describe fecal matter than any published work in North America. We are not high-minded and have never claimed to be. The majority of inciting incidents in this book involved Jeremy finding porn on the Internet, so don't start whining now.

Back to me scheming on how to whore out this book; I knew I could handle the monkeys part. I was confident I could figure out more than a few story lines that revolved around apes, chimps, or something in that ball park. I mostly recycle movie plots and very shitty television and hope no one notices. It was the big breasted women part that was giving me trouble. Then I nailed it. "I'll make Sara grow up to adulthood **real** fast...hmmnn... but no bikini... **Wait!** Dude! I'll have her tossed into some Savage Land like dimension and she'll sport one of those loin cloth jobs... COOL... **now** we're gonna sell some **comics...**"

Then... I pictured a moment between Barry and Sara, and the whole thing came together quite differently from my original greedy ruminations.

The **Gorilla Warfare** story arc was born out of a single image—Barry, dumbfounded, staring up at a full-grown version of Sara. It was over two years ago that the one idea gave birth to six issues of *Barry Ween*. The last three pages were part of the plan from the very beginning. As was Sara dying. As was Barry undoing it all. The cheeseball idea to sell books suddenly became a more important story—one that would allow us to see a completely different side of our little foul mouthed protagonist. It all happened in just a few minutes. Just like that. Sometimes even the worst intentions bring out the best.

The whole point of *Barry Ween* was for me to finally produce some cartoons that were without pretense or self-consciousness. Don't obsess about where you'll publish it. Don't worry about an audience. Don't concern yourself with how inappropriate it is and that your mother will be embarrassed. Bottom line: Just make this the funniest motherfucking comic you can.

I tried. And I believe in many ways I succeeded. But Barry, Jeremy and Sara—these little bastards— they started getting all emotional on me. I mean it.

In truth, I'm not one these intellectual horseshit artists who moans on and on about "finding his voice" or claiming the characters "just write themselves." Anybody who thinks their characters just write themselves should probably get on the same meds as John Nash. The rest of us don't take dictation. We write. Or in my case, as mentioned earlier, I steal from motion pictures and television.

My point, if I have one, is that this ridiculous little exercise has become a lot more. Most importantly, it has grown into something I care very much about.

In all modesty, I think it's the finest work I've done in my life.

Judd Winick
pissy cartoonist
April 2002, San Francisco